Christian Dahl, Tue Andersen Nexö (eds.)
To Be Unfree

Political Science | Volume 9

CHRISTIAN DAHL, TUE ANDERSEN NEXÖ (EDS.)
To Be Unfree
Republicanism and Unfreedom in History, Literature, and Philosophy

[transcript]

Bibliographic information published by the Deutsche Nationalbibliothek
The Deutsche Nationalbibliothek lists this publication in the Deutsche Nationalbibliografie; detailed bibliographic data are available in the Internet at http://dnb.d-nb.de

© 2014 transcript Verlag, Bielefeld

All rights reserved. No part of this book may be reprinted or reproduced or utilized in any form or by any electronic, mechanical, or other means, now known or hereafter invented, including photocopying and recording, or in any information storage or retrieval system, without permission in writing from the publisher.

Cover concept: Kordula Röckenhaus, Bielefeld
Printed by Majuskel Medienproduktion GmbH, Wetzlar
Print-ISBN 978-3-8376-2174-7
PDF-ISBN 978-3-8394-2174-1

Content

Introduction
Christian Dahl and Tue Andersen Nexø | 7

PART 1: CONCEPTUAL VARIETIES OF UNFREEDOM

Statelessness, Domination, and Unfreedom.
Arendt and Pettit in Dialogue
Christian F. Rostbøll | 19

Freedom as Non-Arbitrariness or as Democratic Self-Rule?
A Critique of Contemporary Republicanism
Robin Celikates | 37

The Unlikely Claimant. Sovereignty and
Republicanism in Hobbes
Amnon Lev | 55

Materially Unfree. Corruption as a societal diagnosis
and the political forms of unfreedom
Tue Andersen Nexø | 73

Unfreedom and the Republican Tradition
in the French Revolution
Ruth Scurr | 93

PART 2: CULTURAL REPRESENTATIONS OF UNFREEDOM

Occupy Rome. Citizenship and Freedom in Early Modern
Political Culture, Recent Political Theory, and *Coriolanus*
Oliver Arnold | 119

Unfreedom, Servitude, and the Social Bond
Susan Maslan | 139

Naturally free, politically unfree.
Voltaire's Quakers and the modern discourse of human rights
Ingvild Hagen Kjørholt | 157

Dependency, Corruption, and Aesthetics in Denis Diderot's
Le neveu de Rameau
Anne Fastrup | 177

Baudelaire and the Government of the Imagination
Christopher Prendergast | 199

Unfreedom and the Crises of Witnessing. A Republican Perspective on the African American Slave Narratives
Christian Dahl | 213

About the Authors | 229

Introduction
Republican perspectives on freedom's other in philosophy, history, and literature

CHRISTIAN DAHL AND TUE ANDERSEN NEXØ

Spearheaded by John Pocock (1971, 1975) and Quentin Skinner (1978), the last four decades have seen a large and hugely successful attempt to unearth a republican strand within the long history of European political ideas. During the 1990s this historical interest became the starting point for several attempts to revive republicanism not only as a phenomenon of the past, but as a viable political theory with its own distinct conceptual structure and normative claims about the organization of contemporary society. Absolutely central to this attempt was and is the work of the political philosopher Philip Pettit, especially his book *Republicanism: a Theory of Freedom and Government* (1997, see also 2006, 2012), as well as Quentin Skinner's book *Liberty before Liberalism* (1998).

The titles alone assert that the concept of freedom lies at the heart of both Skinner's and Pettit's attempt to revive the republican tradition. For both thinkers, it is a specific idea about what freedom is – and what it is not – which makes the republican tradition attractive today; neither has shown much interest in reviving some of the tradition's other key normative ideas such as patriotism or civic virtue (as opposed to Sandel, 1996; Viroli, 1995). And despite some minor differences (see Pettit, 2002), their arguments are very similar. The republican concept of freedom, they argue, is distinct from a positive concept of freedom understood as self-realization through the active participation in the self-governance of the political community, but it is also distinct from a liberal concept of freedom understood as the absence of interference – the dichotomy which in political theory had been codified by Benjamin Constant (2010) and Isaiah Berlin (1958). Instead, they propose to think of freedom as the absence of domination.

Since discussions of freedom have presupposed that negative freedom should be understood as non-interference for so long, it has been important for both Skinner and Pettit to show how non-domination and non-interference differ from each other. At its core, their argument has been both very simple and very convincing. A wife can be dominated by her husband, a slave by his master, a political subject by an almighty king without the husband, master or king actually interfering in the wife's, slave's or political subject's life. These are all instances of unfreedom, Pettit and Skinner argue, since the mere fact that someone *can* interfere in your life with impunity is enough to make you unfree, not least because this possibility in itself will modify your behaviour. The wife (or slave, or subject) could very well choose to behave in such a way that that the husband (or master, or king) has no reason to interfere. Thus, domination is not the same as interference. Conversely, laws that are contested and decided through democratic procedures do not reduce our freedom, Pettit argues, even though they do interfere in our lives, since they are not instances of domination. Thus, absence of domination is not the same as absence of interference.

Many consequences stem from the distinction between freedom as non-interference and freedom as non-domination. For instance, while interference is most often thought of as an act or at least a specific event, domination is a state of being. Hence, freedom as non-interference refers to the freedom to act as one pleases, but both Skinner and Pettit are adamant that freedom as non-domination has less to do with a freedom to act than it has to do with a specific social status, the status of living as a citizen among one's equals. At the same time, the example shows how Pettit's and Skinner's distinction between a liberal and a republican concept of freedom – and many of the consequences they draw from it – are in reality premised on conflicting understandings of what it means *not to be free*.

In a sense, this is not surprising, since non-interference and non-domination are both negative freedoms; they describe freedom as the absence of something. Yet the meaning of unfreedom has not been a major theme in Skinner's and Pettit's work. What happens, one could ask, if one changes the conceptual focus, and discusses different forms of unfreedom instead of different concepts of freedom? This book, *To be Unfree*, is an attempt to answer – or propose many answers to – that question. As a collection of essays, it contains contributions from a series of academic fields – literary and cultural history, political science, philosophy and law – united through a keen interest in the republican tradition and attempts to revive that tradition today. Though differing in their methodologies, they are also united in their examination of what it means to be unfree.

CONCEPTUAL VARIETIES OF UNFREEDOM

Discussions of the conceptual varieties of unfreedom fill the first part of this book. Several of these actively challenge Pettit's and Skinner's focus on non-domination. They do so by introducing a somewhat strange question, namely: What is the opposite of freedom understood as self-governance? If self-governance is the state of collective autonomy, of participating in articulating the laws under which one lives, its opposite could be understood as heteronomy, the state of having to live under a law not formulated by yourself. Heteronomy is not unconnected to domination or interference – if you are dominated, you are unable to freely participate in the articulation of the laws of the polity; such a law would of course interfere with your choices – but it is also not identical with them. As Pettit has argued, freedom as non-domination does not lead to an ideal of self-governance, but rather to the ideal of a contestatory democracy. It leads to a constitutional ideal where the right to protest against laws that do not adequately track your interests is of central concern, rather than the right to actually participate in the formulation of these laws (Pettit, 2012). In that sense, heteronomy is not in itself a form of domination. It has specific semantic contours.

Furthermore, not all political participation has to do with the articulation of laws. Participation in the governance of one's polity can also be understood as participation in decisions which are inherent in the administration of laws or concern other types of questions: Should we go to war? Do we consider this man guilty or not? A polity not only makes law, but also exercises political power according to historically specific and particular situations. To be a free citizen thus entails not only a direct or indirect say in the making of laws, but could also entail – for instance – the right to be judged by a jury of one's peers, and the right to be a member of such a jury. Within this broader perspective, the answer to the question "What is the opposite of self-governance?" is exclusion rather than heteronomy. More precisely, heteronomy is one form of exclusion from self-governance, but not the only one. It might be that you are unfree when you are excluded from the institutions of political life as such, or perhaps excluded from the polity as such.

The relationship between domination, heteronomy and exclusion is a starting point for several essays in the first part of this book. In different ways they each argue that absence of domination might be an important political goal – and an important aspect of freedom – but that this absence is inadequate to understanding and securing political freedom. In "Statelessness, Domination, and Unfreedom: Arendt and Pettit in Dialogue" Christian Rostbøll compares the figure of the slave in Philip Pettit's work with Hannah Arendt's writings on the plight of the stateless. Working through paradigmatic figures of the unfree in Pettit's and Arendt's thinking, Rostbøll shows how the figures' semantic differences inform the two thinkers' conception of freedom, but also argues that they should be seen as complementary rather than incommensurable. Just as domination and non-domination are to be understood as forms of social status in Pettit's thinking, for Arendt the stateless is also the status-less, someone accorded no status at all in a polity. Rostbøll argues that the opposite of this state is not so much self-governance, but simply the right to be given full status as a member of society, which is also the right to participate in the governance of the polity. There is a difference between having a right to participate and actually participating. Focusing on freedom's other thus lends a keener sense of the positive aspects of freedom, but also shows that the positive aspects of freedom can be considered from multiple perspectives.

The exclusion discussed in Robin Celikates's "Freedom as Non-Arbitrariness or as Democratic Self-Rule? A Critique of Contemporary Republicanism" is of a different kind – not from the polity as such, but from the processes of government. Celikates argues that one can be unfree within a polity whose laws are formulated to track the interests of its citizens – even though such laws supposedly are non-dominating. How can that be? If we are not allowed to participate in the formulation a law, it will feel as an alien imposition upon us. Furthermore, the implicit distinction between those who formulate the laws and those who only have legal resources to protest against them after the fact reintroduces a fundamental inequality into what is supposed to be a society of free and equal citizens. Because of this, Pettit's focus on non-domination needs to be supplemented with the more positive conceptions of freedom found in a different strand of the republican tradition, which runs from Machiavelli to Claude Lefort.

Even more radical is Amnon Lev's proposal in "The Unlikely Claimant. Sovereignty and Republicanism in Hobbes." Looking at republicanism – and especially at attempts to revive it today – within a history of the secularization of sovereign political power, Lev argues that the focus on non-domination fails to account for the novelty in Hobbes's argument regarding how a modern polity constitutes itself through a primordial act of exclusion from self-governance and submission to the sovereign – as well as the kinds of freedom a Hobbesian sovereign must eventually extend to its subjects. With this in mind, how big of a difference is there between a liberal and a republican form of government, especially if republicanism leads to the ideal of a contestatory democracy, but forfeits the ideal of self-governance? Not much, Lev answers polemically.

The two last contributions in the first part of this book discuss reflections upon unfreedom within the history of republican thought. In "Materially Unfree.

Corruption as a Societal Diagnosis and the Political Forms of Unfreedom in Machiavelli, Davenant, and Bolingbroke," Tue Andersen Nexø argues that the concept of corruption, so dear to the republican tradition from Machiavelli onwards, should be understood as a specific kind of unfreedom: one endemic in the tissue of society – what Machiavelli calls the material of the polity – rather than one that is encoded within a constitutional blueprint. But, whereas corruption in Machiavelli is tightly interwoven with his analysis of how a free republic decays and changes into an unfree tyranny, for the 18th century neo-Machiavellians it becomes a preferred term to diagnose social life under the aegis of a new, fiscal-military state. No longer part of a vocabulary to analyze the fate of the republic in secular time, it instead designates a permanent tension between the form and the material of society.

Focusing on the political debates surrounding the establishment of the first French republic, Ruth Scurr highlights how the specific meaning of republican freedom was, in reality, under constant debate. Rather than the conceptual structure of freedom – should it be understood as self-governance or non-domination? – it is the ways freedom and unfreedom were intertwined that these debates centered on, Scurr argues, and on the ways that freedom in one area of life might entail lack of freedom in another. A rhetoric of political freedom might lead to economic restrictions or legitimize laws restricting social mores. Thus, the idea of the free republic, so easy to defend when contrasted to the unfree Ancien Règime, quickly became a much more complicated phenomenon.

CULTURAL REPRESENTATIONS OF UNFREEDOM

The second part of *To Be Unfree* focuses on how lack of freedom has been represented in European, mainly French, literature and culture in the 17th, 18th and 19th centuries. Some of the essays cite explicit dialogues or lines of influence between the republican tradition within the history of political ideas and works of literature, while others use a republican concept of unfreedom – here understood to encompass both domination and exclusion from self-governance – as an analytical tool to refine our understanding of writers and works which are not typically understood to be part of a republican tradition.

These ways of conceiving a lack of freedom prove to be fruitful in the analysis of literary and cultural history, and certainly more fruitful than a conception of unfreedom as interference. We don't think this is a coincidence. As Quentin Skinner (2008, p. 127cc) has convincingly shown, Hobbes' polemical redefinition of what it means not to be free – where the lack of freedom simply means physical interference – enabled him to counter the republican distinction between the free citizen and the unfree subject. It allowed him to declare the citizens of a republic as unfree as the subjects of a tyrant, since the law of the republic interferes as much as the will of a tyrant in peoples' lives. But there is another consequence of Hobbes' redefinition: effectively, he reifies the concept of freedom. This is abundantly clear from *Leviathan* itself:

"Liberty, or Freedom, signifieth (properly) the absence of opposition; (by opposition, I mean external impediments of motion;) and may be applied no less to irrational, and inanimate creatures, than to rational. For whatsoever is so tied, or environed, as it cannot move, but within a certain space, which space is determined by the opposition of some external body, we say it hath not liberty to go further. And so of all living creatures, whilst they are imprisoned, or restrained, with walls, or chains; and of the water whilst it is kept in by banks, or vessels, that otherwise would spread itself into a larger space, we use to say, they are not at liberty, to move in such manner, as without those external impediments they would." (Hobbes, 1996, chp. 21, p. 139)

As one can see, for Hobbes the paradigmatic figure of the unfree is neither the slave nor the stateless, but rather the prisoner – hindered in his movement not by other people, but by physical objects such as chains and walls. Even more radically, the state of being a prisoner is understood through the properties of flowing water. As a paradigmatic figure, the prisoner is thought of as a physical entity, blocked in his or her movement by other physical things. It is not that interference is not a state of being in Hobbes – the water is continually hindered by "the opposition of some external body" – rather, in the state of being unfree, the subject becomes understood as if he or she were a non-sentient object.

Hobbes does more than invent a concept of freedom that makes the citizen and the subject equally unfree. Through his imagery he changes what in the republican tradition was thought of as a relation between human beings – the social status of being excluded or included, of being dominated or being equal – into a relation between things which can then block or not block each other's movements. This reification makes discussions of freedom and its other strangely distinct from any analysis of the psychological complexities and subtle balances of power inherent in social life. It conceives of the lack of freedom as something that can be discussed independently of any understanding of intersubjectivity. It also makes any discussion of what it means to feel unfree, to experience unfreedom, seem irrelevant to an analysis of what it means not to be free. And all of this is accomplished in opposition to the thinkers in the republican tradition for whom freedom and its other was a question of social and political status – which were, of course, also subjectively felt and experienced. Literature has probably always been engaged with the production of images of individual experience and of the minute ways our self-conception is connected to our position within the structures of intersubjectivity – be it of an intimate or public kind, be it informal or highly ritualized – but in early modern and modern literature this topic was explored with astounding variety, subtlety, and regularity. Furthermore, both early modern and modern literature quite often also functioned as an imaginary space – a playground, so to say – for the examination of philosophical concepts and their consequences, reveling in descriptions of hypothetical sociopolitical situations or forms of social organization whose seriousness would always be up for debate. It is not surprising, then, that a surprising number of literary works from the 17th, 18th and 19th century can be understood as examinations of what it means to be unfree and how being unfree produces its own specific kinds of subjectivity. It is also not surprising that the republican vocabulary of unfreedom as domination and/or exclusion is a much more fruitful beginning point for an analysis of this literature than Hobbes' and the later, liberal tradition's reified understanding of freedom as non-interference.

Conversely, the subtlety and complexity of literary works often shed light back upon a republican tradition and especially upon the current attempts to revive it. They complicate an account of freedom and its other which too often simply notes that lack of freedom has subjective and existential, as well as political, implications, but rarely examine these implications or how the existential and the political interact. This interplay – between literature and political philosophy, between theories of unfreedom and representations of being unfree – is at the core of Oliver Arnold's "Occupy Rome: Citizenship and Freedom in Early Modern Political Culture, Recent Political Theory, and *Coriolanus*." First showing that theories of citizenship – understood as participation in the commonwealth – and theories of freedom were almost inextricable from each other in Elizabethan and Jacobean England – thus complicating any neat distinction between freedom as self-rule and freedom as non-domination – Arnold then discusses two very different attempts to make sense of the relationship between citizenship, freedom, and political representation in England around 1600. Whereas members of parliament would insist that the whole people of England were actually present in parliament through their representatives, Shakespeare's Roman plays argue that political representation actually barred the citizens from active self-governance, Arnold contends. Shakespeare's works do not elaborate upon any political position circulating in Elizabethan England. Rather, his dramas reshuffle components of existing arguments, resulting in a radical and – for his time – strikingly original proposition about freedom and its other.

The genre which has most consistently explored the intersubjective structure generated by the primary social institution of unfreedom, household servitude, is without doubt classical comedy and its modern descendants. Skinner (1998) and Viroli (2012) have already discussed the clever slaves of Plautine comedy as agents who are free according to the liberal concept of freedom as non-interference, but remain unfree according to a republican definition of freedom as non-domination. In "Unfreedom, Servitude, and the Social Bond" Susan Maslan presents Marivaux's comedy *The Slave Island* (1725) as a fable that first reveals servitude as an institution without moral and political legitimacy, and subsequently seeks to demonstrate the impossibility of transcending the intersubjective relations of domination servitude, granted that servitude is synonymous with society itself. Marivaux's comedy can hardly be called republican but, as Maslan demonstrates, it anticipates Rousseau's anti-foundationalist theory of social inequality where the social sphere, not nature, becomes the source of heteronomy.

The dichotomy between natural freedom and political unfreedom uncovered by political theorists of the French Enlightenment is also the topic of Ingvild Hagen Kjørholt's essay "Naturally Free, Politically Unfree: The Quakers in Voltaire's *Lettres philosophiques*". Kjørhagen challenges the widespread association of Voltaire's political philosophy with early modern liberalism by unfolding Voltaire's highly ambiguous portrait of the British Quaker society. On one hand, the Lettres portray the Quaker society as a utopian realization of natural liberty and praise the Quaker's evasion of political interference. On the other hand, Voltaire reveals the futility of the Quakers' quietist attempt to realize their natural liberty at the expense of political participation. Voltaire's *Lettres* also suggests that the mere absence of political dominance does not relieve the Quakers from their political unfreedom, however self-imposed their political exclusion may be. As it will be clear from the contributions of the first part of this book, this is a view that would divide contemporary republican theorists.

With Anne Fastrup's essay "Dependency, Corruption and Aesthetics in Denis Diderot's *Le neveu de Rameau*". we return to the question of servitude. If Marivaux's *The Slave Island* displayed servitude as an inescapable but arbitrary social condition, Diderot's satire reveals an aesthetics of servitude, according to Fastrup. Diderot, a pioneer of aesthetic theory and criticism in the 18th century, develops his social criticism of servility into an aesthetic critique of a variety of performing arts from pantomime to opera. In sharp contrast to later romantic celebrations of artistic freedom, Diderot sees an intimate, but troubling, connection between heteronomy and artistic creativity.

Fastrup's discussion of Diderot's satirical novel and its relation to his aesthetic criticism is consonant with a small, but significant, number of attempts to recover the long forgotten republican impulses behind 18th century aesthetic theory. This recovery also comes to the fore in Christopher Prendergast's discussion of Baudelaire's writings on criticism and aesthetics, which in many ways continue discussions begun by Diderot. Baudelaire, the apogee of post-romantic and post-revolutionary disillusion, came to see poetic imagination not as a source of aesthetic education and liberation, as Friedrich Schiller and Immanuel Kant would have it, but as a despotic power: a source of aesthetic heteronomy. Disillusioned by the revolution of 1848 and the compromised Second Republic, Baudelaire saw how aesthetic concepts associated with republican freedom had been tainted by the liberal individualism of romanticism. As Prendergast points out, this rejection of the aesthetics of liberation is fundamental not only for Baudelaire's critical writings but for a whole current of reactionary thought in modernist writing and art throughout and beyond the 19th century.

Finally, Christian Dahl compares Philip Pettit's theory of freedom to a body of literature which is concerned with unfreedom in its most radical form: slave autobiography from the Antebellum period in the United States. In his essay "Unfreedom and the Crises of Witnessing" Dahl argues that the slave narratives not only served to document and oppose slavery but also to assert the same aspects of freedom that are central to the republican theory of non-domination. Special attention is paid to the importance of discursive control which was not only central to the slave narrators but also to Philip Pettit's theory of freedom and his criticism of competing philosophical theories which focus only on rational and volitional control.

Most of the contributions in this collection were originally presented at the conference "To Be Unfree" held at the University of Copenhagen 4th to 6th of March 2010. We would like to thank all contributors and participants at the conference. In particular our thanks go to Professor Isak Winkel Holm, head of the research network Cultures of Republicanism, which funded the conference and thus made it possible for us to let this varied group of academics meet and enter into dialogue with each other – in Copenhagen as well as in this book. Special thanks also to Professor Christopher Prendergast. Without his advice and help this book would not exist.

References

Berlin, I. (1958). *Two Concepts of Liberty*. Oxford: Oxford University Press.
Constant, B. (2010). *De la liberté des anciens comparée à celle des modernes*. Paris: Fayard.
Hobbes, T. (1996). *Leviathan*, ed. J.C.A. Gaskell. Oxford: Oxford University Press.
Pettit, P. (1997). *Republicanism. A Theory of Freedom and Government*. Oxford: Oxford University Press.
Pettit, P. (2002). Keeping Republican Freedom Simple: On a Difference with Quentin Skinner. *Political Theory* 30, 339-356.
Pettit, P. (2007) Joining the Dots. In G. Brennan et. al. (Ed.), *Common Minds. Themes from the Philosophy of Philip Pettit*. (pp. 215-344). Oxford: Oxford University Press.
Pettit, P. (2012). *On the People's Terms. A Republican Theory and Model of Democracy*. Cambridge: Cambridge University Press.
Pocock, J.G.A. (1971). *Politics, Language and Time: Essays in Political Thought and History*. New York, NY: Atheneum.
Pocock, J.G.A. (1975). *The Republican Moment. Florentine Political Theory and the Atlantic Republican Tradition*. Princeton, NJ: Princeton University Press.
Sandel, M. (1996) *Democracy's Discontent. America in Search of a Public Philosophy*. Cambridge, MA: Harvard University Press.
Skinner, Q. (1978). *The Foundations of Modern Political Thought*. 2 vols. Cambridge: Cambridge University Press.
Skinner, Q. (1998). *Liberty before Liberalism*. Cambridge: Cambridge University Press.
Skinner, Q. (2008). *Hobbes and Republican Liberty*. Cambridge: Cambridge University Press.
Viroli, M. (1995). *For Love of Country. An Essay on Patriotism and Nationalism*. Oxford: Oxford University Press.
Viroli, M. (2012). *The Liberty of Servants. Berlusconi's Italy*. Princeton, NJ: Princeton University Press.

Part 1

Conceptual Varieties of Unfreedom

Statelessness, Domination, and Unfreedom
Arendt and Pettit in Dialogue

CHRISTIAN F. ROSTBØLL

Historical struggles for freedom are often portrayed as born of the unbearable experience of oppression and, therefore, as a matter of casting off a yoke, of freeing oneself from something. This image, even if it does give some insight into the meaning and importance of freedom, gives the misleading impression that freedom is merely the absence of something, and that it can be understood and defined in negative terms only. To avoid this impression, and to appreciate that it is a misleading impression, we need a deeper understanding of the experiences of unfreedom, of what the other of freedom is.

The idea that freedom must be understood in relation to its opposite is prominent in the republican tradition of political thought. Philip Pettit has become the most influential contemporary theorist of republican freedom, and he has systematically developed and defended a conception of freedom as non-domination (Pettit, 1997; 2001; 2008). In the republican tradition, according to Pettit (1997, p. 31), "liberty is always cast in terms of the opposition between liber and servus, citizen and slave." In another strand of republican thinking, a strand that Pettit (1997, p. 8) distances himself from, stands Hannah Arendt for whom the extreme experience of unfreedom lies in being stateless. According to Arendt (1979, pp. 296f.), the plight of the stateless is "deprivation of a place in the world," which is different from the situation of the slave who "still belonged to some sort of human community." We find in these two republican thinkers, then, two contrasting images of unfreedom: slavery vs. statelessness; a contrast that, as I shall show, has important implications for how we may understand freedom. Specifically, it can cast light on and contribute to challenging the common contrast between negative and positive conceptions of liberty. Moreover, it can help clarify the intrinsic and instrumental values of democracy in relation to freedom.

This chapter argues that both the freedom-versus-slavery theme and the phenomenon of statelessness supply important insights into the meaning and importance of freedom. We must, therefore, bring Pettit and Arendt into dialogue, something that is rarely done because of needless divisions in contemporary political theory.[1] Integrating Pettit's insights into domination and Arendt's insights into the plight of being excluded from a community that is responsive to one's opinions and actions requires adjusting each position. The chapter analyzes differences between Pettit and Arendt related to their respective uses of slavery and statelessness as freedom's other. I find three core elements that differentiate the two: First, there is the question of whether unfreedom requires the presence of a dominator (as the slave metaphor indicates), or whether unfreedom is characterized by extreme loneliness (the stateless). Second, there is the issue of whether unfreedom is best understood as a form of status (as the slave does have), or whether it means a lack of status (the stateless is apparently status-less). Third, does unfreedom involve being used as a means by someone else (the slave), or does it mean being superfluous in the eyes of others (the stateless)? The analysis and discussion of these three differences between slavery and statelessness as freedom's other leads to a discussion of the relationship between freedom and democracy. The main question here is whether, or to what extent, or in what way, we should regard freedom as a positive notion. I also discuss whether freedom is intrinsically or only instrumentally related to democracy. I argue for regarding republican freedom as having positive dimensions but in a non-Rousseauian sense.

THE SLAVE AND THE STATELESS

1) The free man and the slave

In Pettit's understanding of the republican tradition, and in his own conception of freedom as non-domination, freedom is understood in contrast to slavery. The condition of the slave is to live "at the beck and call of a master," and to be "in a position where fear and deference will be the normal order of the day" (Pettit, 1997, pp. 32, 64). Even the most fortunate slave, even the slave with the most permissive master, will live a life in unfreedom because she is "depending on [someone else's] grace and favor" (Pettit, 1997, p. 33).The liberty-versus-slavery

---

[1] Pettit's work is mainly discussed among analytical philosophers, while Arendt's work tends to be discussed exclusively by continental philosophers and political theorists.

theme implies, according to Pettit (1997, p. 32), that "the ultimate in unfreedom is having to live at the will of another – the arbitrary will of another – in the manner of the slave; the essence of freedom is not to have to endure such dependence and vulnerability." The slave is the most extreme example of this dependence, because she is the property of another. Pettit gives a compelling picture of the ills that this sort of dependence entails.

The slave metaphor serves also the more systematic purpose of showing the possibility of unfreedom without interference. This is essential, because Pettit believes that freedom as non-domination is different from (and superior to) the alternative conception of freedom as non-interference, which we know from thinkers such as Thomas Hobbes, Jeremy Bentham, and Isaiah Berlin. Freedom as non-domination is, like freedom as non-interference, a negative conception of freedom, but it is concerned with absence of domination rather than absence of interference. For Pettit, the republican tradition's contrast between liberty and slavery and the possibility of living in slavery without being interfered with "is a sure sign of taking liberty to consist in non-domination rather than in non-interference" (Pettit, 1997, p. 32). For "slavery is essentially characterized by domination, not by actual interference: even if the slave's master proves to be entirely benign and permissive, he or she continues to dominate the slave" (Pettit, 1997, p. 32). This proposition, of course, requires a definition of domination as something different than interference. Pettit suggests that A dominates B, if A has the capacity to interfere on an arbitrary basis in certain choices that B is in a position to make (Pettit, 1997, p. 52). "Domination can occur without interference, because it requires only that someone have the capacity to interfere arbitrarily in your affairs; no one need actually to interfere" (Pettit, 1997, p. 23). Thus, the slave metaphor, via the example of the non-interfering master, is used to argue for the possibility of living in unfreedom without experiencing interference.

To view unfreedom and domination as "a generalization of the case of slavery" (Markell, 2008, p. 11) has some important implications. I would like to highlight three elements for our further discussion. First, the slave metaphor suggests that unfreedom involves a relationship between persons akin to that of a master and his slave. To be dominated means "being subject to the alien control of others" (Pettit, 2008, p. 102, emphasis added; cf. 2010, pp. 73, 75). Domination in this view, then, involves the presence of the dominator and unfreedom is part of a human relationship. Second, it is interesting to note that the slave occupies a certain position in society. Being a slave is a form of status (usually one legally defined) and as such slaves have a relation to human society. This is not something Pettit emphasizes, but it is part of what slavery historically has involved, and we will see its relevance in contrast to the phenomenon of statelessness. Third, slaves are used by their masters; they are used to serve the ends of their masters rather than their own. When this idea is generalized, it means that domination involves someone exploiting someone else for her own ends. Unfreedom, in this view, means being used as a means rather than as an end.

2) Statelessness, membership, and humanity

We find Arendt's description of statelessness in the second volume of *The Origins of Totalitarianism* (Arendt, 1979, p. 267cc). The stateless are those persons who do not belong to and who do not have a status in any political community. Arendt's category of the stateless should not be confused with (even if it can inform a discussion of) our days refugees, who since the 1951 Refugee Convention have had a legal status in international law. The stateless in Arendt's discussion are people who have no nation of their own and/or who have been excluded from or stripped of their citizenship and juridical status in any other nation, as the Jews were by the Nazis in the 1930s. Arendt's main concern is understanding what makes the stateless so vulnerable, but we might also understand the situation of the stateless in terms of unfreedom. Arendt's description of statelessness as freedom's other, which pointedly differs from Pettit's liberty-slavery theme, has some interesting implications for freedom's positive dimensions. I shall consider the three elements listed under Pettit above in turn.

It is possible for a stateless person, Arendt notes, to have more freedom of movement than a person within a political community: a lawfully imprisoned criminal, for example. But this negative freedom, this absence of interference, experienced by the stateless "is due to charity and not to right" (Arendt, 1979, p. 296). There is a parallel here between the situation of the stateless and the slave and, thus, an apparent similarity to Pettit's contention that unfreedom does not require interference. Clearly, neither Arendt nor Pettit see freedom as defined by non-interference and, in both cases, slavery and statelessness, unfreedom has something to do with the lack of security against arbitrary interference. But the cases of the slave and of the stateless differ in terms of whether lack of freedom requires the presence of a dominus. What is special about the situation of the stateless is that there is no one (no particular other) who controls or rules her; she is, rather, at the mercy of any would-be dominator. The stateless is also not the property of anyone, as is the slave. The plight of the stateless is not that she has no rights against a particular master, but that she does not have anyone to whom she can address herself; she does not have anywhere where she can press claims. "The fundamental deprivation" of the rightless, according to Arendt (1979, p. 296), "is manifested first and above all in the deprivation of a place in the world which makes opinions significant and actions effective." The predicament of the stateless "is not that they are not equal before the law, but that no law exists for them; not that they are oppressed but that nobody wants even to oppress them" (Arendt, 1979, pp. 295c).

"[I]n the light of recent events [totalitarianism, the holocaust]," Arendt writes (1979, p. 297):

"[...] it is possible to say that even slaves still belonged to some sort of community; their labor was needed, used, and exploited, and this kept them within the pale of humanity. To be a slave was after all to have a distinctive character, a place in society – more than the abstract nakedness of being human and nothing but human [which is the plight of the stateless]."

I get back to slaves being needed and used in the next paragraph; the point I want to note here is that while the slave has a status, the stateless does not; the latter, as Arendt sees it, is status-less. Arendt suggests that the slave gets a character and place in society because of what she does or what she contributes with, her labor. But it should be noted also that the slave's status is defined in legal terms and as such the slave is (in a sense) part of a human community. The slave has a place in and is part of both the socio-economic and the legal structure of society, even if she is excluded from the *polis* or the political life of the community. The stateless, by contrast, has no place whatsoever in any of these human structures. I challenge and qualify this description below, but here we should note the important connection to Arendt's famous idea of "a right to have rights" (1979, p. 296). The right to have rights is a right to membership and is prior to specific rights to life, liberty, and the pursuit of happiness. What the stateless lack, as James Bohman (2008, p. 203) notes, is "the capability to have a status as such," and the right to membership is "a right to the statuses and powers that make our freedom secure and allow us to be free to avoid the ills and evils that result from the loss of such a status." The question that will occupy us below is whether the status of being a member can be understood merely in terms of security against arbitrary interference or whether it also has intrinsic value.

As we just saw, slaves being needed by other human beings is what gives them a place in society. In *The Origins of Totalitarianism*, Arendt describes how the Nazis saw the Jews as "superfluous" (e.g. Arendt, 1979, p. 296), and in a letter to Karl Jaspers she explains that "making human beings as human beings superfluous [means] not using them as means to an end, which leaves their essence as humans untouched and impinges only on their human dignity; rather, making them superfluous as human beings" (Arendt & Jaspers, 1992, p. 166). It is not immediately clear why Arendt thinks being used as a means keeps slaves "within the pale of humanity," while the Jews under Nazism were made "superfluous as human beings." Nor is the distinction between violating human dignity by being used as a means and undermining the essence as human beings by being regarded as superfluous entirely clear. Aristotle, who Arendt is so fund of citing, describes the slave as a "living piece of property" on par with other tools and instruments (Aristotle, 1992, 1253b28-32; cf. Hansen, 1999, pp. 120c). Does this make slaves needed as human beings? Slaves could not act in Arendt's specific sense of self-disclosing action among equals in the public space (Arendt, 1958, pp. 175-247). And action is usually what makes us (fully) human to Arendt; if one only labors, as the slaves does, one does not rise above the sphere of necessity and meaninglessness. How can slaves be part of humanity when they are deprived of the possibility of participating in the most human of human activities? I can see why being needed gives the slave a certain security that persons who are regarded as superfluous lack, since rational people will be inclined to give some protection to what they need over and above what they do not need. But protection based on someone else's need does not imply making the protected part of humanity. Clearly the slave's humanity is not respected in the Kantian sense, which is why Arendt says the slave's dignity is impinged. She must, therefore, have another understanding of humanity in mind when she speaks of what the stateless are excluded from and deprived of. I return to this other understanding of humanity below (in subsection three of the following section).

FREEDOM OF THE CITY

Above I have analyzed three important differences between regarding freedom's other as slavery and statelessness, respectively. I have done so with little comment or criticism of the two theorists. In what follows I discuss the three elements – presence/absence of dominator, status, and being used as a means vs. superfluousness – in more detail. This discussion will require also consideration of further details of the views of Pettit and Arendt. This section will form the background of an examination of the relationship between freedom and democracy in the section "Freedom, Politics, and Democracy".

1) Presence/absence of dominator

In Pettit (2008, pp. 102cc) unfreedom requires the presence of someone who is in position to control certain of your choices, and freedom from domination requires security against such alien control. Moreover, the *only* positive dimension to freedom as non-domination that Pettit allows for is the requirement of the *presence of security* against interference on an arbitrary basis; the positive dimensions involved in participating in politics and self-government are rejected as external to the conception (Pettit, 1997, pp. 51, 27cc). An obvious way to gain freedom on this basis seems to be to escape from the presence of other people who might dominate you; for where could one find more security against arbitrary interference than in the solitude of a deserted island? This issue does not arise in Arendt, it seems, for her description of the situation of the stateless shows not only that without rights one is in danger of arbitrary interference from anyone, but also – and more fundamentally – that one lacks a place in the human world. And lacking a place in the world means in and of itself lacking freedom. Actually, Pettit (1997, p. 66) denies that freedom as non-domination can be achieved by isolation: "Non-domination, as that is valued in the republican tradition, means the absence of domination in the presence of other people, not the absence of domination gained by isolation." The question is whether seeing freedom as social or civil freedom – "the status associated with living among other people, none of whom dominates you" (Pettit, 1997, p. 66) – is compatible with regarding security against arbitrary interference as the *only* positive dimension of freedom. Why is non-domination in the city more valuable, if one rejects the intrinsic values of political participation, as Pettit does?

Perhaps the experience of the stateless can point to another, additional, positive dimension of freedom than slavery does? Pettit (1997, p. 66, emphasis added) merely says that the non-domination "that is valued in the republican tradition [is] the absence of domination in the presence of other people," but it is difficult to see how this can be made part of his definition of non-domination. This is particularly so when the only positive dimension allowed for in his conception of freedom is presence of security against arbitrary interference. Pettit's formulations entail that there could be freedom outside the city, but that this is not the freedom valued by republicans. Arendt's engagement with statelessness, in contrast, suggests more clearly that there can be no freedom outside a political community. Her claim is partly a historical and contingent claim about stateless people lacking legal protection. But when she says that the plight of the stateless shows that one must be a member of a political community in order to have "the very qualities which make it possible for other people to treat him as a fellowman" (Arendt, 1979, p. 300), her point is a deeper one. One may ask whether her position is the stronger one that our humanness is constituted by belonging to a political community or the weaker one that our humanness can appear only in political communities. I think the latter possibility is the more plausible interpretation. The subject that is to be free can appear only in a human world in which others are responsive to one's actions and opinions. In this way there is a further positive dimension to freedom than mere security and protection, a dimension of intersubjective relationships and human responsiveness. In what sense this dimension is political is something to which we return.

2) What kind of status

When we see the position of the slave in contrast to that of the stateless, it becomes clear that the slave has a positive status that the stateless lack. As mentioned, the slave has a position in both the legal and the socio-economic structure of the society in which she lives. The slave experiences domination exactly *because of her position or status* in the social structure of society and not merely because of lack of guarantees against arbitrary interference, as Pettit says. The unfreedom of slaves is a product of the positive privileges that their master have against them. The same is true of Pettit's other examples of dominated persons, the worker in capitalist society and the wife under patriarchy (Pettit, 1997, pp. 138-143). The domination of these categories of people is the product of social structures and institutions, of the capitalist division of labor and the patriarchal family. If this is right, domination does not exist by the mere fact that someone has *the capacity* to interfere arbitrarily in others' affairs but in their accepted right to do so.[2] We must, therefore, distinguish between the mere capacity to interfere arbitrarily and the accepted right (or authority) to do so with impunity.

At first glance, and as Arendt sometimes describes the matter, it appears that the situation of the stateless is to be status-less. The stateless does not occupy a position that gives others the right or authority to arbitrarily interfere in her affairs. The stateless is entirely outside legal and also economic relations. Or so it seems. It is important to remember that even if masters can interfere arbitrarily in the lives of their slaves with impunity, there are limits to how they can treat their slaves. In ancient Athens, for example, masters could not, most importantly, put their slaves to death with impunity (Hansen, 1999, pp. 120c). With regard to the stateless, there are no legal limits on how they can be treated by others, as long as being stateless means lacking the "right to have rights." But can we describe the situation of the stateless as entirely outside of and deprived of human relation-

---

2 As Henry Richardson (2002, p. 34) has argued, kidnappers have the capacity to arbitrarily interfere with people's lives, but we do not for that reason regard them as dominating their potential victims (all of us). Cf. Rostbøll (2008, pp. 48c).

ships, as Arendt does? I would suggest that being stateless is still something one is in relation to something; it cannot be understood in negative terms only.

As we learn from Arendt herself, the situation of the stateless in the interwar period should be seen in relation to the European nation state system. "Only with a completely organized humanity could the loss of home and political status become identical with expulsion from humanity altogether" (Arendt, 1979, p. 297). Not having a nation state, as the Jews did not, is a deprivation in relation to a system that protects people on the basis of their nationality. Moreover, stateless was not merely something Jews (and others) were but rather something that was done to them. So even if the stateless have no status within any particular nation state, they do have a status in relation to nation states and from the perspective of the international system. Stateless is a status in the international political system. And it is a status that one is commonly pushed into. Thus, the difference between statelessness and slavery cannot be understood in terms of the dichotomy between having and not having status in a political community. What matters for freedom is what kind of status in what kind of political community.

3) Superfluousness vs. being used a means

The liberty-slavery theme in Pettit implies that domination and compromising others' freedom is the product of self-interest and partiality and that the misfortune of the unfree is similar to being someone's else's property, that is, being exploited and being used as a means. Arendt's description of the stateless and of how the Jews and others were made superfluous under totalitarianism suggests, by contrast, that deprivation of freedom might be unconnected to self-interest and to some using others for their own ends. Rather, unfreedom is not to be seen and heard, not sharing a world with others. This difference has implications for the respective positive specifications of freedom that we might reach, beginning from either slavery or statelessness. In one, a central issue for freedom is whether one's interests are neglected or not; in the other, the more fundamental issue for freedom is the possibility of acting among others in a shared world. This contrast, as we shall see below, leads to different views of the connection between freedom and democracy, as well as of what kind of democracy is required in order to respect and/or enhance freedom.

While it is true that the stateless discussed by Arendt were not used in the direct material self-interest of particular masters, as slaves are, to regard the Jews as utterly superfluous for the Nazis is misleading. Clearly, depriving the Jews of their rights did have some function for Nazi Germany, for example, as creating the Other of Arian identity. As argued earlier, the stateless is defined in relation to something else, and not only in legal terms, but also in terms of identity. Still, the important insight for our further discussion is that perhaps the issue of being used in the interest of others is not the only or even the most fundamental dimension of unfreedom. To exploit this insight we need to become clearer on what it means to being made superfluous as a human being, than Arendt is. First, is it being made so or being so that constitutes unfreedom? Second, what does it mean to be (or being made) superfluous as a human being? In Kant, being treated as a means implies being treated as someone who does not have ends of one's own, but who exists only for the sake of others' ends. Humanity refers to the rational capacity of setting ends for oneself (Kant, 1996, pp. 74cc).

Arendt must mean something else. Here we must, I think, bring in her notion of natality, the human capacity to insert oneself in the human world through words and deeds. Arendt (1979, pp. 438, 454c) describes the stateless as being deprived of their humanity by being deprived of the capacity to begin. The capacity to begin belongs to all of life not merely to action, but "action has the closest connection with the human condition of natality" (Arendt, 1958, p. 9; see also Arendt, 1979, p. 438). It seems that being denied the right to act politically does not entirely undermine the human capacity to begin something new; only the more radical being made superfluous does so. The ability to begin is more fundamental than the ability to have ends of one's own, because it entails becoming somebody and being acknowledged as somebody who is welcome in a human community (cf. Markell, 2003, p. 180). The capacity to begin, then, requires in the first instance a human community that welcomes one as a member. It is this particular status of being welcome that the stateless lack. The slave is not a full member but also not entirely unwelcome; only those who are regarded as superfluous are not welcome at all.

FREEDOM, POLITICS, AND DEMOCRACY

I have suggested that to understand freedom properly we need a positive dimension beyond and in addition to security against arbitrary interference. This point leads us to a discussion of the relationship between freedom and politics, and in particular freedom and democracy. Now, one may think that the positive dimension of freedom that I am urging is the Rousseauian idea that in order to be free one must be the author of the laws to which one is subject. This is how we have learned to understand positive liberty by Isaiah Berlin (1969). Pettit (1997, pp. 8, 27cc) – and before him Quentin Skinner (1983; 1991, p. 202; 1998; 2002) – has argued that republican liberty is not a positive conception in this sense; a point I shall not challenge here, since I am concerned with a different possibility. Arendt, however, might because of her critique of liberalism and negative liberty be seen as advocating a positive conception of freedom. But if she does so, it is not freedom in the sense of Rousseauian popular sovereignty (Canovan, 1992, p. 212). Rousseau represents for Arendt, just as much as liberalism does, a wrongheaded tradition that regards politics in terms of sovereignty and ruling (Rostbøll, 2006, p. 308; 2010, pp. 32cc). Thus, neither Arendt nor Pettit hold a positive conception of freedom *in the sense of collective self-rule*, nor is that the positive dimension of freedom that I shall explore below.

Another way of regarding the relationship between democracy and freedom is to ask whether democracy is intrinsic to freedom or whether it is instrumental to freedom. To say that the relationship between democracy and freedom is an intrinsic one is to hold that democracy is an inherent part of freedom, and that freedom is not merely an external consequence of democratic decision making. On the intrinsic argument there is something in democracy that makes us free. By participating in (or perhaps by having the opportunity to participate in) democratic politics, citizens are free. To say that democracy is instrumental to freedom is to hold that the value of democracy in relationship to freedom is that of a means that furthers a valuable end. In the instrumental justification, democracy has no value in itself but only the value it derives from being a means to freedom. Now, it seems that the intrinsic argument gives a stronger foundation to democracy than the instrumental one, because the first gives democracy unconditional value while the instrumental connection, by its nature, is a contingent and conditional one.

How can we place the republican conception of freedom in relation to the distinction drawn in the previous paragraph? Pettit explicitly denies that the relationship between democracy and freedom is intrinsic and notes that the importance of democratic control comes "from the fact that it is a means of furthering liberty" (1997, p. 30, emphasis added). Still, Pettit thinks Berlin's famous conclusion that there is no necessary connection between freedom and democracy exhibits a shortcoming of freedom as non-interference (Berlin, 1969, p. 130; Pettit, 1999, pp. 168cc). While Berlin notes that democracies might be better at protecting freedom (as non-interference) than non-democracies, he sees this as a contingent matter. Pettit, in opposition to Berlin, wants to show that democratized states represent a lesser assault on republican freedom than non-democratic ones, and not just contingently but "just in virtue of being democratized" (1999, p. 163). His aim is to show that coercive law and government is not necessarily the enemy of liberty, and that democratization is what is required for law and government not to be dominating or hostile to freedom. What is noteworthy in Pettit's republicanism is the attempt to show such a relationship between freedom and democracy without appealing to the intrinsic value of democratic participation or to the idea that a law given by the people cannot dominate the people. Pettit's position, then, seems to be that the relationship between democracy and freedom is instrumental but nonetheless robust (Rostbøll, 2014).

Let us look at why Pettit thinks the relationship between democracy and freedom is robust (yet not intrinsic). Recall that for Pettit freedom is not defined as absence of interference but rather as non-domination. This means, according to Pettit, not only that there can be domination without interference (as in the case of the non-interfering master), but also that there can be interference without domination. The decisive question is whether the interference is arbitrary or not. What democratic governments do, according to Pettit, is to substitute one form of interference with a completely different kind. And, "interference occurs without the loss of liberty when the interference is not arbitrary and does not represent a form of domination" (Pettit, 1997, p. 35). Interference is non-arbitrary when it is "designed to track people's interests according to their ideas" (Pettit, 1997, p. 149), or more precisely, "to the extent that it is forced to track people's common avowable interests" (Pettit, 2001, p. 139; cf. 1999, p. 176). Thus, democracy is robustly connected to freedom, in Pettit's view, because it is a form of government that is designed and forced to track people's interests as they see them and to interfere exclusively on that basis.

One may ask here whether the emphasis showing the robust relationship consist in that democracy is designed to track people's interests or rather in the idea that democracy is designed to track people's interests. The first possibility entails an outcome based view of democracy that is susceptible to the criticism that democracies cannot provide an infallible method for making non-arbitrary decisions that track and track only common avowable interests (Bellamy, 2008, pp. 164cc). The second possibility has the tendency to turn the view into an intrinsic one. If what makes democracy valuable is that it is designed to treat everyone's interests equally, its value comes not from the fact that democratic decisions actually do so, but rather from the equal status afforded everyone in the democratic process. I believe the latter argument would be the stronger one, but Pettit has excluded himself from endorsing this view because of his rejection of any intrinsic justification of democracy. He fails to see that there are other intrinsic justifications of democracy than Rousseauian and perfectionist ones, the first involving collective self-rule and the latter relying on political participation being the highest form of life.

It is an assumption of Pettit's view of the relationship between democracy and freedom that the core (and only) complaint one can have against one's oppressors or the government is that one's interests are not tracked. He follows the classical view, which has its roots in Aristotle (1992, 1279a22-b10), that deviated forms of government are characterized by the rulers governing in their own as opposed to the common interest. Arendt (1979, pp. 460cc), in contrast, believes that 20th century totalitarianism exploded this distinction between arbitrary and legitimate government because the leaders of the totalitarian movements did not rule in their own interest. She emphasizes over and again that the horrors of totalitarianism cannot be understood in terms of treating others as means or exploiting them for one's own ends. This is relevant for understanding Arendt's alternative view of the relationship between democracy and freedom. To be excluded from a place in the human world and from political participation entails a different and more fundamental unfreedom than one's interests not being tracked and incorporated in political decisions. What exactly this unfreedom consist in and why it is an unfreedom is complicated, but it has to do with the lack of possibility to speak and act, to be heard and seen. And clearly it is actively engaging in these activities, and being responded to when one does so – rather than any consequences that may accrue from this – that is of value and necessary for freedom.

To be heard and seen is related to the capacity to become somebody, to natality or the capacity to begin. In *The Human Condition*, Arendt writes that beginning "is not the beginning of something but of somebody, who is a beginner himself" (1958, p. 177). The ability to begin is a precondition of becoming somebody, of gaining individuality and having and attaining status. When someone begins, she distinguishes herself "instead of being merely distinct" (Arendt, 1958, p. 176). The beginner is not merely ascribed an identity by others but shows in word and deed, by her own initiative, who she is. This possibility of becoming somebody, which the stateless lacked, is prior to and existentially more fundamental than having interests or ends. Becoming somebody is a precondition of having ends at all. Having one's interests tracked in Pettit's sense is also not sufficient for becoming somebody, for in that case one is only a "what," someone who has interests that she shares with many others, and not a "who," which distinguishes her from "anyone else who ever lived, lives, or will live" (Arendt, 1958, p. 8).

Which view of the relationship between democracy and freedom is implied by Arendt's view as outlined above? And what kind of democracy is required for freedom in this view? Freedom entails, as we just saw, becoming somebody, becoming a distinct individual. The stateless, the person outside politics, according to Arendt (1979, p. 302), is "other," but since he is "without a citizenship, without an opinion, without a deed by which to identify and specify himself," he is merely "different in general, representing nothing but his own absolute unique individuality which, deprived of expression within and action upon a common world, loses all significance." What is it, then, that democratic politics does for freedom? It organizes and guarantees a common public space in which people can meet each other, a space "into which each of the free men [can] insert himself by word and deed" (Arendt 1993, p. 148). This helps explain why the value of democracy for Arendt lies in participation, rather than in interest representation. For Arendt (1990, p. 235, pp. 268c) "expressing, discussing, and deciding" are "in a positive sense [...] the activities of freedom," while having one's interests represented through voting is not.

We are now able to see the contours of a core difference between Pettit's and Arendt's view of the relation between democracy and freedom. The difference can be understood in terms of a distinction between control and involvement suggested by Patchen Markell (2008, p. 12). When Pettit says that democracy is robustly connected to freedom, because democracy secures that political decisions track common interests, this is a matter of politics being controlled by citizens' common interests. When the question of the relationship between political power and freedom is phrased as a matter of involvement, the question is: "whatever it is that's happening, and, however it's being controlled, to what extent is it happening through you, through your activity" (Markell, 2008, p. 12). Now, sometimes control and involvement go hand in hand, but it is also possible that "the mechanisms that guard against arbitrariness and subject decisions to control [...] displace involvement" (Markell, 2008, p. 12). While the latter possibility falls out of view (or is not regretted) in Pettit and explains his rather minimalist view of democracy, the issue of involvement is fundamental in Arendt and explains her criticism of representative democracy as "oligarchic" (Arendt, 1990, p. 269).

In Arendt there are two strands of thought – perhaps two positive dimensions of freedom – that goes further than Pettit's account of freedom as non-domination: one concerns membership, and the other political participation. One may argue that Arendt does not sufficiently distinguish the value of being a member of a political community and the value of active involvement in politics. Actually there are two issues here. First, it is unclear whether the value in both cases is merely instrumental (being a means to secure life and liberty) or intrinsic (valuable in itself, as an expression and the essence of freedom). Second, if there is intrinsic value in being a member of a human community, can this be enjoyed only as an active participant in politics? The latter is a controversial view, which seems to exclude the possibility that most people find more fulfillment in the private sphere than in politics. While it is possible to find places in Arendt's writings that commit her to the latter view, I think this objection fails to see the force of her position. Even if most people "would rather cultivate their garden than the common good" (Bellamy, 2008, p. 162), it doesn't follow that having the status of someone's whose actions and opinions are responded to is not intrinsically valuable and part of what freedom means. It might be that this status is not exclusive to politics, but understanding (political) action as Arendt does in The Human Condition helps us understand its distinctiveness and value. Arendt's celebration of political involvement should be seen as the sharpest possible contrast to being stateless, and her point might be that if we don't understand the value of political action, we may not understand the value of being a member of a political community, and therefore may not understand what freedom means and requires (Arendt, 1993, p. 148).

Now, it is an important objection to intrinsic and noninstrumental justifications of democracy that they cannot on their own explain the importance of democratic procedures, for this we need also some idea of which procedures make for epistemically good decisions (Estlund, 2008, ch. 4 & 5). With regard to Arendt's position the problem is that the intrinsic value of political participation might be a mere by-product of aiming at substantial outcomes; political participation requires an instrumental aim to be valuable (Elster, 1997, pp. 19cc). The intrinsic value of political participation is conditional upon its instrumental value. But this does not mean that the noninstrumental value of democracy has no weight of its own. As Elizabeth Anderson (2009, p. 225) has pointed out:

"The proper test of the noninstrumental goodness of an activity is not whether we'd prefer to do it, even if it didn't result in desirable consequences. It is rather whether we'd still prefer to engage in it, even if the same consequences could be brought about by other (passive) means."

Of course, Arendt does not think that the value of belonging to a political community could be achieved by other means, but she goes too far in ignoring the instrumental dimension of democratic politics (Habermas, 1985). Here Pettit's idea that democratic procedures must be designed to track common interests comes into its own. It is an important part of the justification of democracy that it has instrumental value in tending to making non-arbitrary decisions that promote the interests of everyone equally. The dialogue between Pettit and Arendt, thus, points to the need to combine intrinsic and instrumental justifications of democracy.

Conclusion

Arendt's understanding of the experience of the stateless highlights what it means to "lack common liberty held with others" (Bohman, 2008, p. 206) in a way that Pettit's use of the slave metaphor and his conceptualization of non-domination as security against arbitrary interference does not. This difference has implications also for their view of the *raison d'être* of democratic politics, which for Pettit is to secure that interference is non-dominating by tracking common avowable interests, while it for Arendt is to secure the conditions of acting together in common liberty, creating a world where everyone can become somebody by her own initiative. Thus, Pettit's concern for exploitation and control can be traced back to the liberty-slavery theme, while Arendt's concern for involvement can be seen in light of her discussion of totalitarianism and statelessness. The argument of this chapter is that while both the use of the slave metaphor and the description of statelessness are suggestive and lead to valuable insights, they also result in blind spots in Pettit's and Arendt's respective understandings of democracy and freedom and their relationship. Neither the exploitation of the slave, nor the superfluousness of the stateless can stand alone as freedom's other.

The dialogue between Arendt and Pettit has helped us approach an understanding of which positive dimensions republican freedom has and does not have. I have argued that there is a further positive dimension to freedom than mere security against arbitrary interference. The additional positive dimension is the capacity to become somebody by inserting oneself in a common world, which is responsive to one's opinions and actions – and not merely to one's interests. This argument has implication for how we should view the relationship between democracy and freedom. I have suggested some distinctions that make new possibilities apparent, for example, that one can regard democracy as robustly connected to freedom without seeing the connection as intrinsic, and that one can be committed to an intrinsic justification of democracy without this relying on a Rousseauian idea of collective self-rule or on the idea that political participation is the only truly good life. In the end, I argued for (what we might call) a dual justification of democracy and freedom that includes both intrinsic and instrumental concerns. Democracy is valuable both because it affords everyone the possibility of becoming somebody and holding common liberty with others, and because it has the instrumental value of protecting citizens against arbitrary decisions and domination. And, it should be emphasized, the value of holding common liberty with others goes beyond being a means to ensuring that one's avowable interests are tracked on an equal footing with others' interests. We would and should, I propose, still prefer being active members of political communities that welcome and are responsive to our actions and opinions, even if nonarbitrary decision making could be secured by other means.

REFERENCES

Anderson, E. (2009). Democracy: Instrumental vs. Non-Instrumental Value. In T. Christiano & J. Christman (Eds.), *Contemporary debates in political philosophy* (pp. 213-227). Malden, MA: Wiley-Blackwell.
Arendt, H. (1958). *The Human Condition* (2nd ed. 1998). Chicago, IL: Chicago University Press.
Arendt, H. (1979). *The Origins of Totalitarianism.* (New ed. with added prefaces). New York, NY: Harcourt Brace Company.
Arendt, H. (1990). *On Revolution.* Harmondsworth: Penguin Books.
Arendt, H. (1993). What is Freedom? In *Between Past and Future: Eight Exercises in Political Thought* (pp. 143-172). Harmondsworth: Penguin Books.
Arendt, H. & K. Jaspers (1992). *Hannah Arendt, Karl Jaspers: Correspondence 1926-1969* (ed. L. Kohler & H. Saner). New York, NY: Harcourt Brace.
Aristotle. (1992). *The Politics* (trans. by T.A. Sinclair, revised by T.J. Saunders). Harmondsworth: Penguin.
Bellamy, R. (2008). Republicanism, Democracy, and Constitutionalism. In C. Laborde & J. Maynor (Eds.), *Republicanism and Political Theory* (pp. 159-189). Oxford: Blackwell Publishing.
Berlin, I. (1969). Two Concepts of Liberty. In *Four Essays on Liberty* (pp. 118-172). Oxford: Oxford University Press.
Bohman, J. (2008). Nondomination and Transnational Democracy. In C. Laborde & J. Maynor (Eds.), *Republicanism and Political Theory* (pp. 190-216). Oxford: Blackwell Publishing.
Canovan, M. (1992). *Hannah Arendt: A Reinterpretation of Her Political Thought.* Cambridge: Cambridge University Press.
Elster, J. (1997). The Market and the Forum: Three Varieties of Political Theory. In J. Bohman & W. Rehg (Ed.), *Deliberative Democracy: Essays on Reason and Politics* (pp. 3-33). Cambridge, MA: MIT Press.
Estlund, D.M. (2008). *Democratic Authority: A Philosophical Framework.* Princeton, NJ: Princeton University Press.
Habermas, J. (1985). Hannah Arendt: On the Concept of Power. In *Philosophical-Political Profiles* (pp. 173-190). Cambridge, MA: MIT Press.
Hansen, M.H. (1999). *The Athenian Democracy in the Age of Demosthenes.* Norman: University of Oklahoma Press.

Immanuel, K. (1996). Religion Within the Boundaries of Mere Reason. In A. Wood & G.D. Giovanni (Eds./trans.), *Religion and Rational Theology*. New York, NY: Cambridge University Press.
Markell, P. (2003). *Bound by Recognition*. Princeton, NJ: Princeton University Press.
Markell, P. (2008). The Insufficiency of Non-Domination. *Political Theory, 36* (1), 9-36.
Pettit, P. (1997). *Republicanism: A Theory of Freedom and Government*. Oxford, NY: Oxford University Press.
Pettit, P. (1999). Republican Freedom and Contestatory Democratization. In I. Shapiro & C. Hacker-Cordón (Eds.), *Democracy's Value* (pp. 163-190). Cambridge: Cambridge University Press.
Pettit, P. (2001). *A Theory of Freedom: From the Psychology to the Politics of Agency*. New York, NY: Oxford University Press.
Pettit, P. (2008). Republican Freedom: Three Axioms, Four Theorems. In C. Laborde & J. Maynor (Eds.), *Republicanism and Political Theory* (pp. 102-130). Oxford: Blackwell Publishing.
Pettit, P. (2010). A Republican Law of Peoples. *European Journal of Political Theory, 9* (1), 70-94.
Rostbøll, C.F. (2006). Hannah Arendt: Magt som handling i fællesskab. In C.B. Laustsen & J. Myrup (Eds.), *Magtens tænkere* (pp. 293-314). Frederiksberg: Roskilde Universitetsforlag.
Rostbøll, C.F. (2008). *Deliberative Freedom: Deliberative Democracy as Critical Theory*. Albany, NY: State University of New York Press.
Rostbøll, C.F. (2010). *Hannah Arendt*. Copenhagen: Jurist- og Økonomforbundets Forlag.
Rostbøll, C.F. (2014). Nondomination and Democratic Legitimacy. *Critical Review of International Social and Political Philosophy*, special issue on "Freedom and Domination" (forthcoming).
Skinner, Q. (1983). Machiavelli on the Maintenance of Liberty. *Politics, 18*, 3-15.
Skinner, Q. (1991). The Paradoxes of Political Liberty. In D. Miller (Ed.), *Liberty* (pp. 183-205). New York, NY: Oxford University Press.
Skinner, Q. (1998). *Liberty Before Liberalism*. Cambridge: Cambridge University Press.
Skinner, Q. (2002). A Third Concept of Liberty. *Proceedings of the British Academy 117*, 237-268.

Freedom as Non-Arbitrariness or as Democratic Self-Rule?
A Critique of Contemporary Republicanism*

ROBIN CELIKATES

Most republicans share the general view that there is a link between the freedom of citizens and their participation in the self-government of the community of which they are members. How this link is to be conceived, however, remains subject to dispute, and it is this question which I will discuss in what follows. The argument proceeds in four steps. I will start with a quick reminder of the neo-republican argument for the introduction of a third concept of freedom, viz. freedom as non-domination (I). I will then sketch a defence of this argument against a recent criticism raised by the proponents of the so-called theory of pure negative freedom who claim that what counts is actual (and potential) interference, not the mere fact of domination (II). In the third part I will raise a different objection against the neo-republican position as it is elaborated by one of its most prominent representatives, Philip Pettit (III), and I will end by suggesting the superiority of another, more democratic variety of republicanism (IV). In a nutshell, my claim will be that while neo-republicanism brings into view a form of unfreedom ignored by liberal thinkers, especially in the variant put forth by Pettit, it fails to sufficiently take into account a specifically political form of unfreedom due to its problematic, and surprisingly liberal-constitutionalist, understanding of the link between freedom and democracy. On the one hand, neo-republicans supply us with a radical revision of the concept of freedom, but on

---

* I have presented material used in this article at conferences and colloquia in Bonn, Frankfurt/M., Copenhagen, Medellín, Jena, and Flensburg and would like to thank participants in these events for their comments.

the other hand they tend not to be radical enough when it comes to the link between freedom and participation.

A THIRD CONCEPT OF FREEDOM

Under what conditions can we regard ourselves as politically free? What (if any) link is there between freedom and democratic participation? There seem to be three possible answers to this question which allow us to (admittedly, in a very crude way) structure the theoretical landscape: i) There is no link: Being free is neither necessarily nor contingently related to (the possibility of) democratic participation. ii) There is a contingent and external link: (The possibility of) Democratic participation can, under certain circumstances, be a facilitative condition of being free. iii) There is a necessary and internal link: (The possibility of) Democratic participation is a necessary and/or constitutive condition of being free.

Proponents of classical liberalism usually hold thesis i) or ii). Here are just two famous quotes from the many possible examples from authors who favour the negative understanding of freedom as the absence of interference (while many egalitarian liberals, following Rawls, obviously subscribe to a much richer notion of freedom). The first is from Hobbes (1997, ch. XXI, p. 149): "There is written on the Turrets of the city of *Luca* in great characters at this day, the word *LIBERTAS*; yet no man can thence inferre, that a particular man has more Libertie, or Immunitie from the service of the Commonwealth there, than in *Constantinople*. Whether a Common-wealth be Monarchicall, or Popular, the Freedome is still the same." The second is from Isaiah Berlin (1969, pp. 129-130): "It is perfectly conceivable that a liberal-minded despot would allow his subjects a large measure of personal freedom. [...] Freedom in this sense is not, at any rate logically, connected with democracy or self-government."[1] With this understanding, we can regard ourselves as free to the extent that the state respects our rights and does not interfere with our private sphere – and whether this is the case remains independent from the democratic credentials of the state in question. Berlin's statement, however, already opens the door to an instrumentalist understanding of the link between freedom and democratic participation, but this

---

1   Skinner (2008a) argues that Hobbes' position should be understood as an ideological intervention aimed at discrediting the "democratic gentlemen", i.e. the pro-parliamentary critics of monarchy; Tully (2013) argues that we should understand Berlin's influential article in a similar way, namely as an attempt to discredit the "democratic gentlemen" of his day.

contingent link may be rather weak and of no great theoretical or political significance.

Proponents of republicanism usually hold thesis ii) or iii) and I will argue that what kind of republican one is depends on which of these options one subscribes to – what we can call constitutionalist republicans tend to hold ii), while democratic republicans hold iii).[2]

If freedom is understood as the absence of domination, as in Pettit's influential development of this 'third concept' of freedom, the nature of the link between freedom and participation obviously depends on the concrete understanding of non-domination.[3] For the sake of brevity, Pettit's view can be characterized by two core theses (for the latest statement of these see Pettit, 2012, ch. 1.3.-4.). According to the first, unfreedom as dependence and domination can exist in the absence of interference. This can be illustrated by the example of the 'lucky' (n.b.: not 'happy') slave and the non-interfering master: Even if the master is very lazy, or inattentive, or benign and does not interfere much with how his slaves lead their lives, they are still depending on his arbitrary will and can therefore not be regarded as free in any meaningful sense. According to the second thesis, interference does not necessarily amount to domination, and can thus be compatible with freedom. This can be illustrated by the example of the rule of law: Proper laws interfere with the individual's actions but do not dominate it and are thus compatible with its freedom.

Freedom is thus still construed negatively, as an absence – not as the absence of interference, however, but as the absence of domination. Correspondingly, unfreedom does not coincide with interference since there can be both domination (and thus unfreedom) without interference as well as interference without domination (and thus without unfreedom). In opposition to the understanding put forth by Hobbes and Berlin, freedom thus understood is dependent on the type of political system one is living in – it matters greatly whether one lives in Lucca or

---

2   This distinction overlaps but is not identical with the one made by Pettit (2012, pp. 11-18) between the Italian-Atlantic and the Rousseauvian tradition that he characterizes as communitarian and that focuses on freedom as participation rather than non-domination.

3   In what follows, I mainly discuss and criticize Pettit's proposal, which in great detail spells out the consequences of the neo-republican position for democratic theory. Occasionally I also refer to Skinner's work, which is of course equally influential in the neo-republican debate, and seems to avoid some of the problems I will raise with regard to Pettit's position. For some of the differences, which I will not be able to go into in any detail on, see Pettit 2002.

in Constantinople. In this the neo-republicans follow the lead of James Harrington (1992, p. 20) who has replied to Hobbes's quip with the observation that in Constantinople "even the greatest bashaw is merely a tenant of his head, liable to lose it as soon as he speaks or acts in such a way as to cause the sultan offence."

Let us now examine the two core theses in turn. There are two kinds of argument republicans put forth to support the first core thesis. The first kind is psychological: Those who live in conditions of domination (or dependence) tend to pre-emptively adapt to the anticipated reactions of those they depend on and engage in acts of practical self-censorship with the aim of avoiding future interference. As Skinner (2002, pp. 256-257; see also Skinner, 1997, pp. 92-95) notes: "[A] mere awareness of living in dependence on the goodwill of an arbitrary ruler *does* serve in itself to restrict our options and thereby limit our liberty. The effect is to dispose us to make and avoid certain choices, and is thus to place clear constraints on our freedom of action, even though our ruler may never interfere with our activities or even show the least sign of threatening to interfere with them." To pick just one from numerous contemporary examples, in 2010 the German constitutional court (1 BvR 256/08) ruled that a law was unconstitutional that required the monitoring and documentation of communication via phone and email. The defenders of the law argued that law-abiding citizens, in contrast to terrorists and other criminals, have nothing to worry about and would of course not be restricted in their freedom. As empirical surveys have shown, however, a majority of people said that they would refrain from using phone or email to contact psychotherapists or drug help agencies if the new law became effective. Using proto-republican terminology, the court ruled that already "the diffusely threatening feeling of being under surveillance" was incompatible with the basic liberties protected by the constitution, even in the absence of concrete interference (see the court's press release 11/2010).

It is, however, questionable whether this kind of psychological mediation – the psychological fact of being aware of one's dependence on the arbitrary will of others – is really essential for existing forms of domination to count as forms of unfreedom. According to the republican position, it seems that even slaves who are not only lucky but also naïve and unaware of their slavery are nevertheless slaves and thus unfree. It is the mere fact of domination that counts, not the awareness of this fact and the behaviour that results from it. Why this is so can be seen from the following conceptual explication of the first thesis which goes beyond the psychological argument supporting it: Freedom is not just predicated on individual actions, it is – essentially – a status that can be ascribed to a person depending on her standing in relation to other persons, and that can come in degrees depending on both the intensity and extension of non-domination.[4] This status is incompatible with the mere fact of domination, independently of any psychological considerations. As Pettit (2007, p. 715) explains, for actions to count as free they must meet two conditions:

"First, they must be unobstructed; second, they must be unobstructed in virtue of the status enjoyed by the person. Choices that are unobstructed for purely contingent reasons, not because of the status of the agent, will count as unfree. The choice of a free person that is frustrated by a contingent crime will not be free; nor will the choice of the unfree person – in the limit case, the slave – even when that person manages to do as he or she wishes."

As we saw, Pettit's second core thesis holds that interference does not necessarily amount to domination and is, under certain conditions, compatible with freedom. This is so because being dominated means being subject to arbitrary power. And from this it follows that if the interference is non-arbitrary (or uncontrolled, as Pettit (2012, p. 58) now says), it does not dominate me and thus leaves my freedom intact. Now, for Pettit, interference has to meet two conditions in order to count as non-arbitrary. The first condition is procedural: The interference has to be the result of rule-governed procedures that minimize or exclude the influence of the arbitrary will of others. The second condition is substantial: The interference has to track the (qualified[5]) interests and opinions of those affected, and the claim that it does this has to be controllable and contestable by those affected (this gives the substantial condition a procedural twist). According to Pettit, these conditions are supposed to hold under the rule

---

4 See Pettit 2007 as well as Pettit 1997, p. 75: "People will enjoy more and more non-domination both as dominators come to dominate them less intensely and as they come to dominate them across a smaller extent." On freedom as status, see also Skinner 2010, p. 98: "*It is possible to act freely*, they [the republicans] maintain, *if and only if you are a freeman*. If instead you live as a slave, you can never act as a free agent under any circumstances. This is not necessarily because your choices and actions will be impeded, but rather because they will never be the product of your own autonomous will. They will inevitably be a product both of what you will and desire and of what your *dominus* may be willing to permit."

5 Pettit uses a variety of formulations here, ranging from "interests" via "avowed interests" to "common avowable interests" – i.e. from de facto to somehow normatively qualified interests. See Pettit 1999, p. 176: "They are the interests that those who are expected to give a system of government their allegiance may reasonably expect government to track."

of law (so imprisonment will, under these conditions, not constitute domination and accordingly not make the imprisoned unfree, although it will make them "non-free"[6]).

Before turning to the discussion of this second thesis, and to my worry that it leads to a constitutionalist rather than to a democratic version of republicanism which misconstrues the link between freedom and democracy, I will address a critique of the first thesis that freedom consists in the absence of domination which has been put forth by the defenders of a more liberal, or libertarian, negative conception of freedom.

POSSIBILITY, NOT PROBABILITY

The radical and distinctive character of the neo-republican proposal becomes evident in an exchange in which Skinner and Pettit have been criticized from the perspective of the so-called theory of pure negative freedom presented by Carter (2008) and Kramer (2008). According to this theory, what counts when we are interested in freedom is actual and potential interference and not the mere fact of domination. It is the *probability* and not the mere *possibility* of interference that is of theoretical and normative significance. On this probabilistic view, "where A's mere opportunity to exercise power has some degree of probability of being exercised, then B's unfreedom [recte: freedom] is to that same degree limited" (Carter, 2008, p. 70). If, in contrast, after a reliable probabilistic assessment, a slave comes to the conclusion that he can act in a certain way without being interfered with, he is thus free to act accordingly. Put in other words, freedom is, as in Hobbes, a matter of the options I have; but whereas Hobbes thought that the robber, who, by pointing a gun at me, confronts me with the choice 'your money or your life', still leaves me both options (although the costs of accepting one of them are extremely high) and thus does not take away my freedom, according to Kramer and Carter the robber does take away an important option, namely the conjunctive option of keeping my life and my money, and thus it is already his threat (and not only its being carried out) that, if credible, limits my freedom. In assessing the extent of our freedom, probability thus plays a crucial role. This

---

6   See Pettit 2002. With regard to this, Kramer (2003, p. 102) remarks: "Consequently, if the placement of a highly dangerous man in chains or a straitjacket is legitimate because of his uncontrollably violent behaviour, neither of those means of immobilization will deprive him of any liberties. A theory that generates such a conclusion can hardly claim to be cogently illuminating."

also holds for the law which closes off the option to both violate the law and continue to act in ways that will be made impossible by the law's sanctions (e.g. by imprisonment). In cases like these, interference consists in "the undoing of the conjunctive exercisability of many opportunities – opportunities that could have been exercised conjunctively in the absence of the dominant party's sway" (Kramer, 2008, p. 44; see also Kramer, 2003, p. 39). Thus, in order to speak of a restriction of one's "overall negative freedom" there does not have to be an actual interference, since a credible threat is sufficient. The focus will therefore turn on how credible the threat and how probable the threatened interference is. Pointing to the mere fact of domination is not informative. What matters is the likelihood with which this fact will lead to the closing down of certain options or combinations of options.

What can the republicans answer to this challenge? It seems that first of all, following Skinner and Pettit, they should insist that slaves are unfree regardless of the probability with which their masters will interfere. As Skinner (2008b, pp. 88-89) notes: "It is the mere fact that their [the slaves'] master or ruler has arbitrary powers to intervene that takes away their liberty, not any particular degree of probability that these powers will ever be exercised." Pettit (2008) makes a similar point when he speaks of "alien control" the mere fact of which, and not the probability with which it leads to interference, is incompatible with freedom as non-domination. According to the republicans, the pure negative conception of freedom simply misunderstands the existential situation of the slave and ignores that freedom is a question of the status of the agent, and not (or rather: only secondarily) of their sets of options.

Take an example that came up in this debate and imagine that there is a gentle giant who is reliably disposed against using his immense power and who lives peacefully among his fellow human villagers. According to Carter and Kramer the giant's neighbours can sleep without having to worry – so why should they be seen as dominated and thus as unfree? To this, Skinner (2008b, p. 97) replies: "If it is true, as he [Kramer] claims at one stage, that there is *no prospect* of the giant's interfering – if this has somehow been rendered impossible – then [...] the community is wholly free, for it is wholly free of the giant's arbitrary power. If on the other hand the freedom of the community remains dependent, as Kramer says at another stage, on the *disposition* and *inclinations* of the giant, then a republican will want to insist that the community is wholly enslaved. If the giant *could* interfere at will and with impunity, then the community remains in his power; and the essence of the republican argument is that living in such a state of subjection is equivalent to living in servitude."

In order to be free it is therefore not enough to make this sort of dominating interference unlikely, its possibility has to be ruled out: "The point is not just to make arbitrary interference improbable; the point is to make it inaccessible" (Pettit, 1997, p. 74). However, this obviously raises a new problem, namely the realistic worry about how this could ever be achieved: Isn't the minimization of the probability of dominating interference the only thing we can reasonably expect to achieve (see Friedman, 2008; Kramer, 2003, pp. 138-139)? The neo-republican position seems to imply a fantastic notion of freedom that is difficult to reconcile with our ordinary understanding of social relationships. This challenge, however, need not worry neo-republicans too much: They can hold on to the (negative) claim that certain forms of dependence that are irreducible to actual or probable interference are cases of unfreedom – the dependence of employees on the arbitrary will of employers and of women on the arbitrary will of their husbands are paradigmatic examples – without subscribing to the unrealistic ideal of a state of perfect freedom. Such a state in which the possibility of dependencies of this sort would be ruled out once and for all is, indeed, hardly imaginable. Although it might be the case that all we can do is reduce the probability with which agents can get into a position that allows them to dominate others, the existence of certain positions of this type – the slave-holder, the colonial master, the tyrannical husband and employer – is incompatible with the freedom of those subject to such forms of dependence because it is incompatible with their status as free citizens.

NON-ARBITRARINESS AND DEMOCRATIC SELF-RULE

After having sketched a defence of the first core thesis associated with the neo-republican concept of freedom as non-domination as spelled out by Pettit, I now move on to the second thesis and a different kind of critique. As we saw, according to the second thesis, freedom requires the absence of the possibility of arbitrary interference. We also saw that there are two conditions for non-arbitrariness, one procedural and one substantial. Correspondingly, an interference is arbitrary, if it depends on the will of an individual or specific individuals and does not track the interests and opinions of those subject to the interference. This means that it is not dependence as such that is the problem but dependence on the *arbitrary* will of someone else (or *arbitrary* dependence on the will of someone else). Arbitrariness thus becomes the central concern, and this concern also guides the search for institutional remedies that aim at preventing such forms of dependence from arising.

It seems to follow from this that I am not unfree if the norms I am subjected to are not the result of a political process in which I was able to participate as long as they are the result of a process that minimizes or excludes the influence of the arbitrary will of others and that tracks my (considered) interests and opinions in a way that is controllable and contestable. As Pettit (1997, p. 184, my emphasis) himself puts it:

"The promotion of freedom as non-domination requires, therefore, that something be done to ensure that public decision-making tracks the interests and the ideas of those citizens whom it affects; after all, non-arbitrariness is *guaranteed* by *nothing more or less* than the existence of such a tracking relationship. The decision-making must not represent an imposition of their will on us, as the citizens are likely to think about the matter. It must be a form of decision-making which we can own and identify with: a form of decision-making *in which we can see our interests furthered and our ideas respected.*"

Pettit thus seems to assume that there is no intrinsic relation between the genesis and the validity of a norm beyond the demand that the procedure reduce the influence of the arbitrary will of others on the norm that is its result. In this framework, the tracking of interests and the possibility of *ex-post* contestation take the place of *ex-ante* participation – i.e. participation in the process of norm-making itself.

On this basis it is not difficult to see why Pettit's neo-republicanism is of an essentially liberal-constitutionalist type. Although he understands freedom in terms of a status that is fundamentally relational, he tends to construe this status and its institutional presuppositions and implications in a way that does not adequately account for the strong link between freedom and democratic participation. One might respond that Pettit's idea of control can provide an answer to this worry since it requires that those subject to potential interference are "in control." A closer look, however, reveals that "to be in control" of an interference means, for Pettit, that this interference is guided by one's interests and not by the arbitrary will of others. Without losing its efficacy and its freedom-enhancing role, control can remain purely virtual as long as it can be activated if problems arise from the perspective of those who are virtually in control – or so Pettit claims. Control is virtual insofar as it is not activated: "It involves standing back while some other agency actively controls the process but assuming a disposition to amend what the active controller does, should the outcome not prove satisfactory" (Pettit, 2006, p. 302).

This distinction between active and virtual control is mirrored in his distinction between authorial and editorial control. While an author has active control over the text she is writing, the control exercised by an editor is virtual: She can simply accept the text or reject it, but she also has the authority to make certain editorial changes. Even if she doesn't intervene at all, a good editor can influence how her authors write on account of her reputation as a very critical reader so that they try to anticipate her reactions in a way that renders her actual interference superfluous. This analogy is supposed to suggest that the form of control exercised by the editor is different, yet often equally and sometimes more significant, than the authors' control. Applied to the realm of politics it yields the following picture: While initially "the people [trust] the state to ensure a dispensation of non-arbitrary rule" (Pettit, 1997, p. 8), the citizens have to be watchful and check – presumably via some intermediary structure like a vibrant public sphere – whether the state lives up to the assigned task.[7] If necessary, they can then contest the state's claim of having acted in their common interest. Such a contestation consequently has to trigger a review of the policy or law in question by an impartial, but not necessarily democratic body. The citizens thus exert "editorial control [...] to ensure, ideally, that only matters of common avowable interest have an influence on government" (Pettit 2001, p. 163; see also the discussion of active, virtual, and reserve influence in Pettit 2012, p. 156). Out of fear of public protest and sanctions in form of the loss of electoral support, representatives can be expected to aspire to govern in the way suggested by the criteria for non-arbitrariness: As Pettit (2006, p. 310) puts it, any reasonable government will make an effort "to adjust preemptively [to the interests of the people] in the attempt to keep the public happy."

From a perspective inspired by democratic republicanism, this view must seem surprising in several ways. One is more accustomed to hear the argument that the direct participation of citizens is of no great political significance and that what matters are "apt decisions" from critics of republicanism such as Brennan and Lomasky (2006, pp. 233-234): "[I]t is not at all plausible that more participation in setting policy is better than less. What is important is apt decisions, not the number of people who toss in their (more or less uninformed) opinions concerning how to prioritize these tasks. [...] The knowledge that currently complacent citizens will not inevitably remain so is itself a spur to political actors to moderate their activities in order not to rouse the sleeping giant. In this manner,

---

7   It is noteworthy that Pettit does not provide an extensive account of the role of civil society and the public sphere in his "contestatory democracy," leaving us without a clear idea about the process of democratic will-formation. This lacuna might be due to the utilitarian underpinnings of his theory that surface in his idea that the task of politics is to "track" the interests of those affected.

even the apathetic and disengaged are important political actors, albeit *in potentia*. This suggests that the availability of avenues of access to political participation is more important than participation per se." It is of far greater importance, however, that Pettit subjects a fundamental principle of classical republicanism to a radical revision: In place of the principle that the addressees of a law also have to (be able to) conceive of themselves as its authors we now find the principle that they also have to (be able to) conceive of themselves as its editors. This reformulation points to what tends to get lost here: the very idea of democratic self-rule.[8]

As if this would not sufficiently curtail the power of the *demos*, Pettit (1999, p. 180) goes on to characterize popular editorship as the "limited and, of course, indirect power of editorship" which can be invoked ex post within the envisaged institutional fora of contestation (such as committees and ombudsmen). In a more active manner it is at best exercised in an advocatory way through courts such as the US Supreme Court and its powerful instrument of judicial review. Again, it is worth noting that Pettit's position here is much closer to the liberal-constitutionalist case for judicial review than to a democratic-republican position which seems to provide a rather firm basis for a critique of judicial review (see Waldron 2004 and Waldron 2006). Like the liberal-constitutionalist position, Pettit's position seems to be motivated by a fear of the tyranny of the majority which he at one point even calls "the ultimate form of arbitrariness" (Pettit 1997, p. 8). The institutional response to this risk, however, is in danger of creating and heightening the risk of the opposed danger of a tyranny of a minority – a danger also mentioned but not addressed adequately by Pettit. As Bellamy (2007, p. viii) notes: "Far from guarding against a largely mythical tyranny of the majority, the checks imposed by judicial review on majoritarian decision-making risk undermining political equality, distorting the agenda away from the public interest, and entrenching the privileges of dominant minorities and the domination of unprivileged ones." All of these should obviously be great cause for concern from a republican perspective.

Instead of providing a convincing republican case for judicial review and the kind of limited democracy he envisages, Pettit thus tends to reproduce certain positions advocated by liberal constitutionalists such as Ronald Dworkin (1996) for whom it is primarily the constitution and the institutions that protect it that

---

8   This idea should not be understood to imply a collective self that then rules itself – rather, it implies that the citizens are, collectively, making their own decisions and do not have these decisions made by others.

are able to realize the basic principles of democracy. *Democracy in Robes*, however, is not an ideal to which republicans should light-heartedly subscribe.

Pettit's republicanism seems to suffer from two shortcomings: On the one hand, it truncates the ideal of democracy by reducing participation to the participation in the election of representatives (the only form of authorial control Pettit seems to allow for) and to *ex-post* forms of contestation; on the other hand, it limits these forms of contestation to institutionalized procedures in which individual citizens can voice their protest in very mediated ways. This trust in established institutions and the apparent renunciation of more active forms of participation and more activist forms of contestation (such as civil disobedience; see Celikates, 2014) seems to be due to the assumption that the institutions in question are indeed independent and impartial and thus willing and able to secure the interests of the citizens even in the face of representatives who might be prone to neglect or distort them.[9] One does not have to believe in the "iron law of oligarchy" to remain sceptical in this regard. The whole framework also seems to involve a rather undemocratic shift in the burden of proof as citizens are asked to establish in procedures determined by the state that their interests and opinions have not been adequately represented or translated into political decisions. Given the well-known procedural democratic deficits of even well-functioning representative systems such as agenda setting and framing which are compatible with keeping up the liberal-democratic form, one can doubt whether such a form of contestation is very effective when it happens on the state's terms (see Young, 2001).

GENESIS AND VALIDITY

In accordance with his conception of control which already implies that the government, as the object of control, is an institution that is distinguished from the citizens who have to control it, Pettit understands democracy primarily as a combination of electoral and contestatory elements. On this view, participation and democratic self-rule are neither intrinsically valuable nor do they seem to be essential aspects of being a citizen. The inclusion of participatory and democratic elements – such as the election of representatives – in Pettit's republican framework may, of course, make it more likely that individual freedom is secured,

---

9   Pettit (2012, p.138) now acknowledges that "the act of breaking the law [...] may also count as a mode of contestation, a way of opposing laws within the system", emphasizing, however, that opposition has to be limited to "intra-systemic contestation".

and, to the extent that there is a correlation between how people get power and how they exercise it, the first aspect matters as well. But no intrinsic link between freedom as non-domination and democratic self-rule seems to exist. Democracy is called for as a means for securing non-domination, and it may well be that in certain policy areas it is not very good at that and, perhaps, there are other non-participatory functional equivalents that might do an even better job, as Pettit seems to suggest at times when he urges the depoliticization of certain fundamental questions (i.e. the delegation of decision-making power to expert bodies that are neither democratically elected nor democratically controlled, e.g. to central banks) as a means of increasing the quality of decision making and securing non-domination (see Pettit 2004).[10] Waldron (2007, p. 49) therefore seems to be right when he points out that Pettit tends to regard "participation in lawmaking [a]s an anachronistic hangover from the liberty of the ancients, [...] that is not part and parcel of a useful modern conception of liberty as non-domination".

In this sense Pettit opts for the second interpretation of the relation between freedom and democracy that I initially distinguished: Participation can, under certain circumstances, be a facilitative condition of being free but it is not a necessary or constitutive part of the citizens' freedom. This seemingly leaves open the possibility of a paternalistic power that correctly tracks the enlightened interests of its subjects, envisages fora in which citizens can voice their dissent, and thereby governs non-arbitrarily. A similar point is made by Brennan and Lomasky (2006, p. 241) when they observe: "Republican liberty is compatible with extensive paternalistic control. Because the official requirement is to consider the *interests* of citizens, not their *preferences*, there is no limit to the state's authority to override individuals' preferences, just so long as it is deemed to be in their best interest to be deflected from the desired activity." This might be true of Pettit's constitutionalist brand of republicanism but it is certainly not true of its more democratic variants.

For these reasons the neo-republican view of freedom as non-domination has to be complemented by a more positive, democratic conception of freedom as involving, essentially, the possibility of effective *ex-ante* participation in order to

---

10 See Rostbøll 2008, p. 55: "For Pettit, then, whether or not a policy is arbitrary, and hence whether or not it compromises freedom, is a factual issue that can be determined impartially by a small body of people and, hence, without the participation of the people who are subject to the policy." See also Urbinati 2010. Pettit (2012, p. 235) does acknowledge the potential dangers from unelected authorities but argues they can be checked by contestatory mechanisms.

account for a specific variety of unfreedom that tends to get ignored or at least marginalized in Pettit's framework. Whether a (basic) norm is compatible with the freedom of those subject to it, depends on whether the latter have had (the chance to have) a say in the framing of the norm (and continue to have a say in its continuing application), not on whether they would or could – hypothetically or ex post – give their consent to it. Another way to put this is to say that freedom and democracy have an expressive dimension: Those subject to a norm have to be able to understand the norm as the expression of their own activity *as* citizens, i.e. as a result of their political practice. If this turns out to be impossible, they will rightly regard the norm as alien and externally imposed, not as a realization of their freedom, even if it tracks their interests and even if they can formally contest it afterwards. This is the basis for the claim that there is an internal link between the genesis and the validity of political norms which Habermas (1996, p. 121) spells out as follows, in a way that to some might seem surprisingly radically democratic: "Even if each legal subject realizes, in the role of moral person, that she herself *could* have given herself certain basic rights, this moral approval in hindsight will not do; it by no means eliminates the paternalism of the 'rule of law' characteristic of political heteronomy. It is only *participation* in the practice of politically autonomous lawmaking that makes it possible for the addressees of law to have a correct understanding of the legal order as created by themselves."

Political freedom is thus incompatible with uncoupling the validity of norms from their genesis. Pettit (1997, p. 186) therefore tends to miss the core of the idea of democratic self-rule by understanding it "in a modal rather than a historical way" and by claiming that "the self-ruling demos or people may often run on automatic pilot, allowing public decision-making to materialize under more or less unexamined routines." Especially from a republican perspective, however, it must seem rather unlikely that citizens who "run on automatic pilot" will be able to muster the necessary political energy once they find themselves in a situation in which this would be called for. By being the passive observers of politics, a topos of classical republicanism that Skinner has brought back to our attention insists, they will gradually loose the cognitive and practical capacities as well as the motivational resources necessary for an active citizenry.

Even more worrying than this more pragmatic concern is the incompatibility of the outsourcing of self-determination – the reduction of democratic control to editorial control of norms authored by others – with the status of the citizen as free and equal. As Richardson (2002, p. 71) puts it: "when public decision-making emerges from 'more or less unexamined routines,' something importantly different is going on, namely: the people are being ruled by *someone else*.

Whether one is making one's own decisions or is simply under the sway of another is always an issue pertinent to autonomy, individual or otherwise."

Note that the idea that freedom not only requires non-arbitrariness, but also a link between autonomy and democratic participation as well as self-rule does not imply the (confused) thesis that by participating in democratic decision making I am ipso facto free. If I do not belong to the majority but to a minority in a certain decision, it would be mistaken to say that this was, really, my decision. But it is not confused to say that being able to participate in these decision-making procedures is a necessary part of being respected as a free and equal citizen and of collective self-rule.

Pettit's republic comes too close to a system in which the *demos* only plays a passive and secondary role and in which political conflicts which have been regarded as a productive and freedom-enhancing force by republican political theory from Machiavelli via Arendt to Claude Lefort are domesticated and absorbed into state institutions (see Vatter, 2005, McCormick, 2011). This alternative, a more democratic and conflict-oriented variant of republicanism has always insisted on the fact that emancipatory progress is not the work of elected or unelected rulers but of the struggles of the ruled that often have to resort to non-institutionalized forms of political practice. It is in these more intense and active forms of involvement and participation, and not merely in accountability and responsiveness plus control and ex post contestation, that the agency of ordinary citizens expresses itself (see Markell, 2008).

Accordingly, this more democratic variant of republicanism also involves a different conception of citizenship as primarily a positive status that individuals have as members of a community of free and equal citizens who collectively govern themselves. On this understanding, "equal participation in the collective decision-making process [i]s constitutive of non-arbitrary rule" (Bellamy, 2007, p. 218). Non-domination properly understood must thus include the effective participation of equals not just ex post, but ex ante. Thus, "a government of laws, and not of men" could still be regarded as tyrannical if those subjected to it have no direct say in its establishment, however "apt" the laws may be when it comes to tracking their interests. While for Pettit being a citizen seems to consist primarily in enjoying a negative status – namely not being subjected to the arbitrary will of another – from a democratic perspective the link between citizenship and having an effective say is essential: Freedom requires not only non-arbitrariness, but also self-rule. Correspondingly, unfreedom not only consists in not being able to articulate one's interests and to give them weight in public decision-making, it can also consist in only being able to participate under conditions that have been established without one's participation and that one cannot effectively control – if I can only participate on terms and in ways that others have set, this can make me unfree. As James Tully (2008, p. 93) puts it: "If the rules by which the *demos* are governed are imposed by someone else, and even if they have a range of freedoms within this other-imposed regime, they are not self-governing, self-determining or sovereign, and are thus unfree." It is this form of unfreedom that Pettit's neo-republicanism is not sufficiently attentive to, due to its fear of populism, its focus on non-arbitrariness, and its resulting problematic, liberal-constitutionalist construal of the link between freedom and democracy.

REFERENCES

Bellamy, R. (2007). *Political Constitutionalism. A Republican Defence of the Constitutionality of Democracy*. Cambridge: Cambridge University Press.

Berlin, I. (1969). Two Concepts of Liberty. In I. Berlin, *Four Essays on Liberty* (pp. 118-172). Oxford: Oxford University Press.

Brennan, G., Lomasky, L. (2006). Against Reviving Republicanism. *Politics, Philosophy and Economics*, 5, 221-252.

Carter, I. (2008). How Are Power and Unfreedom Related? In: C. Laborde and J. Maynor (Eds.), *Republicanism and Political Theory* (pp. 58-82). Oxford: Blackwell.

Celikates, R. (2014). Civil Disobedience as a Practice of Civic Freedom. In: D. Owen (Ed.), *On Global Citizenship. James Tully in Dialogue*. London: Bloomsbury Press.

Dworkin, R. (1996). *Freedom's Law. The Moral Reading of the American Constitution*. Oxford: Oxford University Press.

Friedman, M. (2008). Pettit's Civic Republicanism and Male Domination. In: C. Laborde and J. Maynor (Eds.), *Republicanism and Political Theory* (pp. 246-268). Oxford: Blackwell.

Habermas, J. (1996). *Between Facts and Norms. Contributions to a Discourse Theory of Law and Democracy*. Cambridge, MA: MIT Press.

Harrington, J. (1992). *The Commonwealth of Oceana*. Cambridge: Cambridge University Press.

Hobbes, T. (1997). *Leviathan*. Cambridge: Cambridge University Press.

Kramer, M. (2003). *The Quality of Freedom*. Oxford: Oxford University Press.

Kramer, M. (2008). Liberty and Domination. In: C. Laborde and J. Maynor (Eds.), *Republicanism and Political Theory* (pp. 31-57). Oxford: Blackwell.

Markell, P. (2008). The Insufficiency of Non-Domination. *Political Theory*, 36, 9-36.

McCormick, J. (2011). *Machiavellian Democracy*. Cambridge: Cambridge University Press.
Pettit, P. (1997). *Republicanism. A Theory of Freedom and Government*. Oxford: Oxford University Press.
Pettit, P. (1999). Republican Freedom and Contestatory Democratization. In: I. Shapiro and C. Hacker-Cordón (Eds.), *Democracy's Value* (pp. 163-190). Cambridge: Cambridge University Press.
Pettit, P. (2001). *A Theory of Freedom*. Oxford: Oxford University Press.
Pettit, P. (2002). Keeping Republican Freedom Simple. *Political Theory*, 30, 339-356.
Pettit, P. (2004). Depoliticizing Democracy. *Ratio Juris*, 17, 52-65.
Pettit, P. (2006). Democracy, National and International. *The Monist*, 89, 301-324.
Pettit, P. (2007). Free Persons and Free Choices. *History of Political Thought*, 28, 709-718.
Pettit, P. (2008). Republican Freedom. Three Axioms, Four Theorems. In: C. Laborde and J. Maynor (Eds.), *Republicanism and Political Theory* (pp. 102-130). Oxford: Blackwell.
Pettit, P. (2012). *On the People's Terms. A Republican Theory and Model of Democracy*. Cambridge: Cambridge University Press.
Richardson, H. (2002). *Democratic Autonomy. Public Reasoning about the Ends of Policy*. Oxford: Oxford University Press.
Rostbøll, C.F. (2008). *Deliberative Freedom. Deliberative Democracy as Critical Theory*. Albany: SUNY Press.
Skinner, Q. (1997). *Liberty before Liberalism*. Cambridge: Cambridge University Press.
Skinner, Q. (2002). A Third Concept of Liberty. *Proceedings of the British Academy*, 117, 237-268.
Skinner, Q. (2008a). *Hobbes and Republican Liberty*. Cambridge: Cambridge University Press.
Skinner, Q. (2008b). Freedom as the Absence of Arbitrary Power. In: C. Laborde and J. Maynor (Eds.), *Republicanism and Political Theory* (pp. 83-101). Oxford: Blackwell.
Skinner, Q. (2010). On the Slogans of Republican Political Theory. *European Journal of Political Theory*, 9, 95-102.
Tully, J. (2008). The Unfreedom of the Moderns in Comparison to Their Ideals of Constitutional Democracy. In: J. Tully, *Public Philosophy in a New Key, vol. 2: Imperialism and Civic Freedom* (pp. 91-123). Cambridge: Cambridge University Press.

Tully, J. (2013). 'Two Concepts of Liberty' in Context (pp. 23-51). In: B. Baum and R. Nichols (Eds.), *Isaiah Berlin and the Politics of Freedom*. London: Routledge.

Urbinati, N. (2010). Unpolitical Democracy. *Political Theory*, 38, 65-92.

Vatter, M. (2005). Pettit and Modern Republican Political Thought. In: M. S. Williams and S. Macedo (Eds.), *NOMOS XLVI: Political Exclusion and Domination* (pp. 118-163). New York: New York University Press.

Waldron, J. (2004). Judicial Review and Republican Government. In: C. Wolfe (Ed.), *That Eminent Tribunal. Judicial Supremacy and the Constitution* (pp. 159-180). Princeton: Princeton University Press.

Waldron, J. (2006). The Core of the Case Against Judicial Review. *Yale Law Journal*, 115, 1346-1406.

Waldron, J. (2007). Pettit's Molecule. In: G. Brennan, R.E. Goodin, F. Jackson, M. Smith (Eds.), *Common Minds. Themes from the Philosophy of Philip Pettit* (pp. 143-160). Oxford: Oxford University Press.

Young, I.M. (2001). Activist Challenges to Deliberative Democracy. *Political Theory*, 29, 670-690.

The Unlikely Claimant
Sovereignty and Republicanism in Hobbes

AMNON LEV

The mantle of republican claimant does not sit easily on Hobbes's shoulders. Without exception, the principal theorists of republicanism have pointed to him as the main culprit in the perversion or loss of political liberty which comes to define political modernity (Pettit, 1997, p. 37; Pocock, 1975, pp. 370-372; Skinner, 2008, pp. xiv, 211-213; Skinner, 2002b, pp. 187). It is in his work that the liberty of the citizen is replaced by the liberty of the subject; it is here that the pursuit of selfish ends replaces the dedication to public life. In this reading, Hobbes' political theory represents the antithesis of republicanism. However, lines may not be as sharply drawn as we are led to believe by the conventional reading. If we consider the format of sovereign power that Hobbes invented, we find that it takes up republican themes, albeit inverting their sense. Understanding how these themes are implicated in the format of sovereignty promises to shed light on the extraordinary success of sovereignty as a format of government. It will also give us insight into the nature of the motive forces that are driving republican theory, driving it like a wedge into the format of sovereign power. But before we can undertake the challenges that republicanism poses to sovereignty, indeed to political theory, we would perhaps do well to reflect on the shifts in our intellectual horizon that have brought to prominence a conception of liberty which, as Philip Pettit tells us, was lost to the point of having become invisible to historians of political thought (Pettit, 1997, p. 50; cf. Skinner, 1997, pp. 117-118n29). Rather than a criticism of republicanism, what follows is an attempt to situate it as an event in the history of sovereign power. As we shall find, this attempt will in turn require us to consider the use which republican theory makes of history, how it uses history and how it depends upon it.

REPUBLICAN THEORY AND SOVEREIGN DISCOURSE

Seeing republicanism as an event presupposes that there is in fact something out there we can identify as republicanism, a conceptual kernel or a set of basic tenets that we can situate in the history of discourse on how man should live together with his peers. However, in the face of the, at times, considerable differences between the contemporary thinkers whose work somehow revolves around republican themes, we quickly despair of finding such a conceptual kernel. Rather than look for a propositional content around which the different trajectories revolve, we prefer to speak of a shared sensibility with certain features of modern political thought as the thread that runs through republican theory. Explaining republican theory from a sensibility shared by all members of a specific group of theorists will obviously fall short of the structural differences between the bodies of work that they have produced. Indeed, what we shall have to say in the following will not do justice to the different aspects of republican theory. This is likely to invite the objection that we are being heavy-handed in our reading, but this is a risk we must accept. Only if we stay at the level of basic intuitions can we come to understand what it is that resonates in republicanism and why it is that republican theorists recognize each other as taking part in a common enterprise.

Looking at the different trajectories that we group together under the heading of republican theory, one is struck by the fact that they all tend to oscillate between, on the one hand, a critique of the liberal account of political life and, on the other hand, a reference to past forms of government that did not revolve around subjection to sovereign power. This feature of republican theory which sets it apart from rival positions in contemporary political philosophy has perhaps not received the attention it merits. We fail to grasp its significance if we understand the use of history simply as an ornament, at best, a supplementary argument. The persuasive power of republican theory hinges on the nexus between critique and historical reference. If the point of the republican critique is that the liberal account of man is reductive as it focuses exclusively on the protection of life and property, it is the reference to history which shows that the liberal account of man, however self-evident it may appear, does not represent the whole truth of his social existence. It simply represents a partial view, and whatever patterns of subjection have grown up around it do not reflect inalterable features of (human) nature.

Judging by the resonance that republican themes have had in political philosophy, this two-pronged attack on sovereign discourse has been very effective. It strips sovereignty of its symbolic power by showing it to be a discursive formation among others.[1] But this unsettling of sovereignty cannot be the last word. If it is a fact that sovereign discourse is only a discursive formation among others – that it has no special claim to represent the truth of man's social existence – it is no less a fact that it has been the dominant discourse of modernity. For almost three centuries, we articulated our notions of political life and political community around it. To find out if this predominance is coming to an end and what that would mean we must first discover why republican theory has proven to be so effective against sovereign discourse. This leads us back to the question of its implication. A formal condition of the effectiveness of republican theory is its relative proximity to that against which it is directed. If republican theory can unsettle sovereign discourse, it is because it subscribes to the underlying account of political modernity that keeps it in place. It subscribes to the idea that political modernity revolves around a nexus of liberty and civil community, both in the sense that authority in a civil community must rest on and reflect liberty and in the sense that civil community represents the natural horizon of liberty.

These ideas are the foundation of sovereign power and so can be used to invalidate its normative claim. In fact, this invalidation would seem to follow as a matter of course. If we accept that civil community constitutes the natural horizon of liberty, the demand that we subject ourselves unconditionally to a sovereign power appears exorbitant, absurd even.[2] It is from this sense of the absurd that republican theory derives its explanatory force. However, there is a blindness in this deconstruction of sovereignty that arises out of a displacement of perspective. To republican theory, these notions of liberty are at the very heart of political modernity, as they are to sovereign discourse; but republican theory

---

1   In the lecture series at the *Collège de France* that stretched from January 7 to March 17, 1976, published under the title of *Il faut défendre la société*, Michel Foucault pursues a parallel strategy of historicizing sovereign discourse. By assigning a position to the universalist discourse of law, sovereignty is to be replaced by "a new form of law;" a law "emancipated from the principle of sovereignty". The problems Foucault unearths as he grapples with sovereignty shall in the following years lead him to the development of the concepts of bio-politics and governmentality. They shall also lead to a turn towards existence which, to some extent, parallels the trajectory of republican theory.

2   The inability to understand the point of sovereign discourse is already evident in Hegel's 1802 article on natural law wherein he dismisses its concepts as having no value other than to satisfy our curiosity as to the history of science, despite the fact that his own political philosophy relies upon the domestication of liberty performed by natural law.

ignores that, to sovereign discourse, these notions were not the self-evident truths we take them to be. They were hard won and their apparent self-evidence is the result of a painstaking process of acculturation that it is the feat of natural law, the format of power Hobbes invented, to have accomplished. Sovereignty had to overcome the millennial belief that the true liberty of man was manifested not within political community, even if in opposition to it, but in the defiant refusal to acknowledge the authority of any government that was of this world.

If we are to understand how sovereign discourse overcame this belief, how it succeeded in domesticating the liberty of man, we must engage with the question of the theological foundations of civil authority. It is here, in this dimension, that we find the source of the power of sovereignty. The question of political theology is not only essential to an understanding of Hobbes' philosophy, as the work of Howard Warrender and, more recently, Luc Foisneau has shown. It is also essential to understanding the critique of sovereignty by republican theory: a critique that depends upon the account that republican historiography has given of the genealogy of political thought. Only on the basis of this genealogy can republican theorists posit the nexus of liberty and civil community as an absolute, thus showing the absurdity of sovereignty's claim to obedience. To assess the merit of this critique, we must bring into focus the continuity of medieval and early modern political thought that republican theory has attempted to block out – an effort, ironically, of a mind with Hobbes.[3] The point is not simply that we

---

3 This blocking-out is reflected in Quentin Skinner's implausible reading of a pivotal figure such as Marsilius of Padua who, with no textual support, is portrayed as a thinker of the Italian city-republic, even if the world in which he tries to articulate a doctrine of civil community, making him a precursor to Hobbes, is unmistakeably that of medieval scholastic philosophy, as recent and not so recent scholarship has established. See Skinner (2002a), pp. 18, 22. To fit Marsilius into the republican narrative, one must disregard not only explain why the *civitas* remains subordinate to the imperial order of Roman law, depending on it for its cohesion; one must also disregard the bulk of his treatise, more precisely, the second discourse that contains his ecclesiology. Various attempts have been made to dissociate the first from the second discourse, supposedly not representative of Marsilius' actual views (Alan Gewirth, Cary J. Nederman). Recent scholarship has, on the contrary, emphasized the unity of the *Defensor Pacis*, noting its Romanist tendency, to which Georges de Lagarde and Jeannine Quillet pointed, and drawing attention to its proximity to certain positions of medieval orthodoxy. See Boureau (2006), p. 17; Garnett (2006), pp. 52-54, 68. A more nuanced view of the nexus of medieval and early political thought is indicated in Pocock (1997), pp. 66-67, but the indication is not further explored.

need to correct republican historiography. The point is that to understand how we can talk about political liberty today, we must rid ourselves of the notion that it is a natural fact of modern life, a structural feature of how we organize ourselves as communities. Only if we come to understand how political liberty was created discursively, can we come to understand how discourse continues to condition its exercise.

GOVERNING THE COMMONWEALTH

Only recently have we thought to raise the question of liberty in connection with Hobbes' treatise on the commonwealth. For centuries, it was seen as a manifesto of subjection, certainly not without cause. Governed as it was by the imperative of putting an end to war, there seemed to be no place in Hobbes's universe for man's liberty. This impression is misleading, despite having been the conventional reading for centuries. Liberty is absolutely pivotal to the government of the commonwealth, but Hobbes can only develop a theory of liberty in the margins of his work. In a sense, he is every bit as much a victim to the spell of self-preservation as we are. Having constructed society around the concern for survival, he cannot move beyond the primordial situation of sovereignty to consider the life that unfolds within the commonwealth. Consequently, he cannot develop the considerations that are to govern the exercise of sovereign power. But such considerations exist. Having brought sovereign power into existence, Hobbes must show how it should be exercised so as not to be lost. This requires him to accommodate liberty in the government of the commonwealth.[4]

What is often overlooked is that liberty does not disappear with man's passage into society. This persistence of liberty makes sense once we take into consideration the theological foundations of power in Hobbes' work. As Howard Warrender showed, the foundation of power proposed by Hobbes makes implicit reference to the voice of God, the only voice capable of commanding in the state of nature (Warrender, 1957, pp. 200, 207-209). God commands man to construct the sovereign of whom he shall henceforth be a subject. This is the passage from the Immortal to the Mortal God of which Hobbes speaks (Hobbes, 1994, p. 109). What drives man to subject himself to a sovereign power is not self-preservation, as we are wont to believe; self-preservation is a duty towards man's creator, not towards man himself. The constitution of sovereignty rests on an obligation that

---

4 This point has been made by various scholars in recent years. See Foisneau (2000), pp. 116-117; Sorell (2004), pp. 191-192.

wends from the innermost recesses of man's being. The indications contained in Warrender's work have been developed by other scholars, perhaps most impressively in the work of Luc Foisneau who has shown how Hobbes worked out the idea of sovereignty in a confrontation with and transposition of the scholastic notion of divine omnipotence (Foisneau, 2004, pp. 215-255, especially pp. 231-236). Republican theorists, most famously Quentin Skinner, have contested this reading of Hobbes. The gist of Skinner's argument is that no-one in Hobbes's own time, neither his followers nor his critics, picked up on the theological aspect of his theory. To impute to Hobbes a theory that was not only without resonance in his own time but, furthermore, he did not think to invoke in replying to his critics, is, Skinner argues, so historically implausible that, for this reason alone, the theological reading of Hobbes's theory of political obligation must stand as discredited. However plausible it may be as a reading of the *Leviathan*, it comes at the price of removing "most of the points of contact between Hobbes and the intellectual milieu in which he lived and worked" (Skinner, 2002b, p. 285, cf. p. 282).

As Skinner himself seems to have retreated from this rather excessive emphasis on context over the last decade, there is perhaps no need to rehearse the argument further beyond pointing out that Skinner is unable to maintain the line of demarcation between secular and religious argument, as he would have to in order to keep in place the republican genealogy of modern political thought. In Skinner's account of the event he singles out as the relevant context of Hobbes' theory of political obligation – the engagement controversy – the distinction between religious and non-religious positions tends to break down. Not only did the "theologians" continue to take part in the controversy, even after it had supposedly metamorphosed from its initial, religious phase, but "lay apologists" also continued to invoke the providence of God in support of the "very different" arguments which they advanced in support of engagement (Skinner, 2002b, pp. 299, 303).

Taking into consideration the theological dimension of sovereign power in Hobbes' work not only allows us to make sense of this interplay of religious and secular arguments. It also allows us to make sense of what happens inside the commonwealth where subjection is, in fact, not total. As we have seen, Hobbes' foundation of sovereign power is based on a parallel between God and the civil sovereign, but this parallel is not perfect. The sovereign commands as of right, but his right is not absolute. As a subject, man has a right he does not have as a man, that is, as a subject of God: the right of self-defence (Hobbes, 1969, p. 88;

Hobbes, 1966, pp. 177-178; Hobbes, 1994, pp. 82, 204.).[5] Subjection to sovereign power and the right of self-defence both reflect divine injunction. Man subjects himself to the sovereign because God commands him to preserve his life. Subjection rests on the obligation of self-preservation. But as self-preservation is the basis of man's political being, self-defence is not only a right of which he cannot be stripped; it is also an obligation he cannot shirk. It is the last vestige of the direct dominion that God exercised over man in the state of nature. As such, it reflects a religious dimension of human existence that cannot be appropriated by the sovereign; the only sacral dimension of human existence Hobbes recognizes. A good part of his work on the citizen, *De Cive* from 1641, is taken up by arguments to show that the political teachings of the Gospel consist simply in the injunction to obey ones temporal lords; faith commands nothing more than belief in the teaching that Jesus is the Christ; an argument Marsilius already used to counter the political ambitions of the Roman Church (Hobbes, 1966, pp. 281-281; pp. 420-428; Hobbes, 1994, p. 402-410; Marsilius, 1932, pp. 4-5). As the right of self-defence reflects God's direct dominion, it takes precedence over all other legal and moral considerations. It applies even to the criminal who has been justly condemned to death for his crime. Not only does he have a right to defend himself; he even has a right to join with his like in armed combat against the commonwealth (Hobbes, 1994, pp. 143, 204).[6]

The importance of the matter is evident: recognizing that the individual has a right of self-defence poses an absolute limit to sovereign power.[7] Perhaps more

---

5 I cannot agree with Luc Foisneau who seems to view the original compact as being founded on the unlimited power of the civil sovereign over the life and death of his subjects. See Foisneau (1997) pp. 300-302.

6 The opposition of sovereign power and the direct dominion of God over man can also arise in the shape of the martyr, who sacrifices his life for the glory of God and in defiance of the civil sovereign. Hobbes renders martyrdom political insignificant by his insistence that only him to whom the divine precepts have been supernaturally revealed must respect them as law in the proper sense of the term, in their immediate form (Hobbes, 1994, p. 259). As the Son of God has already come, Hobbes can thus limit the category of martyrs to those who have seen Christ in the flesh (pp. 340-341). On this point, see Kodalle (1972), pp. 126, 155-158.

7 The right of self-defence mirrors the sovereign's right to punish. As all sovereign rights arise through authorization by the subjects, we would expect the right to punish to be limited by their inalienable rights. But Hobbes vacillates on this point. At times, he extends the authorization of the sovereign to encompass the right to punish (Hobbes, 1994, p. 111); at other times, he conceives of the sovereign's right to punish

importantly, it also draws attention to the fact that, unlike God, the civil sovereign does not have an unconditional claim to obedience.[8] But more is at stake in the question of self-defence than the limits of sovereign power. As self-defence reflects the persistence in society of God's dominion over man, it imports into society the logic that governed interaction in the state of nature. Only this time, the relevant interaction is not that between men but that between subject and sovereign. By submitting to the Leviathan, man receives assurance against the threat that his fellow men pose to him by their very existence; but what of the threat that the existence of a sovereign power poses to him?

As man subjects himself to the sovereign in order to preserve his life, it follows that any threat to his life from the sovereign liberates him from his bond of allegiance and reinstates him in the unlimited right that he enjoyed prior to his passage into society. On first reading, we would thus incline towards seeing self-defence as a legal safe-guard, posing a limit beyond which the sovereign cannot go. This is certainly the most obvious reading. But something more is going on in Hobbes' text. The primacy of the obligation of self-preservation, in relation to which man is under the direct dominion of God, means that the very existence of sovereign power poses a threat to his existence. As there is no power on Earth to which man and Leviathan are both subject, and as man is sole judge of what is necessary to preserve his life where no common coercive power exist that can give him assurance, his interaction with the sovereign will, if it is left to run its natural course, invariably reproduce the oppositional patterns of the state of nature. His right to self-defence cannot be limited to certain categories of sovereign acts, as no power exists that can give him assurance that all other sovereign acts will not eventually be to his detriment. On the contrary, he must perceive every act by which sovereign power sustains itself as a threat to his own existence because it can be used against him. Man's right of self-defence must be, as his right

---

as an unfounded remnant of the right of nature (p. 204). The indeterminacy reflects the theoretical impossibility of reconciling sovereign power and the right of nature once they are brought into contact. Cf. Terrel (1994), pp. 243-244; Zarka (1995), pp. 242-245.

8   This view put Hobbes at odds with the English royalists who denied the right to self-defence against the King. See for example Clarendon (1676), p. 87. On the relationship of Hobbes to the royalist factions, see Hoekstra, (2004) pp. 37-38, 45-46; Lessay (1988), pp. 63-66; Sommerville (1992), pp. 35-37; Tuck (1993), pp. 312-313, 325-326.

of nature is, without limits.[9] The impossibility of assigning any limits is reflected in Hobbes' observation that the motive for which man transfers his right of nature to the sovereign is "nothing else but the security of a man's person, in his life and in the means of so preserving life as not to be weary of it" (Hobbes, 1994, p. 82). The passage confers an almost hedonistic quality on a right that is only formally a subject of choice. Man must not only be secure in his existence; he must also be satisfied with it. This shifts the perspective of the construction of commonwealth from the *existence* to the *perception* of sovereign power. Hobbes cannot alleviate the fear that sovereign power inspires by somehow curtailing it. Within the limits that set by the right of self-defence, sovereign power must be absolute. Hobbes can only alleviate this fear by instituting a system of screens and mirrors in which man is not confronted with sovereign power. He lives his life in a sphere from which sovereign power *seems* to be absent, even if its jurisdiction is not.

If we inquire further into Hobbes' construction of the commonwealth, we find at its centre a sphere of individual action where man is free to do as he pleases and where the presence of sovereign power is not felt. The primary signification of this liberty is corporal liberty, the liberty from chains and prison (Hobbes, 1994, p. 136). This determination corresponds to the primary objects of the right of self-defence: life and physical integrity. It circumscribes a sphere of action attached directly to the individual. But as we proceed, we find that liberty's domain extends beyond this narrow definition:

"The liberty of the subject lieth, therefore, only in those things which, in regulating their actions, the sovereign hath praetermitted [omitted] (such as is the liberty to buy, and sell, and otherwise contract with one another; to choose their own abode, their own diet, their own trade of life, and institute their children as they themselves think fit; and the like)." (Hobbes, 1994, p. 138)

The liberty of the subject comprises more than his life and his movements. It encompasses a series of contingent, yet essential aspects of human life: property,

---

9   This dimension disappears from view in the work of Jean-Jacques Rousseau, for whom the alienation of man's being to society comprises the whole of his former, natural state, including the biological fact of being alive which, to Hobbes, is the umbilical cord that tied the subject to the man. To Rousseau, the sovereign is entitled to demand that a citizen lay down his life in the interest of the state. With the passage into civil society, biological existence ceases to be a "bounty of nature;" henceforth it is a "conditional gift of the state," one that can be taken away (Rousseau, 1964, p. 376).

the choice of abode, diet, trade and the up-bringing of one's children. The rather off-hand manner in which Hobbes determines the liberty of the subject should not mislead us about its significance. The imperative of edifying and consolidating a sovereign power means that Hobbes can only introduce these aspects of human existence in the margins of his theory of commonwealth. They are nonetheless essential to the workings of the society that unfolds under the rule of the sovereign. Through the cursory indications of Hobbes we begin to perceive that it is not mere existence but life that unfolds within the commonwealth. Around the kernel of natural right – life and physical integrity – a wider sphere of human existence lies. The activities that take place within this arena have all been "praetermitted" by the sovereign; in other words, they have not been made the object of sovereign decision. Man's action within this sphere is not determined by law, not because law has lost its force, but because it is not immediately present. The "praetermitted" actions fall below the threshold of law: "As for other liberties [than the liberty to defend oneself against attack], they depend on the silence of the law. In cases where the sovereign has prescribed no role, there the subject hath the liberty to do or forbear, according to his own discretion" (Hobbes, 1994, p. 143). The juridiction of sovereign power is unchanged; its impact on human existence is not. Man is legally bound to obey the sovereign in all aspect of his existence, but sovereign power is not manifested in all dimensions of the commonwealth. It is hidden from view such that man feels at liberty, despite the fact that, as a matter of law, he is not.

The relationship of subject and sovereign is mediated by a triadic structure that can be teased out of Hobbes' text: 1) at the core, a sphere that attaches immediately and directly to the individual. This sphere revolves around the life and bodily security of the individual and it is governed by the right of nature. 2) A wider sphere, in which man is free to live as he pleases, provided that the laws are silent. And 3) the sphere of law, seen as the expression of sovereign will. Of these spheres, only the first and the third, respectively the spheres of natural right and civil law, are engaged in the institution of the commonwealth. They are, by their very nature, contradictory but must nonetheless be brought to coincide in theory if the commonwealth is to maintain itself. In the account that Hobbes gives of the genesis of the commonwealth, he relies on the fiction of the state of nature to align the complete liberty that is the essence of the right of nature on the total submission that is the essence of civil law. This does not address the question of how men are to live together once they have made the passage into society. If the existence of sovereign power is a condition for peace, it is the existence of a sphere of individual liberty unchecked by sovereign power that allows Hobbes to show how natural right and civil law might align in government.

Within the commonwealth, the coincidence between natural right and civil law cannot be complete because, on the terms stipulated by Hobbes, the passage into society is never complete. Man will always carry within himself a dimension of liberty that the civil sovereign cannot appropriate. But the nexus of natural right and civil law can be managed so that the non-coincidence is not (too) manifest. A balance between natural right and civil law can be struck if society is constructed in such a way that, for the most part, man will not have to act under a direct threat to his life, nor under the compulsion of civil law. If he perceives himself to be acting freely, according to his own will and to his own desires, the existence of sovereign power will not be seen to constitute a threat to his freedom, and the opposition between natural right and sovereignty will not be felt to be a problem, even if it cannot be resolved.[10]

REPUBLICANISM: A PLACE IN HISTORY?

Is a society where man is free only where he does not proclaim his freedom a republic? Surely not. But if the commonwealth is not a republic, this place where man is free to "do or forbear, according to his own discretion" where the laws are silent" (Hobbes, 1994, p. 143), is, in certain respects, indistinguishable from it.[11] The subject is free to direct his actions towards the common good as expressed in the civil laws. He is, in other words, free to be a republican. More to the point, the constitution of the commonwealth means that he has good, even compelling, reasons to make this choice. If he does not, the distribution of liberty between social spheres around which Hobbes constructs his theory of commonwealth will eventually collapse and ordered society with it. This, it will be objected, is immaterial. Prudential considerations on how power should be exercised cannot bridge the gap that separates a republic from a society in which liberty is real only as a fiction might be real. And yet, the republic still moves within the orbit of the commonwealth. Its movement is prefigured in the format of the commonwealth. Hobbes renders liberty through the use of fictions because he knows that the idea of political that liberty he has at his disposal - the liberty of the Ancients – cannot be real; it cannot be realized in the modern world because political liberty cannot maintain the cohesion of society. What Hobbes

---

10 For a further analysis, see Amnon Lev, 2014, pp. 78-80.
11 Pocock (1975) notes the singular community of spirit that unites Hobbes and Harrington, the theorist of absolute sovereignty and the theorist of participatory virtue, pp. 397-400.

accomplishes by his theory of commonwealth is to introduce a measure of (civil) liberty into a society where (political) liberty has no place. He does so by maintaining a precarious balance between the imperatives of order and liberty. In a sense, the commonwealth is nothing but this precarious balance which is defined in legal terms as the fact that the civil laws and the laws of nature "contain each other, and are of equal extent" (Hobbes, 1994, p. 174).[12]

Within the confines of the relationship of subjection that opens up social space in the theory of Hobbes, a balancing act is carried out in which contradictory imperatives are aligned. Only if we take into consideration the plasticity of Hobbes' format of political thought, its remarkable capacity of accommodating opposites, can we make sense of the extraordinary success of sovereignty as a format of government. Liberalism has been so resistant to sovereign discourse because it refuses to trade liberty off against something else. Republican theory does not. On the contrary, it articulates its concept of liberty in and through an act of balancing that is a strict parallel to that carried out by Hobbes. Republican liberty is a middle between positive liberty, the liberty of the ancients, and negative liberty, that of the moderns (Pettit, 1997, pp. 18-19). Pettit implies, rather than establishes, a parallel between the republican conception of liberty and the city-republic as the intermediary between the ancient and the modern form of political organization. But if we look closer at what he actually does with this dichotomy, it becomes clear that while he sees positive and negative liberty as attributes of distinct forms of political existence, they are not tied to distinct forms of political organization. Rather, they are seen as aspects of modern political community, the polar opposites between which society exists, and, as such, they are simultaneously present therein: "[The republican conception of liberty] is negative to the extent that it requires the absence of domination by others, not necessarily the presence of self-mastery ... The conception is positive to the extent that ... it needs something more than the absence of interference; it requires security against interference, in particular against interference on an arbitrary basis" (Pettit, 1997, p. 51). Positive and negative are simultaneously present in society; they are present in the balance that is struck between them.

---

12 This relationship of mutual containment comprises two aspects: 1) the laws of nature only become laws in the strict sense through the commands of the sovereign power. 2) Obedience to civil law is itself a dictate of the law of nature. If justice, that is, the performance of covenant and giving to every man his own, is a dictate of the law of nature, honouring the obligation to obey the civil law which the subject takes upon himself as he passes into society is equally a dictate of the law of nature (p. 175).

Republican liberty *is* this balance which Pettit attempts to translate into a republican theory of government in the second part of his book.

The structural parallel between sovereign discourse and republican theory does of course not cancel out the distance separating the political communities which they advocate. And Pettit is right to point out that the republican conception of liberty could not have been articulated within the format of sovereignty. However, the structural parallel means that there is no formal difference between the two discourses. As an event, republicanism unfolds within the forms of sovereign discourse. The point of equilibrium is elsewhere but the basic operation is the same. This explains why Pettit can leave it to the state, the form of political organization that has always served as the vehicle of this operation, to realize the republican programme (Pettit, 1997, pp. 47-48.).[13] The difference between the discourse of republicanism and that of sovereignty, which sets them apart as formats of government, arises out of the way power is exercised in their respective political communities. The exercise of power that corresponds to the republican idea is found in the early modern forms of government to which republican theory makes reference. Crucially, it also informs the theory of government associated with sovereign power. One is hard put to indicate how a transition into a republican form of government would change our present form of political organization. Most of all, the contestatory democracy that Pettit advocates as an alternative to our present-day democracy looks like the 19th century ideal of liberal democracy as described by John Stuart Mill, only with the addition of a vaguely defined institutional set-up to allow for a vaguely defined form

---

13 This confidence is also evident in Quentin Skinner's work, as his 2008 British Academy lecture illustrates. He proposes to reinstate the fictional concept of the state, the origin of which he locates in Hobbes' work, as it might serve to support a notion of the common good (Skinner, 2009 p. 362). Skinner does not indicate what might propel us to believe once again in this fiction. From his account, which emphasizes the distinctness of the Leviathan from the ruler and the ruled (pp. 345-347) it is not quite clear why we ever did. If the fiction of the state was able to inspire belief, it is, we would argue, only because of the almost palpable presence of the people in the constitution of sovereignty. The people is certainly not present in the exercise of sovereign power, but the incomplete nature of the foundation of sovereignty which calls for constant re-enactment means that, at all times, the people hovers just above sovereign order. It is perhaps not irrelevant to note that the wilting away of the idea of the state which becomes visible in Hegel's philosophy – an avatar of the fictional theory, as Skinner notes – goes hand in hand with a hardening of the fluid nexus between the body of the commonwealth and its representation into stark opposition.

of contestation distinct from that which takes place before the courts and the public (Pettit, 1999, pp. 179-180). It is no coincidence that the ideal of 19th century liberal democracy provides the best match for what we might term the form of republican theory: a learned battle of ideas between men, and now women, of substance about the most substantial of matters.

In a sense, Pettit concedes the points, arguing that the novelty of his theory lies not in constitutional forms but in its practice of power. If what it endorses are "established institutional ideals like the rule of law, the separation of powers, and democratic accountability," it supports "those ideals on a distinctive basis and sometimes offer[s] quite unorthodox reformulations of their content" (Pettit, 1997, p. 172). But is this not an accurate description of the modern state composed of a political sphere that is governed by law and a civil society out of which new forms of life emerge that animate the whole? Seen in this perspective, there is not much to separate the republican form of government from that which it is supposed to replace. It is, quite literally, a matter of opinion whether Pettit is right when he tells us that his "unorthodox reformulations" are not "platitudinous." It is a matter of whether we feel them to be so. Contestatory democracy differs from liberal democracy only for those who feel the need to engage in contestation. The reference to feeling confers a hortatory quality on republican discourse; it also means that republican discourse comes up short when seen only as theory. We may know in our hearts that republican rule would be different, but we cannot say wherein its difference consists. If this failure of language would be inconvenient for any political theorist, it is certainly not less so for one who claims to bring back an essential dimension of human life that had not only been lost to political thinkers and activists for centuries, but had even become invisible to historians of political thought.

MAKING SENSE OF POLITICAL THOUGHT

The prominence of history in republican theory is not unrelated to this linguistic short-circuit, this incapacity to show in what sense republican rule would be different from the sort of rule which has grown out of the history of sovereign power. History provides this difference. It is in and through its reference to presovereign forms of government that republican theory demonstrates that it is indeed different. History serves a dual purpose: it destabilizes sovereign discourse and it keeps republicanism from becoming entangled in the history of sovereign power. In the indeterminacy that attaches to republicanism, in its oscillation between what belongs to and what does not belong to the history of sovereign power, we find a structural precondition of yet another feature of republican theory: a feature that is a cause and a reflection of what we have termed the indeterminacy of republicanism. If the truth of republicanism is manifest only within our hearts, it is there that it has its locus. This is perhaps why republicanism is so concerned with meaning, more precisely, the meaning we attribute to political thought. Whereas liberalism and communitarianism advance theories on the order of things, on the rights and duties of the state and citizens, republicanism strives to *think* about political community, and promote this activity. It reacts against the sense that political thought has become an otiose and scholastic endeavour. This fear is reflected in the remark with which Skinner concludes his lecture on Hobbes and republican liberty: that while Hobbes may have won the battle, it is still worth asking if he won the argument (Skinner, 2008, p. 216). Common sense indicates that it is pointless to pursue an argument if the battle has been lost, but it is precisely this seemingly self-evident reaction republicanism seeks to combat. It should matter what we do when we think about the conditions of the life we lead in common with others. As Emile Perreau-Saussine (2007) noted, republican theory is not really a political proposition; it is a call to action, an existential appeal to engage with the questions of political life (pp. 109-110, 119-121).

It is by this appeal that republican inserts itself into the landscape of contemporary political philosophy. Liberalism stands guard over liberty to protect it against state intervention; republicanism enjoins us to do noble things with this liberty. What concerns Pettit are not the limits placed on the exercise of liberty, nor is it the procedures that are meant to ensure the non-arbitrary nature of such limitations. His primary concern is the right of each man to relate as an equal to others, irrespective of differences in power, wealth, or social status. These concerns are shared by liberal theorists, but Pettit takes them further. Not content with the formal equality of the citizen, it is his material sense of equal worth that occupies him.

There is something compelling about republican theory's insistence that political thought is not only, and not primarily, concerned with finding solutions to problems of communal life; that it is also about how we live our lives. Yet, for all its appeal, the resonance of republicanism in contemporary political theory should perhaps give us pause to wonder. Teaching people to walk with their heads held high is indeed a noble endeavour. It must be the aim of any political theory to enjoin us to think and to live politically. But in a world where the communities that define us have stretched to include individuals whose plight will not be ended through an ever so vigorous exercise of political liberty, there is quite a bit of self-indulgence in the excessive concern with the earnestness and the nobility of our actions. Having to "toady" to the high and mighty, an example to which Pettit returns repeatedly, is certainly something no man or woman should have to do, but a political theory that sees this as more than a marginal problem has perhaps shaded over into something that has more to do with care for oneself than with concern for the matters of the city. The possibility of this drift is inherent in political life. Political life is always also a matter of sense. Republicanism is right to remind us of this. We may need to remind ourselves that we loose the meaning of what a political life must be about if we become to concerned with the sense of it.

REFERENCES

Boureau, A. (2006). *La Religion de l'État*. Paris: Les Belles Lettres.
Clarendon, E.H. (1676). *A brief view and survey of the dangerous and pernicious errors to church and state in Mr. Hobbes's book entituled Leviathan.* Oxford.
Foisneau, L. (1997). "Obéissance politique et mortalité humaine selon Hobbes" in Foisneau, Luc (Ed.), *Politique, Droit et Théologie chez Bodin, Grotius et Hobbes*. Paris: Éditions Kimé.
Foisneau, L. (2000). *Hobbes et la toute-puissance de Dieu*. Paris: Presses Universitaires de France.
Foisneau, L. (2004). "Leviathan's *Theory of Justice*" in Sorell, Tom & Luc Foisneau (Eds.), *Leviathan After 350 years*. Oxford: Oxford University Press, pp. 105-122.
Garnett, G. (2006). *Marsilius of Padua & "The Truth of History."* Oxford: Oxford University Press.
Hobbes, T. (1966). *De Cive* in *Opera philosophica quae latina scripsit*, I-V (Ed. W. Molesworth). Aalen: Scientia Verlag.
Hobbes, T. (1969). *Elements of Law Natural & Politic* (Ed. Ferdinand Tönnies), London: Frank Cass & Co. Ltd.
Hobbes, T. (1994). *Leviathan* (Ed. Edwin Curley), Indianapolis/Cambridge: Hackett Publishing Company.
Hoekstra, K. (2004). The *de facto* Turn in Hobbes' Political Philosophy. In T. Sorell & L. Foisneau (Eds.), *Leviathan After 350 years*. Oxford: Oxford University Press, pp. 33-73.
Kodalle, K.-M. (1972). *Thomas Hobbes – Logik der Herrschaft und Vernuft des Friedens*. München: C.H. Beck'sche Verlagsbuchhandlung.

Lessay, F. (1988). *Souveraineté et legitimité chez Hobbes*. Paris: Presses Universitaires de France.
Lev, A. (2014). *Sovereignty and Liberty. A Study of the Foundations of Power*. Abingdon: Routledge.
Marsilius of Padua (1932). *Defensor Pacis* (Ed. Richard Scholz), Hannover: Fontes Iuris Germanici Antiqui, Hahnsche Buchhandlung.
Perreau-Saussine, E. (2007). Quentin Skinner in Context. *The Review of Politics*, 69, pp. 106-122.
Pettit, P. (1997). *Republicanism. A Theory of Freedom and Government*. Oxford: Oxford University Press.
Pettit, P. (1999). Republican Freedom and Contestatory Democratization. In I. Shapiro & C. Hacker-Cordon (Eds.), *Democracy's Value*. Cambridge: Cambridge University Press.
Pocock, J.G.A. (1975). *The Machiavellian Moment*. Princeton: Princeton University Press.
Rousseau, J.-J. (1964). Du Contract Social. In *Œuvres Complètes*, vol. 3. Paris: Éditions Gallimard.
Skinner, Q. (1997). *Liberty before Liberalism*. Cambridge: Cambridge University Press.
Skinner, Q. (2002a). *Foundations of Modern Political Thought*. Cambridge: Cambridge University Press.
Skinner, Q. (2002b). *Visions of Politics: Hobbes and Civil Science*. Cambridge: Cambridge University Press.
Skinner, Q. (2008). *Hobbes and Republican Liberty*. Cambridge: Cambridge University Press.
Skinner, Q. (2009). A Genealogy of the Modern State. In *Proceedings of the British Academy*, 162, pp. 325-370. Oxford: Oxford University Press.
Sommerville, J.P. (1992). *Thomas Hobbes: Political Ideas in Historical Context*, Basingstoke: Macmillan Press.
Sorell, T. (2004). The Burdensome Freedom of Sovereigns. In T. Sorell & L. Foisneau (Eds.), Leviathan *After 350 years*, Oxford: Oxford University Press.
Terrel, J. (1994). *Hobbes – Matéralisme et Politique*. Paris: Librairie Philosophique J.VRIN.
Tuck, R. (1993). *Philosophy and Government*, Cambridge: Cambridge University Press.
Warrender, H. (1957). *The Political Philosophy of Hobbes. His Theory of Obligation*, Oxford: Oxford University Press.

Zarka, Y.C. (1995). *Hobbes et la pensée politique moderne*, Paris: Presses Universitaires de France.

Materially Unfree

Corruption as a societal diagnosis and the political forms of unfreedom in Machiavelli, Davenant, and Bolingbroke

TUE ANDERSEN NEXØ

The following essay will examine a semantic change in one of the republican tradition's key terms, "corruption." This change can be traced back to oppositional polemics against the political order in England in the first half of the eighteenth century, polemics which more often than not were articulated through a republican vocabulary. It occurred, I argue, as a reaction to the very gradual birth of the modern state in England after the Glorious Revolution. Behind this exercise in historical semantics run two other, more theoretical arguments. The first is that a republican understanding of corruption is tightly interwoven with an understanding of the subjective state of not being free. The second, which will only be hinted at, is that the diagnosis of "universal corruption", so called by Lord Bolingbroke, is semantically distinct from other attempts to describe the social ills of modernity. As such, it might be worth retrieving again today.

In that sense, my essay is a late addition to attempts in the past twenty years to make the republican tradition relevant for contemporary political debates. The different attempts to revive the republican tradition have also, however, almost exclusively focused on what one could call republicanism's normative vocabulary. Michael Sandel (1996) has attempted to reintroduce a republican concept of civic virtue; Quentin Skinner (1998) and Philip Pettit (1997) have challenged a liberal conception of freedom as absence of interference, replacing it with a concept of freedom as absence of dependence or domination; the Italian philosopher Maurizio Viroli (1995) has argued for a republican concept of "patriotism" as an alternative to both cosmopolitan and nationalist currents in contemporary political thinking. This essay instead examines the potential in a less discussed term (but see Lessing, 2011; Viroli, 2012) within the diagnostic vocabulary of the republican tradition.

CORRUPTION OF THE REPUBLIC IN MACHIAVELLI'S *DISCOURSES*

There is a great deal of literature on the phenomenon of corruption within the disciplines of economy and political science, especially within the studies of developing third-world economies. But as Seumas Miller (n.d.) – one of the few contemporary philosophers who has written on corruption – has pointed out, this literature is only rarely interested in analyzing different concepts of corruption. Typically, it has been defined as a form of economic criminality, the paradigmatic example of which would be the civil servant taking bribes in order to give someone preferential treatment. In a classic essay with the very telling title, "Corruption and Political Development: A Cost-Benefit Analysis," J.S. Nye (1990) defines corruption as "behavior which deviates from the formal duties of a public role because of private-regarding (personal, close family, private clique) pecuniary or status gains; or violates rules against the exercise against certain types of private-regarding influence" (Nye, 1990, p. 966).[1] In another classic study, *Corruption and Government: Causes, Consequences, and Reform*, Susan Rose-Ackerman discusses acts of corruption as examples of "unproductive rent seeking" (Rose-Ackermann, 1995, p.4, but see Johnston, 2005, for a partial repudiation of this view); it has as its primary societal consequence a clogging up of the smooth workings of a wealth-producing, efficient market. This definition is primarily legal and economic. Corruption is an illegal act performed for private benefit; its consequence is the hampering of economic development and the societal production of wealth.

This is not how "corruption" was used in the republican tradition, at least not in one of its most important texts, Machiavelli's *Discourses*.[2] However, even

---

1 Nye continues: "This definition [...] excludes any consideration of whether the behavior is in the public interest, since building the study of the effects of the behavior into the definition makes analysis of the relationship between corruption and development difficult" (Nye, 1990, p. 966). It is clear from the essay that "development" for Nye means economic growth.

2 Earlier Italian thinkers had mentioned moral corruption as a threat to a free republic, but the concept is developed with far more semantic specificity in Machiavelli's *Discourses* (Skinner, 1978, vol. 1, p. 165). One of the few attempts to systematically

though "corruzione" is a key concept in Machiavelli's analysis of the historical examples from Titus Livius, and in the different political lessons he draws from this analysis, he never defines what corruption means, nor does he explicate the premises of its use. From the examples in *Discourses* it is clear, however, that for Machiavelli corruption does not describe single acts and is not conceived within a legal or economic framework. Instead he uses it as a political diagnosis. Drawing on the word's etymological roots in rot and decay and, specifically, upon the Greek historian Polybius' description of the decay of the different forms of government (Sasso, 1987), Machiavelli uses corruption to signify a kind of rot in the tissue of society, in the material which the political constitution is to give form.[3] This rot is in *Discourses* connected to the Aristotelian distinction between having regard for the common good and only having regard for private gain, but it is not just to be understood as an individual moral failing, nor is it to be understood as a general lack of common ethos or as the simple existence of diverging opinions or political conflict. On the contrary, Machiavelli famously emphasizes that conflict – in *Discourses* between "i grandi" and "i popoli", the patricians and plebeians of the roman republic – is necessary to keep the republic strong and vigorous. In a passage which both shows how corruption is a decay of the societal "material" understood as the collection of people whose lives the laws of the political community are to regulate, and that corruption is not connected to the absence of conflict, Machiavelli declares in the end of *Discourses* I.17 that "dove la materia non è corrotta, i tumulti ed altri scandoli non

---

examine Machiavelli's use of "corruzione" is found in Alfredo Bonadeo's *Corruption, Conflict and Power in the Works of Niccolò Machiavelli* (1973). However, Bonadeo is more interested in Machiavelli's discussions of the causes and consequences of corruption than he is in an analysis of the concept itself. For the differences between what is sometimes called a liberal and a republican concept of corruption, see also Sara M. Schumer (1979); Peter Bratsis (2003) criticizes what he calls a "bourgeois" concept of corruption, but does not engage with the republican tradition.

3   The relevant passage in Polybius is this: "Just as rust is the corruption inherent within iron, and woodworm and grubs are the corruption inherent within timbers, and just as iron and wood, even if they remain unaffected by all external sources of harm, are still destroyed by these things that form within them, in the same way every political system has a source of corruption growing within it, from which it is inseparable" (Polybius, 2010, p. 378). It is worth noting that Polybius' metaphors imply an image of society as something made out of organic material, but nevertheless created by humans; speaking of societal corruption does not lead to a conception of the political community as a living organism.

nuocono; dove la è corrotta, le leggi bene ordinate non giovano, se già non sono mosse da uno che con una estrema forza le faccia osservare, tanto che la material diventi buona." (Machiavelli, 1997, p. 244); "when the material is not corrupt, tumults and other troubles do no harm, but, when it is corrupt, good legislation is of no avail unless it be initiated by someone in so extremely strong a position that he can enforce obedience until such time as the material has become good" (Machiavelli, 1997, p. 159).

How should we then understand this decay of the social fabric? I would like here to turn to an early essay, "Civic Humanism and its Role in Anglo-American Thought," by J.C.A. Pocock. In this essay Pocock tries to articulate the meaning of corruption in the writings of Machiavelli and his contemporary Francesco Guicciardini. First of all, Pocock writes that they both understand corruption as the absence of civic virtue. But this absence is understood as more than the individual citizen's inner lack of a moral compass, his inner choice to disregard the common good of the republic. On the contrary, civic virtue is dependent upon the fact that citizens are equal to one another; its absence, correspondingly, is caused by relations of inequality in the social fabric of the republic: "To lose one's due share of authority, or to have more than one's due, amounted to a loss of virtue, and since virtue consisted in a relation between equals its loss was not private but mutual" (Pocock, 1971, p. 89; see also Pocock, 1975, p. 184).

That corruption also entails a mutual loss of civic virtue can and I think should be understood in two ways: one weak, which regards the individual consequences of intersubjective inequality; one strong, which regards the political consequences of it. The development of one's "civic virtue," understood as a property of the individual, is dependent upon the fact that you are enmeshed in relations between equals. Only then are you able to identify with your co-citizens, only then are you free to identify with the common interests of the political community. But, at the same time, Pocock assumes – like Hannah Arendt – that Machiavelli's concept of "virtù" has as much to do with "virtuosity," the ability to act quickly and adequately, to navigate difficult circumstances, as it has to do with moral virtue (Arendt, 2006, p. 151). A virtuous republic is not (just) a republic whose citizens are morally virtuous, it is also a republic which possesses virtuosity. Understood this way, civic virtue can be recognized as the ability of a political community to act adequately, to navigate difficult circumstances. It is the republic's ability to uphold itself as a free political community within the vicissitudes of secular time.

According to Pocock, Machiavelli thus has a threefold understanding of civic virtue. It is a moral compass, but it is also dependent upon the way the individual is positioned within intersubjective relations, and it is also connected to a diagnosis of the health of the political community as such. This is mirrored in Pocock's description of the civic humanist understanding of corruption:

"[Corruption is] first, the degenerative tendency to which all particular forms of government are prone; second, the specific cause of that degeneration, which is the dependence of some men upon other men when they should be depending upon all and upon themselves; and third, the moral degeneration of the individual who, in these circumstances, is prevented from developing his virtue by identifying his particular good with the good of all. The climax of this corruption arrives when he finds his world controlled by an irrational Fortune instead of by the virtue of political man. Time, which cannot be conceptualized as qualitative change, is now in command." (Pocock, 1971, p. 88)

Like civic virtue, corruption is scalable at a subjective, an intersubjective, and an institutional level. At each level it is the antithesis of civic virtue. Furthermore, Pocock gives the intersubjective level precedence – it is the cause both of the individual's "moral degeneration" and of the "degenerative tendency" of the forms of government.

In the ideally virtuous republic the citizens are equal in the sense that they are only dependent upon themselves and upon the political community in its totality, Pocock writes. In the republican tradition this has often been articulated as the fact that the *res publica* should be governed not by men, but by laws, which the citizens themselves have chosen or at least consented to. But Pocock's exact formulation does not point toward the form and structure of government. It relates to the tissue of intersubjective relations. This tissue is corrupt when it is dominated by relations of dependency, which give some men unbridled power over other men, and leave these other men unfree, at least if we accept the argument by Quentin Skinner (1998) and Philip Pettit (1997, p. 21cc), namely that a fundamental premise in republican thought is the definition of freedom as non-dependency or non-domination. Both Skinner and Pettit understand domination as a consequence of unbridled inequality, of relations of dependency leading to situations where the powerless are forced to constantly take the interest and demands of the powerful into consideration. This means that they are not free to follow their own interests, but also that they are not free to take into regard the common good. However, neither Pettit nor Skinner connects this analysis of what it means to not be free with the republican concept of corruption. In my interpretation, corruption for Machiavelli is a diagnosis of political unfreedom understood materially, as a phenomenon regarding not the formal rights of the citizen or the structures and procedures of the government, but the interpersonal relations which in a sense precede the political forms – our laws and institutions

– which are, at least in the public, political realm, to be given form by our laws and institutions. In such an interpretation one should note that the "materia" of the republic is not its population understood as an aggregate of individuals, but its population understood as individuals always already enmeshed in intersubjective relations. To follow the vocabulary of Pettit, a republican concept of corruption entails an anthropology, which is neither collectivistic nor atomistic, but rather holistic (Pettit, 1993, p. 166).

It is these relations of inequality which cause both institutional and moral degradation. How this happens can be seen in an example from *Discourses* I.18, where Machiavelli discusses the Roman way of choosing consuls and more generally how a corrupted material can subvert the structures of government:

"Non dava il popolo romano il consolato e gli altri primi gradi della città, se non a quelli che lo domandavano. Questo ordine fun nel principio buono, perché e' non gli domandavano se non quelli cittadini che se ne giudicavano degni, ed averne la repulsa era ignominioso; sí che, per esserne giudicati degni, ciascuno operava bene. Diventò questo modo, poi, nella città corrotta, perniziosissimo: perché non quelli che avevano piú virtú, ma quelli che avevano piú potenza, domandavano i magistrati e gl'impotenti, comecché virtuosi, se ne astenevano di domandarli per paura." (Machiavelli, 1997, p. 246)

"The Roman people had never given the consulate or any other important office in the city except to such as had applied for the post. This institution was at the outset good, because only such citizens applied for posts as judged themselves worthy to fill them, and to be rejected was looked upon as ignominious; so that everybody behaved well in order to be judged worthy. This procedure, when the city became corrupt, was extremely harmful; because not only those who had more virtue, but those who had more power, applied for magistracies, and the powerless, though virtuous, refrained from applying through fear." (Machiavelli, 1970, pp. 161-162)

In the corrupted city filled with people with too much and too little power, a once good institution degenerates so that the powerful apply for positions they are not suited for and the virtuous dare not apply out of fear. As Pocock emphasizes, an individual enmeshed within a corrupt social tissue cannot live in any meaningful way, and therefore cannot see himself as a free and equal citizen. He cannot develop his virtue by identifying his own interests with the common good. Whereas those with too much power become deluded by arrogance and ambition, by their regard for their own particular fate, the powerless become fearful and servile. They are forced to constantly track the interests of those particular persons above them, and are therefore not able to act according to their moral compass.[4] The result is the degeneration, or, more precisely, the subversion of a governmental form: the procedure through which consuls and other magistrates are chosen.

One can ask, however, whether Machiavelli actually insists on giving the intersubjective scale causal precedence. Many formulations in *Discourses* point instead to a kind of interdependence between the three levels. "Cosí come gli buoni costume, per mantenersi, hanno bisogno delle leggi; cosí le leggi, per osservarsi, hanno bisogno di buoni costume," ("just as for the maintenance of good customs laws are required, so if laws are to be observed there is need of good customs") Machiavelli writes in a discussion of the impossibility of rectifying "una città corrotissima" (1997, p. 245; Machiavelli, 1970, p. 160). In other instances it seems that the degeneration of individual morality is named as a cause of corruption rather than its consequence. This seems to be the case, for instance, in Machiavelli's discussions of luxury. It would be more precise, then, to think of the three scales as interdependent. It is possible for imbalances in the institutional structure of a polity or corrupt moral norms to produce social inequality, and thus corrupt the social tissue.

There is also something slightly misleading in Pocock's formulation at the end of my quote. Superficially, its meaning is clear: just as civic virtue is an index of the ability to cope with secular change, corruption produces an inability to withstand change, an inability to be in command of one's own fate. But that the subject of this inability is "political man" is simultaneously a fruitful and a not very precise suggestion. For even though Machiavelli doesn't exactly ignore the subjective experience of life within a corrupt state – the ending of *Discourses* I.10 is as much an indictment of corruption as it is an indictment of tyranny – his main focus in *Discourses* is upon how to establish and maintain a free republic in secular time. Corruption, understood as a kind of rot in the tissue of society, is only discussed in order to analyze such a republic's material condition of possibility. In fact, rather than making all constitutional forms unstable – which is what Pocock with an allusion to Polybius suggests: corruption is "the degenerative tendency to which all particular forms of government are prone" – in *Discourses* corruption is uniquely connected with the transition from republic to

---

4 This aspect of not being free is only hinted at by Philip Pettit in his first major discussion of freedom as non-domination (see Pettit, 1997, p. 61), but is explicitly spelled out in his later restatement of his position in the essay "Connecting the Dots". He also makes it clear why this becomes visible through a definition of freedom and its opposite as non-domination and domination: it is often in order to *avoid* interference that the powerless are forced to track the interests of the powerful (Pettit, 2006, p. 306).

monarchy or tyranny. In *Discourses* I.55 Machiavelli writes that the provinces of Naples, the Papal States, the Romagna, and Lombardy are inherently corrupt, both because the inhabitants are prone to idle luxury, and because many powerful nobles have retainers and other people who are beholden to them. Therefore, they are "al tutto inimico d'ogni civilità" ("entirely inimical to any form of civic government"):

"La ragione è questa, che dove è tanto la materia corrotta che le leggi non bastano a frenarla, vi bisogna ordinare insieme con quelle maggior forza; la quale è una mano regia che con la Potenza assoluta ed eccessiva ponga freno alla eccessiva ambizione e corruttela de' potenti." (Machiavelli, 1997, p. 311)

"The reason for this is that, where the material is so corrupt, laws do not suffice to keep it in hand; it is necessary to have, besides laws, a superior force, such as appertains to a monarch, who has such absolute and overwhelming power that he can restrain excesses due to ambition and the corrupt practices of the powerful." (Machiavelli, 1970, p. 246)

Absolute monarchy, where one man rules beyond any law, seems to be the adequate political form to a corrupt societal tissue, where men are not equal, but everyone is enmeshed in particular relations of inequality. But would such a monarchy be stable? Would it be able to cope with the contingencies of secular time? A possible answer is given in a short discussion from *Discourses* I.17. The subject is, again, whether a corrupt people can establish a free republic:

"E debbesi presopporre per cosa verissima, come che quell principe con tutta la sua stirpe si spenga, mai non si può ridurre libera; anzi conviene che l'un principe spenga l'altro; e sanza creazione d'uno nuovo signore non si posa mai, se già la bontà d'uno, insieme con la virtù, non la tenesse libera; ma durerà tanto quella libertà, quanto durerà la vita di quello." (Machiavelli, 1997, p. 243)

"It should be assumed, then, as a basic and established principle, that to a state which has been under a prince and has become corrupt, freedom cannot be restored even if the prince and the whole of his stock be wiped out. On the contrary, what will happen is that one prince will wipe out another, and without the creation of a new lord it will never settle down unless indeed the goodness of some one man, conjoined with virtue, should keep it free. Such freedom, however, will last only as long as he lives." (Machiavelli, 1970, pp. 157-158)

As the adequate form of a corrupted societal tissue, absolute monarchy – or tyranny – seems to rise from its own the ashes. In that sense, it is both constantly changing and strangely stable. If nothing else, passages like these show how far from Polybius Machiavelli's conception of the relationship between corruption and political decay really is.

But, even though the introduction of "political man" seems misleading, it is also potentially fruitful. The experience of life as a subject within a corrupt society might only be passed in glancing by Machiavelli, but it could be developed in ways that not only point to questions of fearfulness and arrogance, but also to questions of temporality. This is one of the semantic developments which happened in early eighteenth century England.

ENGLAND, FINANCE, CORRUPTION

It is well known that a republican concept of corruption played an important role for the political opposition against the English monarchy in the decades after the Glorious Revolution. There has been relative scarcity, however, in actual analyses of what corruption meant in the polemical texts of the period. Even though it is generally acknowledged to be used as part of an attack against a specific set of governmental practices and institutional innovations, for some reason it is also generally assumed that grumblings about societal or political corruption in early eighteenth century English texts are part of a more or less nostalgic attack against the transformation of eighteenth century England into a wealthy, but socially differentiated, commercial society.[5]

---

5   This is the case in what is still the most thorough examination of the use of corruption in post-interregnum English republicanism, chapter 12-14 in J.G.A. Pocock's *The Machiavellian Moment*. Pocock emphasizes that corruption is used to criticize the consequences of the establishment of the national debt and the emergence of "paper credit" as a regular feature of society, and also emphasizes that it is connected to an analysis of how paper credit allows the executive to bribe members of parliament. But at the same time he repeatedly connects corruption to attacks upon a commercial society where cultural and social differentiation threatens archaic republican virtue. The germ of this – in my view, misunderstood – reading is found in his analysis of Machiavelli's attacks upon the professional army (Pocock 1975, p. 200). But Machiavelli does not criticize the professional soldier simply because he is an index of societal specialization – in that case he might as well have attacked professional cloth-makers – he finds him problematic because the army is the ultimate source of political power

I want to challenge this last part of the argument. Drawing on an often explicitly Machiavellian vocabulary, these texts should instead be seen as attempts to diagnose the political problems inherent in, and the societal consequences of, what John Brewer (1989) coined the birth of the English "fiscal-military state" (see also Scott, 2000). As such, subtle, but important changes in their use of "corruption" can be traced. Corruption was still understood as decay in the societal tissue. The interplay between institutional form, intersubjective relations of dependency, and moral degradation was repeatedly stressed. But even though eighteenth century English writers still used corruption to diagnose how private relations of dependency subverted the political constitution and the nation's ability to act forcefully, at the same time the concept gradually disconnected itself from tyranny and absolute monarchy as political forms. In fact, it was no longer used to analyze the movement from one constitutional form to the other. Instead, it was used to describe the consequences of a new type of power that had to do with the economic heft of the state apparatus. It was used to discuss how the administration of taxation, the establishment of salaried positions within the army, and the establishment of the national debt led to a kind of imbalance between the parts of England's mixed constitution, and also to a deformation of the relationship between citizen and government. It became, one could say, a key term in the diagnosis of societal life in a nation where the citizens were dependent upon a state which is almost, but never quite, modern. At the same time, the texts increasingly glanced at the subjective experience of societal corruption. Ironically, Pocock's "political man," who was not very prominent in Machiavelli, is found in these later texts.

Since questions about state finances and military power were closely connected in the late seventeenth century, it comes as no surprise that references to corruption show up in pamphlets from the 1670s, 1680s, and 1690s whose main focus is the absolutist threat inherent in the establishment of a standing army under monarchic command. It is perhaps more surprising that there is scarcely any difference in the arguments of these pamphlets before and after the Glorious Revolution. In texts such as Andrew Marvell's *An Account of the Growth of Popery and Arbitrary Government* (1677), Algernon Sidney's *Discourses Concerning Government* (1681), Robert Molesworth's *An Account of Denmark as it was in 1692* (1694), John Trenchard's *An Argument, Shewing that a Standing Army is Inconsistent with A Free Government, and absolutely destructive to the Constitution of the English Monarchy* (1997), and in Andrew Fletcher's *A Dis-*

(See also M. M. Goldsmith, 1991; Nicholson, 1996; Pocock, 1971, esp. page 93; Worden, 1991, 1994).

course of Government with Relation to Militias (1698) the analysis of what Pocock has called corruption by the executive is wholly subservient to the fear that an English monarch will use the power of a standing army to change the English constitution (Pocock 1975, p. 420). Only intermittently, the army and the court are seen, not as the institutions of sovereign power, but rather as institutions that grant the monarch too much economic influence over his parliament and his subjects.

This changes with Charles Davenant's two satirical pamphlets, *The True Picture of a Modern Whig* from the summer of 1701 – which was quickly printed in 6 editions – and *Tom Double Return'd out of the Country: Or, the True Picture of a Modern Whig, set forth in a Second Dialogue* from 1702.[6] According to these pamphlets, the English constitution was not threatened by a standing army, but by a set of new financial instruments invented to administer the public debt. This debt exploded after the Glorious Revolution, mainly because William III engaged England in a protracted and costly war against France, leading to a tripling of governmental expenditure in the decades following the revolution, sharp rises in taxation, and the introduction of new types of financial instruments to borrow money (Brewer 1989; Dickson 1967; see also Harris 2007, p. 491). After 1688, the English parliament borrowed money through state lotteries and the selling of annuities, both of which produced paper credit, which could be resold thus creating a market for "paper money." The security for these papers lay in the revenue from future taxation, effectively forcing the hand of later parliaments. Furthermore, in 1694, the Bank of England was established in order to lend money to the English government. From 1695 to 1700 a group of Whig noblemen, Davenant's "modern Whigs" – who had been active in the ousting of James II, but had now, as they held positions at William III's court, become much less beholden to the principles of pre-revolution Whiggism – dominated the cabinet of William III.

Tom Double, the very energetic anti-hero of Davenant's two satirical pamphlets – his interlocutor Mr. Whiglove is mainly there to ask questions and listen, both are called "under-spur-leathers to the late Ministry" on the title page of *A*

---

6   Though not as well known as many of the other neo-Machiavellian writers in seventeenth and eighteenth century England, Davenant was one of the leading political and economic thinkers of his day. According to Pocock (1975, p. 436cc) economic activity – trade – was seen by Davenant as something that both strengthened and corrupted the political nation; Pocock does not, however discuss what corruption meant for Davenant. Kustaa Multamäki (1997, p. 67cc) insists on the continuity between Davenant's and Machiavelli's concepts of corruption. He does not examine the semantic changes occurring in Davenant's pamphlets.

True Picture of a Modern Whig – willingly admits to have been part of every corrupt practice of the government since the revolution. He has sold positions at court for money, clipped money as a collector of taxes, attempted to buy an election in order to become member of parliament, and was and is deeply involved in the buying and selling of governmental papers of credit. Through these, he boasts, the whole of London – but not the countryside, alas – has been corrupted. They have invested in governmental debt and are now committed to defending the policies of the modern Whigs:

"[R]esolving, as we always did, to play a corrupt Game, it was highly necessary for us to form to our Selves a Strength that at all times might protect us in the Thefts and Depredations we propos'd to make upon the Publick; and could we have braver or bolder Troops to Fight in our Defence, than as it were an Army of Men with their Pockets full of Bank-Bills, Bank Stock, Malt and Lottery Tickets, Exchequer Bills, *East India* Stock, and who bore in their Hands Tallies instead of Staves and Truncheons?" – "having dipt London so deply in all these Loans; for the great Affection our Friends bear to their Tallies, Stocks, and Riches of the like kind in which they abound, subjects 'em entirely to our direction, and makes 'em have no more concern for the *Publick* of England, than they have for the Publick of *Japan*." (Davenant, 1701, pp. 39, 42. See also Davenant, 1702, page 26.)

The economic dependence of those who invest in government debt forces them to track the interest of those in power, and not the interests of the nation. But since the people are also members of the electorate, and thus not entirely powerless – formally, they decide who should sit in parliament – it is necessary for the corrupt politicians to court them and track their interests, too.[7] Enmeshed in corrupt, interpersonal relations, not only are the powerless dependent on the powerful, but the powerful turn out to be dependent upon the powerless, as well, thus not only unwilling to, but in a sense also unable to, follow the laws of the country or, for that matter, take regard of the common good. They are also unable to control their own fate, something that might have to do with the fact that Davenant wrote at a moment where the Whig "cabal" had just been ousted from power. In fact, most of *The True Picture of a Modern Whig* and *Tom Double Return'd*

---

7   See Davenant 1701, p. 34: "Every little Scoundrel got an Estate. We suffer'd 'em to drink up the People's Blood till they were out of Breath, and till their Eyes grew Red. In short, all Men cheated to what degree they pleas'd, which was wink'd at in hopes to make and secure a Party. Therefore all the busy Proling Fellows both in Town and Country, who hope to advance themselves, wish to see our Noble Friends restor'd to their former Power."

out of the Country lets Tom account for the different strategies he and the other modern Whigs have used to keep their power and what they will do to regain it. But while Mr. Whiglove at the end of *The True Picture of a Modern Whig* seems to despair, Tom Double simply accepts that the future is out of their control:

"[L]eave the rest to Providence: Many things may happen to relieve us, some great Calamity may befall the nation; you shall see us lift up our Heads once more upon any fatal and publick Disaster." (Davenant, 1701, p. 58)

According to Tom Double, one strategy to regain power would be the abolishment of parliament and the introduction of absolute monarchy. However, in Davenant's two pamphlets the professional soldier and a standing army are not in themselves depicted as a threat to the English constitution. On the contrary, the soldiers are "brave Fellows and love their Country" (Davenant, 1701, p. 52), and are thus subject to Tom Double's scorn and pity – and a source for further profiteering, since the English government were habitually unable to pay its arrears in specie. "Poor silly Rogues! their Honour forsooth led 'em to fight for England abroad, but I play'd a much wiser Game, by joining with those who in the mean while were plundering their Country at home," as he declares (Davenant, 1701, p. 31, see also 29, 36). But just as Tom Double inverts the logic of public credit – one shouldn't increase public debt in order to finance wars, one should start wars in order to increase public debt, he argues (Davenant, 1701, p. 11) – he inverts the relationship between arbitrary government and corruption. Corruption is no longer a precondition for arbitrary government, arbitrary government is a means to continue the possibility of corrupt profiteering. It is, in fact, only because England is not yet wholly corrupted – according to Davenant, the countryside has not yet been entirely penetrated by the corrupt practices of the modern Whigs – that it might be necessary to have parliament dissolved and let the monarch rule "by his own will, and with a Standing-Army" (Davenant, 1701, p. 43).

In his polemic and highly entertaining pamphlets, Davenant argues that the expansion of the post-revolutionary English government and its new financial instruments corrupted the English polity. But his argument also produced subtle changes in the meaning of corruption. It made the connection between corruption and tyranny purely contingent: were it possible to corrupt the English countryside, there would be no need for arbitrary government. Furthermore, the individual consequences of living enmeshed in corrupt relations begin to change. Corruption seems not just to make the powerless but everyone dependent upon some particular other, thus forcing them to track the particular interests of someone else. Corruption's moral threat to the powerful is thus no longer arrogance and ambition, but the prospect of making them unfree. Machiavelli repeatedly asserted that a good monarch, at least for a time, could counteract the effects of a corrupt societal tissue. According to the logic of Davenant, this is no longer a possibility. Finally, life enmeshed within a corrupt social tissue is not just characterized by moral degradation, but also by a certain kind of temporality. Even though Tom Double is energetic and nimble, he and his kind are utterly unable to control their own fate. What in Machiavelli seemed the fate of a corrupt political community – its inability to sustain itself in secular time – is now seen as an aspect of subjective life within the corrupt polity.

Many of these changes are also found in the polemical texts of the very vocal opposition against Robert Walpole, who functioned as England's first "prime minister" in the 1720s and 1730s. As is well known, Walpole kept himself at power by using the economic resources of government to gain allies and manage parliament (Black, 2001). Even though he also kept England out of major wars and politically stable, a number of contemporary pamphlets, periodical essays – the most important was *The Craftsman* – and a series of literary satires by John Gay, Jonathan Swift, Henry Fielding, and Alexander Pope consistently described him as the orchestrator of a fundamentally corrupt society (Goldgar, 1976; Nicholson, 1994). At the same time these literary satires were at pains to portray life within the corrupt polity as utterly controlled by the contingencies of fortune, darkly suggesting how the English people not only willingly debased itself – "See all our Nobles begging to be slaves! / See all our Fools aspiring to be knaves!" as Alexander Pope wrote in his "Epilogue to the Satires, Dialogue I" (1737), a poem where the moral code of London is declared to be that "Not to be corrupted is the shame" – but was also, as is seen in John Gay's *The Beggar's Opera* and in Henry Fielding's *Jonathan Wild*, driven through life by contingent, almost random events.

This aspect is visible in, but not the primary concern of, Lord Bolingbroke's *A Dissertation upon Parties*, which was published as a series of letters in *The Craftsman* from October 1733 to January 1734 and again in the fall of 1734.[8]

---

8 There is an unfortunate tendency to dismiss Bolingbroke's writings as overly strategic, suffused with nostalgia and/or derivative of earlier writers in the English, republican tradition (See Kramnick 1968; Burtt 1992; Skinner 2002). Only Burtt emphasizes any semantic changes within Bolingbroke's republican vocabulary. Bolingbroke narrows the meaning of virtue down to mean support for the existing constitution, which are defended by Bolingbroke himself and his fellow patriots, Burtt asserts (Burtt 1992, p. 90). Accordingly, corruption simply means support for Walpole's government. It is

Instead, Bolingbroke develops the dissociation of corruption and tyranny which Davenant's text had begun. Throughout the nineteen letters, Bolingbroke structures his argument by a distinction between two types of governmental overreach. Before 1688, Bolingbroke writes, political conflict in England stood between those who defended the liberty of the citizens expressed – among other things – through parliament, and those who defended the royal prerogative and divine authority. This battle regarding political sovereignty and constitutional form, its expression open disagreement, implicitly assumed that the basis of political power was military and physical force. Now, however, the conflict stands between those who support the current English constitution, and those who argue that it is necessary for the smooth functioning of the political nation that the government manages parliament as well as possible (Bolingbroke, 1997, p. 95, 186). Hence, the main threat to the English constitution is the economic power of the government – Bolingbroke bluntly dismisses the threat of a standing army as irrelevant for contemporary English politics (Bolingbroke, 1997, page 93) – and governmental overreach does not result in open conflict, but rather in political and social corruption.

"In a word, they began to see that the foundations were laid of giving a great power to the crown indirectly, as the prerogative, which they had formerly dreaded, could give directly, and of establishing universal corruption," Bolingbroke writes – "they" designating patriots who formerly fought the prerogative, and were now part of the opposition against Walpole (Bolingbroke, 1997, p. 173). This indirect power is founded upon the institutional inventions in the decades following the Glorious Revolution. Walpole's power derives from his management of governmental debt, which not only allows government to grow larger, thus creating more salaried positions and other funds with which to corrupt representatives in parliament and other politically important people, but also changes the nature of England's larger economy, burdening tradesmen and farmers with high taxes while letting those who place their fortunes in the papers of public credit earn vast amounts of money. The price for this, however, is their dependency upon the government, a dependency which makes them utterly unable to control their own fate: "The main springs that turn, or may turn, the artificial wheel of credit, and make the paper estates that are fastened to it, rise or

---

not important for my reading of Bolingbroke's text to judge whether he was sincere or insincere in presenting his argument, but I do think Burtt's misrepresents the argument of *A Dissertation upon Parties*, which pivots around the fact that corruption is a type of threat the existing English constitution has no safeguards against.

fall, lurk behind the veil of the treasury", as Bolingbroke writes (Bolingbroke, 1997, p. 182).

But, like Davenant, Bolingbroke never argues that corruption will in itself lead to a change in the constitutional form of the nation. He does not even hint at the fact that it would weaken the government's ability to act forcefully. Instead his two final letters continually slip into a kind of subjunctive mode, where the crown becomes ever more powerful and thus ever more able to manage parliament either by bribing the electorate or giving salaried positions to members of parliament, and where the twin threats of overtaxation and financial speculation lead to an ever more corrupt social tissue. It is clear that this is a threat to the English constitution, but it is not clear that this threat should be understood as the threat of constitutional change. In a somewhat confused earlier passage, Bolingbroke describes the political consequences of corruption as something which is both like and unlike tyranny:

"[F]or a prince, or his minister, to become our tyrant, there is no need to abolish Parliaments; there is no need that he who is master of one part of the legislature, should endeavour to abolish the other two, when he can use, upon every occasion, the united strength of the whole; there is no need he should be a tyrant in the gross, when he can be so in detail, nor in name, when he can be so in effect; that for Parliaments to establish tyranny, there is no need therefore to repeal Magna Carta, or any other of the great supports of our liberty. It is enough, if they put themselves corruptly and servilely under the influence of such a prince, or such a minister." (Bolingbroke, 1997, p. 95)

Corruption by the executive leads to a political situation which is effectively tyrannical, but is not tyranny as a constitutional form. When parliament has been corrupted, when it willingly puts itself under the influence – makes itself dependent upon – "a prince, or such a minister," the crown can effectively reign supreme. But the formal protections of liberty are not destroyed: Parliament is not dissolved, the Magna Carta is not repealed. With Davenant, the relationship between tyranny and corruption had become contingent; with Bolingbroke it is as if corruption is the name of a different kind of unfreedom, one for which he has no name, but is yet not quite like tyranny. This is so because Bolingbroke's tyranny of corruption is a form of dominion the subjects willingly submit to. Parliament willingly submits to the overtures of Walpole, the people willingly submit to the overtures of economic reward through investments in governmental bonds. As Bolingbroke writes in his first letter: "He that is corrupted, co-operates with he that corrupts. He runs to his arms at the first beckon; or, in order sometimes to raise the price, he meets him but half way" (Bolingbroke, 1997, p. 3).

But it is also so because corruption no longer bears any relation to changes in constitutional form, such as it did in Machiavelli. Instead, "universal corruption" is the name of a potentially permanent tension between the political form and the societal tissue of a polity which according to Bolingbroke is particular to the modern fiscal-military state. It diagnoses a governmental form which becomes stronger and more stable the more corrupt its citizens become. And it diagnoses the historical situation where we are formally free, Bolingbroke argues, if not materially so.

Coda

It is entirely possible to argue that Bolingbroke's and Davenant's polemical diagnoses are guided by short-sighted, polemical interests or are inadequate descriptions of the changes of eighteenth century England. But taken as a semantic figure, their diagnosis of societal corruption does not function as an attack upon commercial society or social differentiation, as it has often been read. In fact, questions of commerce are rarely mentioned in Davenant's pamphlets or *A Dissertation upon Parties*; luxury is only mentioned in passing and is wholly subsumed by an analysis of the consequences of the establishment of the fiscal-military state; the problem of corruption is never that different social groups develop their own, particular perspective upon society. Put more generally, their – and the republican – use of corruption as a critical diagnosis simply does not relate to some degradation of the subject inherent in trade. Nor does it relate to any idea of *homo economicus*, to any idea of capitalism's inherently degrading instrumental rationality. On the contrary, it presupposes that man is a political being – to be more precise, it presupposes what Phillip Pettit has called a "holist social ontology". On this basis it designates the interplay between institutional imbalance, interpersonal relations of dependence, and subjective moral degradation. This degradation takes on the form of having to continually track the interest of some particular other, to let oneself be dominated by him or her, thus being unable to take regard for the common good. In eighteenth century England, it furthermore takes on the connotation of not being able to control one's own fate, and to designate the state of being materially unfree, a mode of societal and subjective unfreedom emanating not from constitutional form, but from the structure of the social tissue of the polity, which undermines the freedom supposedly secured by constitutional form.

In this sense the concept of corruption might be worth retrieving today.

References

Arendt, H. (2006). *Between Past and Future*. New York: Penguin Books.
Black, J. (2001). *Walpole in Power*. Stroud: Sutton.
Lord Bolingbroke (Henry St. John). (1997). *Political Writings*. Cambridge: Cambridge University Press.
Bonadeo, A. (1973). *Corruption, Conflict, and Power in the Works and Times of Niccolò Machiavelli*. Berkeley, CA: University of California Press.
Bratsis, P. (2003). The Construction of Corruption, or Rules of Separation and Illusions of Purity in a Bourgeois Society. In *Social Text*, vol. 21, no. 4, pp. 9-33.
Burtt, S. (1992) *Virtue Tranformed. Political Argument in England 1688-1740*. Cambridge: Cambridge University Press.
Brewer, J. (1989). *The Sinews of Power. War, Money, and the English State*. London: Unwin Human Ltd.
Davenant, C. (1701). *The True Picture of a Modern Whig*. London.
Davenant, C. (1702). *Tom Double Return'd out of the Country*. London.
Dickson, P.G.M. (1967). *The Financial Revolution in England. A Study in the Development of Puclic Credit*. London: Macmillan.
Euben, J.P. (1989). Corruption. In *Political Innovation and Conceptual Change*, ed. T. Ball, pp. 220-246. Cambridge. Cambridge University Press.
Goldgar, B.A. (1976). *Walpole and the Wits*. Lincoln, NE: University of Nebraska Press.
Harris, T. (2007). *Revolution. The Great Crisis of the British Monarchy 1685-1720*. London: Penguin Books.
Johnston, M. (2005). *Syndromes of Corruption: Wealth, Power and Democracy*. Cambridge: Cambridge University Press.
Lessing, L. (2011). *Republic, Lost. How Money Corrupts Congress – and a Plan to Stop It*. New York: Hachette Book Group.
Machiavelli, N. (1970): *The Discourses*. London: Penguin Classics.
Machiavelli, N. (1997). *Opere*, vol. 1. Torino: Einaudi-Gallimard.
Miller, S. (n.d.). Corruption. Retrieved from plato.stanford.edu/entries/-corruption/
Multamäki, K. (1997). *Towards Great Britain. Commerce and Conquest in the Thought of Algernon Sidney and Charles Davenant*. Helsinki: The Finnish Academy of Science and Letters.
Nicholson, C. (1994). *Writing and the Rise of Finance. Capital Satires of the Early Eighteenth Century*. Cambridge: Cambridge University Press.

Nye, J.S. (1990). Corruption and Political Development: A Cost-Benefit Analysis. In *Political Corruption. A Handbook*, ed. Arnold J. Heidenheimer et. al. pp. 963-983. New Brunswick: Transaction Publishers.
Pettit, P. (1993). *The Common Mind.* Oxford: Oxford University Press.
Pettit, P. (1997). *Republicanism. A Theory of Freedom and Government.* Oxford: Oxford University Press.
Pettit, P. (2006). Connecting the Dots. In *Common Minds. Themes from the Philosophy of Philip Pettit*, ed. G. Brennan et.al. pp. 215-344. Oxford: Clarendon Press.
Pocock, J.G.A (1971). *Politics, Language, and Time.* Chicago, IL: Chicago University Press.
Pocock, J.G.A. (1975). *The Machiavellian Moment.* Princeton, N. J.: Princeton University Press.
Sandel, M. (1996). *Democracy's Discontent.* Cambridge, MA: Harvard University Press.
Sasso, G. (1987). *Machiavelli e gli antichi,* vol 1. Milano: Riccardi Ricciardi Editore.
Scott, J. (2000). *England's Troubles.* Cambridge: Cambridge University Press.
Schumer, S.M. (1979). Machiavelli: Republican Politics and its Corruption. In *Political Theory* vol. 7, no. 1, pp. 5-34.
Skinner, Q. (1978). *The Foundations of Modern Political Thought* vols. 1-2. Cambridge: Cambridge University Press.
Skinner, Q. (1998). *Liberty before Liberalism.* Cambridge: Cambridge University Press.
Skinner, Q. (2002). *Visions of Politics* vols. 1-3. Cambridge: Cambridge University Press.
Viroli, M. (1995). *For Love of Country.* Oxford: Oxford Clarendon Press.
Viroli, M. (2012). *The Liberty of Servants. Berlusconi's Italy.* Princeton, N. J.: Princeton University Press.
Worden, B. (1991). English republicanism. In *The Cambridge History of Political Thought 1450-1700*, ed. J.H. Burns. Cambridge: Cambridge University Press pp. 443-477.
Worden, B. (1994). Republicanism and the Restoration. In D. Wootton (Ed.) *Republicanism, Liberty, and Commercial Society* (pp. 139-193). Stanford, CA: Stanford University Press.

Unfreedom and the Republican Tradition in the French Revolution

RUTH SCURR

During the French Revolution, a consensus emerged about the need for a republican form of government, even though there was little agreement as to how such a form of government should or could be established, and even less convergence on whether or not it would be necessary to introduce some forms of unfreedom to secure a free republic (Nicolet, 1982). Disagreement as to what exactly republican government involved – in both theoretical and practical terms – drew on a long established tradition of political thought, within which Montesquieu and Rousseau were especially important. But as the intense politics of the Revolution unfurled, attention shifted towards describing forms of unfreedom – constraints or sacrifices that might be involved in successfully instituting a stable republic.

This article considers three approaches to the absence of freedom, or the presence of unfreedom, in the early republican debates of the 1790s: political, social and economic. In each of these spheres the question of republican exclusivism (i.e. the claim that the republic is the only legitimate form of government) was central. Participants in the debates of the 1790s asked themselves whether it is possible to be free – politically, socially or economically – inside the republic in ways that are simply not accessible through any other form of government. Unsurprisingly, given the definitive collapse of the French monarchy in 1792, there was a proliferation of positive answers to this question. These answers went beyond a pragmatic acceptance of the republic as the de facto and necessary form of government in the revolutionary circumstances after 1789. Moderates and radicals alike drew on a rich inheritance of republican ideas to make sense of the practical predicament of stabilizing France and establishing a new constitution and government compatible with the Declaration of the Rights of Man and Citizen.

In the struggle to achieve a viable form of government after 1789, fraught questions arose regarding the political, social and economic limits within which a republic might be secured. The Revolution began with the abbé Sieyès's assertion of the inclusive nature of the Third Estate's sovereign and constituting power, but before long it resolved into a series of intense disagreements about how to delineate restrictions to political, social and economic freedom in circumstances where tensions between public and individual interest were difficult to describe in theory and even harder to resolve in practice.

CONSTITUTIONAL UNFREEDOM: THE CONTRAST BETWEEN REPUBLICAN AND MONARCHICAL GOVERNMENT

In 1789, no one in the National Assembly thought France could become a Republic. Instead, the representatives to the Third Estate, who had redescribed themselves as representatives of the nation, with the right to exercise constituting power, were aiming to establish a constitutional monarchy, in the place of the absolute monarchy that had existed under the *ancien régime*. However, between 1789, and the execution of Louis XVI in January 1793, there was a steady rise in republican exclusivism. One turning point in this debate was the Flight to Varennes, which occurred on the night of 20th June 1791, when the National Assembly was still trying to finalize a new constitutional monarchy for France. The King and royal family who had been more or less forced to remain in Paris since the autumn of 1789, finally decided to try and escape to the western border, where a growing number of émigrés had congregated. The attempt failed, the King was recognized, and brought back to Paris in shameful silence. The mayor of Paris (Jean Sylvain Bailly), still hoping he could save the constitutional monarchy, initially tried to claim that the king had been kidnapped, but no one could believe it. There was uproar in the Assembly, and no one could make himself heard. According to Madame Roland's contemporary account, her husband Roland, Robespierre, Pétion and Brissot – all by this time well established in their revolutionary political careers – discussed together how to react to the King's attempted flight. Was this the end of the monarchy? Was a republic now possible – or even necessary – in France? Robespierre, with his habitual grimace, and bi-ting his nails, asked: "What is a Republic?" (Roland, 1821, p. 299; Furet and Halévi, 1996) In the circumstances, this was very far from being a simple-minded question – it went right to the heart of the new dilemma facing France: if the constitutional monarchy that the National Assembly had been arguing over for so many months wasn't going to work, what exactly was the alternative?

Thomas Paine was one of the people who tried seriously to address this question. He did so by starting a new journal with his friend the Marquis de Condorcet, a journal named for, and devoted to, the Republic. In their journal, Condorcet published a satirical letter from a fictitious young engineer, offering to build a royal automaton – a mechanical king – to place at the head of government (Condorcet, 1847, pp. 239-241). This mechanical King, accompanied by a mechanical court, would go to Mass and celebrate Easter at the appropriate time, would converse with foreign Kings at the appropriate level, and would cost the state considerably less than its actual flesh and blood monarch, Louis XVI. The mechanical King could sanction laws, and appoint ministers, following the advice of the legislative assembly. He could even be declared inviolable and infallible. Behind Condorcet's mischief was his sincere belief that what was really important in politics could be rationally ordered through the principles of social science, and a well-designed constitution would have no place whatsoever for the independent or arbitrary will of a monarch (Baker, 1975; Badinter, E. and Badinter, R., 1988). Condorcet envisaged that the monarch would be replaced by an elected executive council, responsible to the National Assembly. Interestingly, the famous constitutional theorist, the abbé Sieyès, saw difficulties with this way of reorganising executive power through an executive council. He elaborated them in 1791 in a public exchange not with Condorcet, but with Condorcet's co-editor, Paine.

The first issue of the journal Condorcet started with Paine considered whether republican government is necessarily limited to small states. Paine thought not: on the contrary, the true republican system of election and representation was the only known, and in his view the only possible, way of establishing a proportion between wise government and the extent of a country (Paine, 1894, pp. 4-8; Claeys, 1989). He argued that the word "republic" expressed the definitive idea of all legitimate government concerning a nation's public affairs, or *respublica*. Historical examples of republics such as Holland and Venice were misleading and more accurately described as aristocracies: the only legitimate form of government was republican.

Paine contrasted the old hereditary form of government with a new representative form. The former was illegitimate and tyrannous in its very nature, whilst the latter delegated power for the common benefit of society. On this account, self-interested hereditary kings caused wars through their passions and vanity, whilst public-interested representative governments were more likely to transcend national prejudice, encouraging universal society as the means of universal commerce. No one could rightfully impose future rulers on later generations:

there was something pernicious in the very notion of personally inherited political power.

In the protracted discussion of a new constitution that occupied the National Assembly from 1789-1792, it was Sieyès who best highlighted the relation between accountability and unfreedom: i.e. the need for constraint on individual ministerial wills within a carefully formed executive branch of government. Sieyès replied to Paine in the newspaper *Le Moniteur* on 6 July, addressing the problem of monarchical government in which the king's role is both a public function and an inherited position. He agreed that when the term "republican" was used in its widest possible sense and understood to indicate a government that was a *respublica*, (as opposed to something privately owned by a privileged elite), it was certainly accurate to say that all legitimate government must be republican (Sieyès, 1989, vol.2, ss. 29-30)

Yet it was equally true, Sieyès insisted, that the term "republican" could also be attributed a far narrower meaning than the term "representative". In this sense, deciding the form of government was a matter of determining the structure of executive power. It was possible to support a monarchical rather than a polyarchical organisation of executive power and still be a republican in the broad sense of the term. Sieyès argued that the choice between a monarchical and a republican form of government was the choice between accountable government on the part of individual ministers, chosen and constrained by the will of an unaccountable elector (the monarch), and decisions formulated by a majority who had no clear legal accountability to anyone else. There is a direct connection between accountability and unfreedom in regard to individual ministerial wills. But beyond this there was still a question as to whether or not the role of the unaccountable elector could be inherited. Sieyès, like Paine, explicitly stated that the notion of inherited public power was irreconcilably at odds with the laws of true representation. It would be far preferable to find a way of electing the king that could combine all the advantages of inheritance (especially the avoidance of civil war), with all the advantages of election. Contemporary circumstances, however, were too precarious to risk this type of constitutional upheaval. The point of Sieyès's argument was to show the importance of homogeneity within the executive power. He supposed that the unaccountable elector could maintain unity within a plural ministerial body that was strictly accountable.

For Sieyès, the choice between a monarchical and republican form of government was a choice about the nation's use of its constituting power, and not a choice about the nature of that power. Sieyès thought that there was a sense in which Paine's conflation of representative and republican government had obscured these issues (Sieyès, 1989, vol.2, ss. 29-30). Paine had been right to emphasise that the choice between a representative government and any other sort of government was the choice between liberty and despotism, between the nation's exercise of its own constituting power, and an unacceptable appropriation of that constituting power. However, the choice between monarchy and polyarchy was the choice between two distinct ways of structuring executive power. In this context, Sieyès clearly indicated his own preference for monarchical government. In his famous exchange with Thomas Paine in 1791, he ostensibly defended a monarchical form of government claiming that,

"Ce n'est ni pour caresser d'anciennes habitudes, ni par aucun sentiment superstitieux de royalisme, que je préféré la monarchie. Je la prefére, parce qu'il m'est démontre qu'il y a plus de liberté pour le citoyen dans la monarchie que dans la république. Tout autre motif de détermination me parait pueril. Le meilleur régime social est à mon avis celui où, non pas un, non pas quelques-uns seulement, mais où tous jouissent tranquillement de la plus grande latitude de liberté possible."

"It is not out of fondness for ancient customs, or any superstitious royalism, that I prefer monarchy. I prefer it because it seems to me that there is more freedom for the citizen in a monarchy than in a republic. Any other means of deciding seems puerile. The best social regime in my view is the one under which all enjoy the greatest possible extension of freedom." (Forsyth, 1987, p. 177)[1]

And yet, Sieyès at this time had pronounced reservations about the legitimacy of inherited power. He recognised that Louis XVI, following the Flight to Varennes, was no longer a viable component of the new constitution. And he was certainly aware of Condorcet's recent, highly publicised, conversion to the republican cause (Forsyth, 1987, p. 177).

Properly understood, Sieyes's preference for a monarchical, as opposed to a polyarchical form of government, links his early revolutionary thought to his constitutional arguments in 1795 and 1799 when he experimented with a variety of different models for obtaining a unified chief executive inside a republican form of government. A remark Sieyes made in a manuscript of 1795 can be applied to the constitutional struggle in France at any point between 1789 and 1799:

"Résoudre ce grand problème: comment se procurer dans un État tous les avantages de l'élection d'un chef sans avoir à en redouter les inconvénients, et tous les avantages de

---

1 All translations are my own unless specified otherwise.

l'hérédité sans aucun de ses innombrables dangers? Alors seulement votre constitution portera en elle-même le principe de sa proper conservation."

"Resolve this great problem: How to procure within a state all the advantages of the election of a head without becoming a prey to all its inconveniences, and all the advantages of heredity without its immeasurable dangers? Only then will your constitution carry within itself the principle of its own conservation." (Forsyth, 1987, p. 182; Sieyès, 1999, vol.1, p. 514)

Arguably, this was a question that Paine's avid promotion of republican government, in the wake of Louis XVI's flight to Varennes, simply failed to register or address.

SOCIAL UNFREEDOM: THE DISPUTE OVER THE ROLE OF VIRTUE UNDER REPUBLICAN GOVERNMENT

Montesquieu's reflections on virtue were the starting point for the debates on virtue during the French Revolution. He had defined virtue within a republic as the love of the republic, a product of feeling rather than of knowledge. In *The Spirit of the Laws*, he described the virtues that sustain republics but are redundant inside monarchies, in heroic terms:

"[…] l'amour pour la patrie, du désir de la vraie gloire, du renoncement à soi-même, du sacrifice de ses plus chers intérêts, et de toutes ces vertus héroïques que nous trouvons dans les anciens, et dont nous avons seulement entendu parler."

"[…] love of the homeland, desire for true glory, self-renunciation, sacrifice of one's dearest interests, and all those heroic virtues we find in the ancients and know only by hearsay." (Montesquieu, 1950-1961, Part 1, Book 3, Chapter 5, p. 69)

In these terms, the problem the French Revolution posed was the problem of finding a new definition of virtue suitable to large, modern commercial states; or else the problem of finding an alternative to virtue to act as the principle (or spring of action) in modern regimes. What constraints on individual freedom would be required to secure virtue inside a modern republic? Once France officially became a republic in 1792, the question of publicly orientated virtue and its role inside republican regimes moved to the centre of political and constitutional discussion. What were the causal antecedents of public virtue? What was its political significance? How was virtue possible inside the modern as opposed to ancient republican form of government? Did virtue have a part to play in providing a social framework within which individuals could be given both the opportunity to become autonomous and the opportunity to exercise their autonomy? How should the relation between the presence (or absence) of virtue and the existence of freedom (or unfreedom) be understood?

In what has become the most famous of all his speeches, delivered at the height of the Terror on 7th May 1794 (or 18 Florèal, in the Revolutionary Calendar), Robespierre set out the foundations for the worship of The Supreme Being in France (Robespierre, 1910, vol.10, p. 442-465). In this speech – at the climax of his revolutionary career – Robespierre attempted to show how the religion of patriotism that had been implicit in the Revolution ever since the great Festival of Federation on the first anniversary of the Fall of the Bastille, might now be developed, institutionalised and used to secure the social foundations of the still very precarious new Republic.

As he spoke, Robespierre raised a question that pinpointed precisely a fundamental contrast between himself and those who had hoped earlier in the Revolution that recent advances in moral, social and political understanding, might be systematically applied in designing a new form of government for France:

"Le fondement unique de la société civile, c'est la morale! Toutes les associations qui nous font la guerre reposent sur le crime: ce ne sont aux yeux de la vérité que des hordes de sauvages policés et de brigands disciplinés. A quoi se réduit donc cette science mystérieuse de la politique et de la législation? A mettre dans les lois et dans l'administration les vérités morales reléguées dans les livres des philosophes, et à appliquer à la conduite des peuples les notions triviales de probité que chacun est forcé d'adopter pour sa conduite privée, c'est-à-dire à employer autant d'habileté à faire régner la justice que les gouvernements en ont mis jusqu'ici à être injustes impunément ou avec bienséance."

"Morality is the unique foundation of civil society. All associations that make war rely on crime: before the eyes of truth they are nothing but policed savage hordes and disciplined brigands. What does this mysterious science of politics and legislation come down to, if not the application to the behaviour of peoples of the trivial notions of probity that everyone is forced to adopt for his private conduct?" (Rapport du Comité de Salut public du 18 floréal an II [7 May 1794]).

These unassuming, ordinary, intuitive notions of probity first encountered and recognised in private life, but afterwards collectively applied, were Robespierre's direct substitute for more systematic or scientific approaches to the general predicament of governing France at the end of the eighteenth century – and the specific predicament of rescuing the Revolution. The contrast was stark. On the one hand, experts like the abbé Sieyès, the Marquis de Condorcet, Pierre-Louis Rœderer, and so on, pioneers of the social sciences who entered the Revolution with high hopes for what might be achieved politically through specialist knowledge. And on the other hand, Robespierre arguing that goodness in human beings is easy, not difficult, to recognise – and that such simple goodness is all there ever is to hope for or rely upon in collective life.

After the fall of the Constitutional Monarchy in 1792, Robespierre became closely associated with Saint-Just whose conception of society vacillated between virtual anarchy and a schoolmaster state (Hampson, 1988, 1991). Saint Just affirmed the emergence of individual rights inside the modern republic, in contrast to their marked absence in the ancient republics of Athens and Sparta. But he also lamented the decline in patriotism and the rise of self-love, egoism or private interest, concomitant with individual rights. Saint-Just was fascinated by the role of political institutions in reconciling individual with public interest. Before the nature and implications of Saint-Just's plethora of republican institutions for the moral education of the people became apparent in practice, his enthusiasm was greeted with excited approval by more moderate, liberal-minded theorists. Pierre-Louis Rœderer, for example, friend and intellectual associate of the abbé Sieyès, commented that Saint-Just was someone who had outlined at last to the National Convention (in April 1793), the need to insert something between precepts and powers in the forthcoming republican constitution (JP, 25 April 1793; Forsyth, 1989). Between the Declaration of Rights and the constitution, between principles and laws, there was a widely acknowledged need for institutions that would shape the wills and habits of citizens in accordance with the general interest.

However it very soon became clear that behind Saint-Just's proposals for republican institutions, there lay a model of what society ought to be that departed radically from the expectations of Rœderer, Condorcet, Sieyès, Brissot and others. Saint Just, echoing Montesquieu, argued that government should rely on a principle or spring of social harmony. But he also invoked Rousseau's argument in the *Social Contract* that the Legislator should mould Man as he needed him to be (Rousseau, 1962, vol.1, p. 478). And during the summer of 1793 he claimed that if the people who had been given a *patrie* were not happy with it, there must be something wrong with them (Hampson, 1988). There was a surprising and shockingly short step between the view that social harmony could not exist independently of political institutions, and the view that individuals should be altered to fit with the institutions they had acquired. By February 1794 Saint-Just was claiming: "Il s'est fait une révolution dans le gouvernement; elle n'a point pénétré l'état civil" ("There has been a revolution in the government, but it has not penetrated into civil society". Saint Just, 1834, p. 215). But the penetration of government into civil society in any directly authoritarian sense was the precise inverse of the schemes for enhancing co-operation and spontaneous social harmony that Sieyès Condorcet, Brissot, Rœderer, and many others had tried to develop before the outbreak of the Terror.

Another way of seeing Robespierre's decisive dismissal of social science during the Terror recognises the strength of his claim that the sole resources for securing the new republic were virtue and terror: "virtue without which terror is destructive; terror without which virtue is impotent" (Robespierre, 1910, vol. 10, p. 357). Early practitioners of social science were convinced that there were more reliable institutional alternatives to Robespierre's alarmingly narrow account of society and politics. Sieyès and others thought that carefully designed representative institutions would minimize the importance of good men in politics and make even a government of fallible and potentially corrupt human beings wholly compatible with the pursuit the of the common good. Robespierre's fierce rejection of any such grounds for reassurance might have made good political sense in far more peaceful times, but in revolutionary circumstances its power was overwhelming. What it lacked was an answer to the urgent questions: when (and how) could the Terror ever hope to end and the reign of virtue begin? How, in short, could virtue be reliably generated or constructed inside the new republic if it did not already exist as a demonstrable capacity among citizens? It is in the struggle to answer this question that the problem or reconciling Robespierre the "man of virtue" with Robespierre "defender of the Terror" arises. On Furet's analysis it is the language of moral politics that effects the reconciliation, linking the aspirations of 1789 to the later bloodshed (Furet, 1978). Older Marxist interpretations looked to the embattled circumstances of the Revolution to explain Robespierre's acceptance of the Terror as political necessity. These judgments each have some force. But Robespierre's rejection of the standing and self-sufficiency of early social science, and its aspiration to minimize the role of virtue in politics, also played a significant part in his defense of the Terror.

ECONOMIC UNFREEDOM: THE DISPUTE OVER FOOD AND REPUBLICAN RIGHTS TO SUBSISTENCE

On 21 September 1792, prompted by Danton, the Convention decreed that property rights would be "eternally maintained" (AP(51), p. 71). On 18 March 1793, the death sentence was imposed on anyone who dared to propose a law subversive of territorial, commercial or industrial property (AP(60), p. 292). And once again, on 21 September 1793 as the Terror swept over France, the threat of arbitrary land redistribution was repudiated. These were unequivocal rejections of social levelling and radical redistribution of wealth. However, the status of property rights was persistently questioned, and like the Constituent Assembly and the *ancien régime* governments before it, the Convention was beset by demands to regulate the grain trade and prevent hunger. Those who opposed government intervention in the supply and demand of subsistence goods, premised their arguments on the view that fear of famine was both unnecessarily alarmist and the major cause of shortages in the grain supply. In doing so they drew on the long history of demands to liberalise the grain trade in France, and echoed the established economic concept of *une disette factice* (AP(53) p. 130; Kaplan, 2013).

In November 1792, the Convention heard Fabre d'Eglantine read a report on behalf of the committees for agriculture and commerce, which recommended significant government intervention in the trading of subsistence goods (AP(53), pp. 130-132).[2] Acknowledging the importance of property rights, the report argued that subsistence goods were a special case with a unique relation to public order (AP(53), p. 131). All those in possession of grain should declare the amount currently at their disposal to specially appointed district commissioners. Working from these lists, municipal authorities could demand the immediate sale of grain in specified markets whenever this was judged necessary. Exportation of grain from France should be prohibited under all circumstances, but circulation of grain inside France should be unhindered. The government should take steps to purchase a substantial quantity of grain from abroad. This report prompted a protracted debate that called into question the relation between government and society in the new republic.

In keeping with the history of the grain trade debate, opinion was split over the question of free trade. On 3 November, the Convention formalised this division by decreeing that all those concerned about subsistence should be divided into two groups: those in favour of unlimited freedom of trade, and those who proposed restrictions on the grain trade. One side appealed directly to the arguments of the *économistes* (or Physiocrats), Turgot and Adam Smith, whilst the other highlighted concerns over public order in the tradition of the abbé Terray

---

2   Fabre d'Eglantine, (Philippe-Nazaire-François) 1750-1794; poet and Jacobin member of the Paris Commune; elected to the Convention; a key figure in the creation of the Revolutionary Calendar (adopted by the Convention on 5 October 1793 and abolished on 1 January 1806); associated with Danton and turned over to the Revolutionary Tribunal on 17 January 1794.

and his predecessors. The revolutionary context affected both sides of the debate without altering its central point of contention: the theory and practice of free trade. Féraud, for example, quoted Turgot's seventh letter to the abbé Terray opposing the revocation of the 1764 edict on liberalising the grain trade, and argued that attempts since 1790 to regulate the domestic grain market and supplement it by importation, must be abandoned before the revolution could be brought to a satisfactory conclusion. He embellished his argument with the rhetoric of violence: "Je maintiens donc qu'en décrétant des entraves, vous décrétez la famine, vous assassinez le peuple" ("I maintain that in decreeing barriers, you decree famine, you kill the people," (AP(53) p. 435).

On the other side, Beffroy countered the claim that the subsistence problem was produced by the Revolution itself. In real terms, genuine and imagined food shortages had identical effects, he argued, and the good of society must be upheld over the interests of liberty and property (AP(53), p. 438).[3] In rejecting the freedom to export grain he quoted Montesquieu's distinction between the fruits of the earth and manufactured commodities: "Les richesses de la terre appartiennent à chaque État; toutes les autres sont au monde entire" ("The riches of the earth belong to each state, and all others to the whole world," AP(54), p. 669).

Beffroy challenged the credibility of appeals to the *économistes*, since their theories were tailored to benefit the treasuries of antiquated despotic governments. Indignantly, he claimed that the *économistes* offered a system for increasing the wealth of a minority when what was needed was the means of providing subsistence for all. If the price of grain could be kept as low as possible, farmers and landowners would not become rich, but this was a small price to pay for natural justice: "Les mœurs y gagneront: le riche aura quelques plats de moins sur sa table, mais le pauvre mangera du pain. Tout le monde vivra." ("Mores will gain: the rich will have fewer dishes on the table, but the poor shall eat bread. Everyone will live," AP(54), p. 670)

Fayau went further in claiming that speculators on the value of subsistence goods must be eradicated from the republic.[4] For him, the rich and poor were two separate nations at war in France:

---

3 Beffroy (Louis-Etienne, de Beauvoir) 1755-1825; elected to the Convention from the Aisne; voted for the King's death.

4 Fayau (Joseph-Pierre-Marie) 1766-1799; elected to the Convention from the Vendée; a Montagnard who voted for the death of the King; later sent on mission back to the Vendée.

"Je vous demande, législateurs, si vos armées campaient dans un pays où des hommes riches auraient des grains sous les verroux, si vos soldats, après la victoire, avaient encore faim, respecteriez-vous cette prétendue liberté des propriétés?"
"I ask you, legislators, if your armies camped in a country where rich men have grain under lock, if your soldiers after the victory were still hungry, you would respect this alleged freedom of properties?" (AP(53), p. 660)

Saint-Just's intervention was a generalised indictment of the entire economy, and a demand for better laws (Soboul, 1908, vol. 124). Arguing for free trade in domestic grain and a ban on exportation, he insisted that inflation must cease and the public debt must be repaid, before the market in grain could be properly stabilised. It was Robespierre, however, who offered the most emphatic characterisation of the government's role in guaranteeing subsistence for all. On 3 December 1792, he argued that the food shortages afflicting France were the result of administrative mismanagement (AP(54) p. 45; Mathiez, 1958, p. 118). He aimed to turn the arguments of those in favour of liberalising the grain trade against free trade itself:

"Dans tout pays où la nature fournit avec prodigalité aux besoins des hommes, la disette ne peut être imputée qu'aux vices de l'administration ou des lois elles-mêmes; et les mauvaises lois et la mauvaise administration ont leur source dans les faux principes et dans les mauvaises mœurs."

"In any country where nature provides lavishly for human needs, scarcity can only be attributed to defects in the administration or the laws themselves, and bad laws and maladministration have their source in false principles and immorality." (AP(54) p. 45)

Robespierre associated the Constituent Assembly with the reviled policies of the *ancien régime*:

"J'ai vu naître la législation de l'Assemblée constituante sur le commerce des grains; elle n'était que celle du temps qui l'avait précédée; elle n'a pas changé jusqu'à ce moment parce que les intérêts et les préjugés qui en étaient la base n'ont point changés."

"I saw the birth of the legislation of the Constituent Assembly on the grain trade, it was only that of the time which had preceded it, and it has not changed until now because the interests and prejudices upon which it was based have not changed." (AP(54) p. 45)

In Robespierre's view, liberty of commerce had been defended to the absurd and disgraceful extreme of using violence against the people. He raised two major objections against the advocates of free trade. The first of these objections was that trade in subsistence goods must be treated differently from trade in non-subsistence goods, since the former was essential for the survival of the people. The second objection was that even if the arguments for free trade in subsistence goods made some sort of sense in times of public order, they did not do so under revolutionary circumstances. Robespierre formulated his argument in terms of the rights of man living in society:

"La première loi sociale est donc celle qui garantit à tous les membres de la société les moyens d'exister: toutes les autres sont subordonnées à celle-là; [...] Il n'est pas vrai que la propriété puisse jamais être en opposition avec la subsistance des hommes."

"The first social law is that which guarantees all members of society the means of existence: all others are subordinate to that; [...] It is not true that the property can never be in opposition human subsistence." (AP(54) p. 45)

The conclusion of this argument was that subsistence goods must be the common property of society; private property must be composed only of what was surplus to fundamental human requirement. Robespierre proposed that legislation regarding trade in subsistence goods should guarantee all members of society enough food to sustain their existence; should guarantee proprietors and cultivators of the land their returns; and should allow any surplus to be freely traded. He appropriated the term "circulation" for the economic system that he proposed, arguing that proprietors have no right to hoard their grain since this was dis-ruptive of the desiderated circulation of subsistence goods inside the nation. His proposals for avoiding secrecy, unlimited liberty and impunity in the conduct of those involved with the grain trade were recommendations for the type of poli-cing which existed under the *ancien régime*. Robespierre's appeal to the patriotism of the people, his request for calm and sacrifice in the face of subsistence shortages, was a clear echo of the eighteenth-century grain trade debates.

On 8 December 1792, the Convention finally adopted a decree in favour of unlimited freedom of trade, with an important codicil banning exportation of grain until the domestic price was comparatively low. This project was a conscious imitation of the English system to which the *économistes* had referred so often. Before passing its decree, the Convention heard a long summary of the history of the grain trade from Creuzé-Latouche, who presented the case for unlimited freedom.[5] He pointed out that the attempt to dismiss the doctrines of the *économistes* on the grounds that these were invented to serve the *ancien régime*, could also be turned against those who proposed policing the grain trade. There was not a single new policing strategy that the Convention had been invited to consider which had not already been tried and abandoned before the Revolution. In making his case, Creuzé-Latouche tried to overcome the Convention's tendency to discuss the grain trade in terms of property rights. There was no doubt that if all the grain in France was owned by a minority who refused to sell it, *le salut public* would require an overthrow of property rights (AP(54) p. 685). But this was far from being the current situation.

Rœderer adopted the Convention's division between those favouring unlimited freedom of trade in subsistence goods, and those who proposed restrictions. He extrapolated from these polarised positions two distinct approaches to social organisation and the problem of inequality. The *économistes* represented theories constructed in terms of production; and the *niveleurs* represented theories constructed in terms of distribution:

"On peut réduire tous les systèmes connus à deux: celui des économistes, qui n'ont vu que les dangers provenant de la nature; celui des niveleurs, qui n'ont vu que les dangers provenant de l'état social."

"One can reduce all known systems to two: that of the economists, who see nothing but the dangers arising from the nature, and that of the Levellers, who see nothing but the dangers from the social state." (Rœderer, p. 144, vol.8, 1853-59)

Physiocracy was a system that focused on production and left distribution undisturbed. It argued that questions of distribution and inequality could be resolved by restructuring the production side of the economy in line with the natural order of things. The *niveleurs*, in contrast, proffered no elaborate theory of production but focused on agitating for changes in distribution. In his lectures Rœderer hoped to provide an alternative interpretation of the principle of equality that would be less disruptive of property. There was no doubt in his mind that the principle of equality had decisively buried Physiocracy's outmoded political agenda:

---

5   Creuzé-Latouche (Jacques-Antoine) 1749-1800; Poitevin magistrate with strong interest in political economy and legal ethics. See his publication of 1793, *Sur les Subsistances*.

"Le système des économistes ne doit pas nous occuper un moment; encore qu'il ait été décoré du titre imposant de *physiocratie*, de gouvernement de la nature, de principes de l'ordre naturel et essentiel des sociétés politiques, les niveleurs en feront justice. Ce système tombera sous leurs coups, car leurs principes sur l'égalité sont excellents; ce sont les conséquences qu'ils en infèrent qui sont mauvais [...]"
"The system of the economists should not occupy us for a moment, even though it was awarded the imposing title of Physiocracy, government of nature, the principles of natural order and essential political societies, the levelers will do it justice. This system will fall under their blows, because their principles of equality are excellent, it is the consequences they infer which are bad [...]" (Rœderer, vol.8, p.145, 1853-59)

Before 1789, the Physiocratic notion of linking political rights to the ownership of land seemed a viable project. Rœderer, however, had already rejected it in his revolutionary pamphlet of 1788, *De la Députation aux États Généraux* (Rœderer, vol.7, pp.558-574, 1853-59). Here he argued that since investment of capital is necessary for the production of wealth from the land, and since capital is often possessed by non-landowners, investors could not justly have fewer political rights than landowners. He repudiated the Physiocratic tendency to define nationhood in terms of land. Whereas the Physiocrats had once claimed that small trading countries, such as Holland and Geneva, were not true nations, but part of the amorphous *république commerçante universelle*, Rœderer argued that the stability of these countries suggested that land was not in fact essential to the creation of a strong political system. Engaging the terms employed by the Physiocrats, he defined *propriété foncière* as land and *propriété mobilière* as the land's produce, arguing that the latter rather than the former provided the essential foundation of society. Criticising Turgot's belief that a man without land is a mere traveller in the state, not a real citizen, Rœderer insisted that in such a system, virtue, honesty and knowledge count for nothing except in combination with one particular form of wealth. In his *Mémoire sur les Municipalités,* Turgot had limited his discussion of the rights of non-landowners to their eligibility for membership of the provincial assemblies, from which it seemed reasonable to exclude all but the landowners since these assemblies were exclusively designed to administer the direct taxes imposed on land. Rœderer argued that it was inappropriate to extrapolate from the provincial assemblies to a national representative body. He also dismissed the example of America, where vast expanses of unappropriated land offered opportunities for capital and labour investment that could not be matched in an old country like France. In contrast, France needed investment in manufacture. For these reasons, Rœderer's *De la Députation aux États Généraux* differed significantly from the vast majority of other revolutionary pamphlets which typically argued for doubling the delegates of the Third Estate and voting by head. By contesting the long established connection between political rights and landownership, Rœderer hoped to find a way to represent all the interests of the Third Estate. His experience with tariff reform had proved that the Third Estate, far from being a homogeneous class, was potentially (and actually) divided against itself. He warned that if the delegates to the Third Estate were exclusively chosen from landowners, the *États Généraux* would not be genuinely representative of the nation.

By 1793 Rœderer was confident that the connection between political rights and landownership had been broken. But the design of legitimate representative republican government was still undecided. In this context, he was concerned to protect property rights against political encroachments justified in terms of equality. He characterised the *niveleurs*, or levellers, as having a conception of social organisation in sharp contrast to that of the Physiocrats. They understood the machinations of human vice, but knew nothing of the economics of farming. They noticed only the social danger of inequality between persons, and because property threatened the equality of individuals they were hostile to it. Faced with the objection that the retraction of property rights would diminish production, the *niveleurs*, as Rœderer characterised them, claimed: 'Fewer riches, and more *mœurs*'. When pressed further by the argument that a lower level of production is an undesirable outcome because it will support only a reduced population, he imagined the *niveleurs* arguing that a smaller population will be a more contented one. But he noted that even they were embarrassed by the practical reality of reducing an existing population, and instead resorted to claiming that, whatever the circumstances, the land could not be made more productive. And this, Rœderer pointed out, merely begs the question.

There were two components to Rœderer's critique of the arguments he attributed to the *niveleurs*. The first focused on the influence of the political thought of Mably, and the second on the influence of Rousseau. The second was explicitly connected to Rœderer's criticisms of Robespierre during the Convention's constitutional debates. Whilst he in no way confused Robespierre with the more radical and anarchic opponents of property, Rœderer's lectures were intended to show how menacing any kind of encroachment on individual property would be for the economic foundations of modern government.

In attacking property, he claimed, the *niveleurs* were contravening the fundamental, natural rights of man. Inspired by Mably, they were gravely mistaken in arguing that property is solely a social institution, subordinate to the interests and needs of society. He characterised this system of social organisation in terms of four principles: firstly, the dissolution of all wealth possessed by individuals at the time of their death; secondly, the limitation of wealth to a fixed level beyond which all earnings should become state property; thirdly, the redivision of existing wealth between all citizens; fourthly, the transformation of privately owned land into public property, and the division between citizens of the produce of the earth by a centralised public authority.

Rœderer's criticism of these premises was founded on his view that to attack property was in fact to attack capital. It was also to attack commerce and all forms of work not directly focused on the common interest, (since the demand for equality would require the levelling of both landed and moveable property). The abolition of property in land, however, would be sufficient to ensure the destruction of all forms of capital, since it would reduce every individual to the possession of nothing other than his or her subsistence: there would be no surplus, no capital and no exchange.

Rœderer presented Rousseau as a defender of private property. He claimed that, contrary to appearances, complex societies combining agriculture, manufacture and commerce conformed to the principle set down by Rousseau, which states that the land belongs substantially to no-one in particular, because its products are available for the whole world:

"[...] dans la réalité, la terre n'appartient qu'au travail de l'homme, elle n'est qu'en dépôt entre les mains de celui qui en est appelé propriétaire [...]"

"[...] in reality, the earth belongs only to human labor, it is merely deposited in the hands of he who is called owner [...]" (Rœderer, 1853-1859, vol. 8, p. 155)

Rœderer argued that in the state of nature a person's labour was free; so any product resulting from it was the property of the labourer. To contest this was to contest a person's right to live. However, whilst this argument supported the right to own the fruits of one's labour (*propriété mobilière ou propriété des fruits*) it was less clear how it could support the right to own land. Rœderer insisted that the need to own the product of the land generates the need to own the land itself, and in cases of first occupancy those who labour on the land rightfully lay claim to it. On this account, society is not established in order to feed individuals, but to guarantee their opportunity for labour to secure their subsistence. According to Rœderer, Rousseau's *Discours sur l'inégalité des conditions*, had been misinterpreted and turned into an attack on property rights (Roussesau, 1962, vol.1, pp. 125-220). Recent interpretations of this text had gone so far as to suggest that Rousseau believed property in land to be damaging to a well-ordered society. In contrast, Rœderer insisted that Rousseau understood the ownership of land to be the key principle of civil society: the very feature that distinguishes civilisation from the life of the savage. In support of his interpretation, Rœderer quoted directly from Rousseau's *Discours sur l'économie politique*:

"Le fondement du pacte social est la propriété; sa première condition, que chacun soit maintenu dans la paisible jouissance de ce qui lui appartient."

"The basis of the social pact is property, the first condition is that everyone is maintained in the peaceful enjoyment of what belongs to him." (Rœderer, 1853-59, vol. 8, p. 239; Rousseau, 1962, vol.1, p. 259)

Finally, Rœderer argued that the way to recapture for civil society the best aspect of the state of nature, (the fact that the fruits of the earth belong to all and the land itself to no one), was to rely on the principle of labour. When there was a division of labour, there would be an abundance of produce to share out amongst everyone. Private ownership of land was the pre-condition for the division of labour, and it would result in more produce for all:

"[...] ainsi, dans le régime actuel, non-seulement le travail est assuré d'obtenir, comme dans l'état de nature, une part des fruits de la terre, mais encore d'obtenir une part infiniment plus considérable, parce que ses produits sont plus abondants [...]"

"[...] and so, under the current system, not only is work guaranteed to get, as in the state of nature, a part of the fruits of the earth, but also to obtain a much more considerable part, because its products are more abundant [...]" (Rœderer, 1853-59, vol. 8, p. 240)

Rœderer claimed that land is acquired before the social contract is formed; rights to it pre-date society and cannot be over-ridden. He argued that the purpose of society is to protect man's ability to fulfil his needs through work, not to satisfy those needs directly. It was inconceivable that any society could have the power to fulfil individual needs in the absence of private interest to cultivate the land. Falling back on utilitarian justifications for private ownership, he pointed out that systems of common cultivation were notoriously inefficient because each individual tried to work as little as possible and consume as much as possible. Improvements in talent, power and methods of working were impossible, he argued, when land is commonly owned and innovations in the division of labour are prohibited.

On 24 April 1793, Robespierre proposed several amendments to the new declaration of rights under discussion in the Convention, hoping to correct what he took to be an inadequate theory of property. Like Harmand earlier in the debate, Robespierre decisively rejected the notion of absolute equality of wealth as illusory, even less beneficial to individuals than to the public good (AP(63), p. 197; Cobban, 1971, p. 166). It was more important to render poverty honorable than to proscribe wealth. According to him, the *comité de constitution* had operated with an erroneous theory of property. When it defined liberty it correctly limited this by the rights of others, so why did it not do the same for property? Property, Robespierre insisted, was a social institution. Whilst the committee had drafted many articles to ensure the exercise of the right to property, there was not one word about the legitimacy of this right. To redress this oversight, Robespierre suggested the following articles:

"Art.1. La propriété est le droit qu'a chaque Citoyen de jouir & de disposer de la portion de biens qui lui est garantie par la Loi.
Art.2. Le droit de propriété est borné, comme tous les autres, par l'obligation de respecter les droits d'autrui."

"Art.1. Property is the right of every citizen to enjoy & to have the portion of property that is guaranteed to him by law.
Art.2. The right to property is limited, like all others, by the obligation to respect the rights of others." (AP(63) p. 198)

In both his public lectures and the *Journal de Paris*, Rœderer discussed Robespierre's suggestion that the Convention should apply limits to property rights. Against Robespierre he argued that true limits to individual freedom must be defined by both the liberty and the property of others. Rœderer pointed out that the argument that a right to property cannot include the right to steal or usurp was extremely superficial and virtually self-evident. If property was the right to steal, how could it also be the right to possess? Rœderer concluded that Robespierre, perhaps without realising it, simply did not recognise the nature of the natural right to property. Instead, Robespierre was defending an insecure right, precarious, variable and subject to the civil law and the magistrates. According to Rœderer the cause of Robespierre's mistake was his view that property is a social institution, and therefore an arbitrary phenomenon, grounded in social contingency and not in inalienable natural right. Rœderer quoted directly from Robespierre's recent speech in the Convention, arguing that it was premised on the principle that landowners did not have the right to starve non-landowners by withdrawing consumable produce from the market. The conclusion that Robespierre drew from this premise was that property rights must be limited. In contrast, Rœderer argued that landowners lacked both the inclination and the power to starve their fellow citizens. Instead they were actually and rationally inclined to put as much produce as possible into the market, in order to increase their profits.

Rœderer's conclusion was sharply at odds with Robespierre's: an unlimited right to *la propriété foncière*, he insisted, was the key to securing for the propertyless their rights to subsistence. Was it common to see stretches of uncultivated land that belonged to powerful landowners? Or to see these landowners hurling their grain into the rivers? Or to find them hoarding their harvests for ten, five or even three years? On the contrary, each year these landowners cultivated a hundred times the amount of grain that they, or their families and dependants, could manage to consume. Why then did the landowners produce a surplus? Rœderer's answer centred on man's need for enjoyment (*jouissances*), that increases in direct relation to the development of his intelligence, and on his need to have something to exchange in return for the manufactured goods that could provide new and different sources of enjoyment. This, he claimed, was the true source of the security of poor labouring men who live alongside the rich. Since property was the means of guaranteeing the rights of those who own nothing at all, it should not be limited, but protected by the full and combined forces of the law, *mœurs* and public opinion.

Conclusion

By the 1790s, political, or constitutional, unfreedom arising from historical precedents derived from the *ancien régime* had been comprehensively dismissed through the assertion of the Third Estate's sovereign power. Under the impetus of the abbé Sieyès's argument, first the National Assembly (in 1789), then the National Convention (in 1792), had entered fully into the exercise of constituting power on behalf of the sovereign people. The legitimate exercise of this power did not, in and of itself, resolve the problem of designing a stable republican government for France; and there was a recurring tendency to focus on the design of the legislative to the neglect of the executive branch of government. The spectre of inherited political power – the constraint placed on the current generation's freedom by its predecessor – that haunted Thomas Paine was no more welcomed by his French republican counterparts. Sieyès, however, considered that there were more urgent technical questions to be addressed in the difficult task of rendering modern government both efficacious and accountable. Most importantly, the question as to how the executive power might be rendered accountable through the imposition of constraints on ministerial wills.

Social unfreedom was discussed in connection with the presence (or absence) of sociability and the need for institutions to shape the manners or mores of a republican people. On the one hand, there were attempts to use early social science to delineate the extent to which society might be left to cohere freely by itself without intervention from repressive political institutions. On the other, there was widespread interest in designing institutions to encourage or nurture individual sentiments and habits suited to a republic. Virtue and probity were central to these debates. The traditional republican notion of citizens schooled in prioritizing the public over personal interest, needed to be reconciled with the reality of a large scale commercial state. Saint-Just meanwhile, with his emphasis on regeneration, gave new and alarming meaning to Rousseau's maxim that it might be necessary for the people to be "forced to be free" under a republican government.

Economic unfreedom – at its most extreme equating with hunger in the absence of basic subsistence – was discussed in the shadow of well-worn 18th century debates about state responsibility and freedom of trade. Moderate republicans, defending the feasibility of large-scale representative government compatible with the division of labour, vigorously defended property rights as the basis for all forms of freedom and prosperity. More radical republicans evoked the safety of the people as a justification for government intervention and redistribution in circumstances where people were starving. In the 1790s, as in earlier and later epochs, hunger was the most compelling definition of unfreedom: no freedom without food.

REFERENCES

(AP), *Archives Parlementaires de 1787 à 1860, Debats Législatifs et Politiques des chambres Françaises*, sous la direction de M.J.Mavidal et de M.E.Laurent, Première Serie, 1787-1799, 82 vols., Libraire administrative de Paul Dupont, Paris, 1885.

Badinter, E. and Badinter, R. (1988). *Condorcet, 1743–1794: un intellectuel en politique*. Paris: Fayard.

Baker, K.M. (1975). *Condorcet: from Natural Philosophy to Social Mathematics*. Chicago, IL: University of Chicago Press.

Condorcet, J.A.N. de Caritat (1847). *Lettre d'un jeune mécanicien aux auteurs du Républicain*, 16 Juillet, 1791. Le Républicain, no.3, in Œuvres de Condorcet, vol. 12. Paris: Firmin Didot Frères Librarire.

Claeys, G. (1989). *Thomas Paine: social and political thought*. Boston, MA: Unwin Hyman.

Forsyth, M. (1987). *Reason and Revolution: the political thought of the Abbé Sieyès*. Leicester: Leicester University Press.

Forsyth, M. (1989). *Pierre-Louis Rœderer: The Spirit of the Revolution of 1789 and other writings of the revolutionary epoch*. Aldershot: Scolar Press.

Furet, F. (1978). *Penser la Révolution française*. Paris: Gallimard.

Furet, F. and Halévi, R. (1996). *La Monarchie Républicaine: la constitution de 1791*. Paris: Fayard.

Hampson, N. (1988). "La Patrie", in C. Lucas (Ed.), *The French Revolution and the Creation of Modern Political Culture*, vol.2, pp.125-139. Pergamon Press: Oxford (1988).

Hampson, N. (1991). *Saint Just*, Basil Blackwell: Oxford.

(JP). *Journal de Paris*, 1 January 1777-30 September 1811.

Kaplan, S.L. (2013). *Bread, Politics and Political Economy in the Reign of Louis XV*. London: Anthem Press.

Mathiez, A. (1958). *Etudes sur Robespierre*. Paris: Editions sociales.

Montesquieu, C.-L.S. (1950-1961). *De L'Esprit des loix* [1748], ed. J. Brethe de la Gressaye. Paris: Société Les Belles Lettres.

Nicolet, C. (1982). *L'idée Républicaine en France (1789–1924): essai d'histoire critique*. Paris: Gallimard.

Paine, T. (1894). *To the Authors of Le Républicain* [1791]. The Writings of Thomas Paine. Ed. by Moncure Daniel Conway, vol.3. pp. 4-9, New York: G.P. Putnam's Sons.

Robespierre, M. (1910-2007). *Œuvres de Maximilien Robespierre: Édition du Centenaire de la Société des études robespierristes*, 11 vols.. Paris : Société des études robespierristes.

Rœderer, P.-L. (1853-9). *Oeuvres du comte P.-L. Rœderer*, 8 vols., ed. A.-M. Rœderer. Paris: Typographie de Firmin Didot Frères.

Rœderer, P.-L. (1989). *The Spirit of the Revolution of 1789 and other writings of the revolutionary epoch* [1789–1815], ed. M. Forsyth. Aldershot: Scolar Press.

Roland, Madame (1821). *Mémoires de Madame Roland: avec une notice sur sa vie, des notes et des eclaircissemens historiques*, vol. 1, Paris: Baudouin, frères.

Rousseau, J.J. (1962). *The Political Writings of Jean Jacques Rousseau*, ed. C.E.Vaughan, 2 vols. Oxford : Blackwell.
Saint-Just, L.A. (1834). *Œuvres de Saint-Just*, Prévot, Libraire Éditeur: Paris.
Sieyès, E.-J. (1989). *Œuvres de Sieyès*, 3 vols. Paris: Edhis.
Sieyès, E.-J. (1999). *Des Manuscrits de Sieyès. 1773-1799*, Published by Christine Fauré, Jacques Guilhaumou, Jacques Vallier and Françoise Weil. Paris: Champion.
Soboul, A. (1908). *Annales historiques de la révolution française*, vol. 124.

Part 2

Cultural Representations of Unfreedom

Occupy Rome

Citizenship and Freedom in Early Modern Political Culture, Recent Political Theory, and *Coriolanus*

OLIVER ARNOLD

The two most ambitious recent arguments about the currency of republican values in early modern England privilege either citizenship or liberty: Patrick Collinson's claim that "citizens...concealed within subjects" pursued lives of meaningful political participation in the "monarchical republic" of Elizabethan England does not depend on establishing the subject-citizen's liberty (2002, p. 412);[1] according to Quentin Skinner and Philip Pettit, seventeenth-century resistance to arbitrary power turned on a distinctly republican definition of freedom as the absence of domination that neither promoted active citizenship as a "bedrock value" nor required for its maintenance widespread participation in political life (Pettit, 1999, p.8). On the one hand, many monarchical republicans in Elizabethan England did not link liberty and the *vita activa* – John Case, for example, defined "citizen" merely as "a participant in civil authority" – or figured active citizenship and obedience as continuous (Peltonen, 2002, pp. 103-104). On the other hand, the neo-Romanists of Stuart England believed that all the participation in the world – serving as a bailiff; sitting in the House of Commons; issuing judgments from the bench – did not make a person who is under domination free. Put another way, Collinson's citizen-subjects located virtue and happiness

---

1 For a lucid account of the scholarship on "monarchical republicanism," see Peltonen (2002, pp. 85-107). Collinson (2002) identifies a wide range of activities as republican: the inhabitants of Elizabethan Swallowfield agreeing to constitute their town as a "self-governing republic"; Lord Burghley drafting plans for an acephalous one-year "Interreyn" between Elizabeth's demise and the settling of the succession; engineers offering initiatives that serve "the public interest" (pp. 20, 32-33, 53-54).

in productive *service* to the commonwealth; the men who would not brook Charles I's tyranny located dignity and happiness in the *possession* of liberty. These influential approaches to English political history haven't paid much attention to one another because the first story seems to end when the second story begins: as James and, especially, Charles, indulged themselves in exercises of arbitrary power, Members of Parliament, political philosophers, and leading citizens from England's towns – the kind of men who, under Elizabeth, might have prized the *vita activa* – embraced liberty as the preeminent republican value. The relation between liberty and the *vita activa* was, in fact, far more complicated for both Elizabethan and seventeenth-century Englishmen. In *De Republica Anglorum* (1563-65), for example, Sir Thomas Smith's most stirring celebration of liberty is occasioned by – and never quite displaces – a commitment to active participation in the commonwealth:

"[T]orment or question which is used by the order of the civill lawe and custome of other countreis to put a malefactor to excessive paine, to make him confesse of him selfe, or of his felowes or complices, is not used in England, it is taken for servile. For what can he serve the common wealth after as a free man, who hath his bodie so haled and tormented, if he be not found guiltie, and what amends can be made him? [...] The nature of our nation is free, stout, haultaine, prodigall of life and bloud: contumelie, beatings, servitude and servile torment and punishment it will not abide. And so in this nature and fashion, our aunciente Princes and legislators have nourished them, as to make them stout hearted, courageous, souldiers, not villaines and slaves, and that is the scope almost of all our policie." (Smith, 1583, pp. 85-86)

Earlier legal theorists had excoriated torture as barbarous and ineffective (Sir John Fortescue, 1997, pp. 31-34); Smith sharpens this long-standing critique by appealing to the most powerful brand of early modern English exceptionalism: the claim that the English were the freest of modern peoples, cherished liberty most, and abhorred bondage with unequalled passion. For Smith, not abiding "servile torment" is a particular manifestation of the free nature that defines Englishness.

In Smith's England, "the scope almost of all [...] policie" is the cultivation of free men rather than "villaines and slaves." On the one hand, then, Smith is a precursor of Skinner's and Pettit's seventeenth-century neo-Romans, who define liberty as the absence of domination: the "opposition between slavery or servitude [...] and freedom," according to Pettit, "is probably the single most characteristic feature of the long rhetoric of liberty to which the experience of the Roman republic gave rise"; "[c]ontrasting liberty with slavery is a sure sign of taking liberty to consist in non-domination" (Pettit, 1997, p. 32). On the other hand, Smith is a monarchical republican: princes *and* legislators work collectively for the common good; and he values service to the commonwealth (at least) as highly as freedom. "[W]hat can" the victim of torture "serve the common wealth after as a free man"? The answer is "nothing." Torture is bad because it deforms the victim's capacity for active participation: if such a man "be not found guiltie," he will regain the legal condition of "free man" – he will once again be *sui iuris* – but he will be disabled from serving the commonwealth.

If Smith, a key figure in Collinson's story, entangles freedom and active citizenship, so too does the MP Thomas Hedley, an important protagonist in Skinner's intellectual history of liberty. In a 1610 speech in the House of Commons, Hedley warned that James I's assertion of an absolute prerogative to levy impositions in the absence of Parliament's consent would transform England into a slave state:

"But it is not so much to lose all a man's wealth as the power of holding it, for that is nothing else but bondage, or the condition of a villein, whose lands and goods are only in the power of his lord, which doth so abase his mind [...] that he is neither fit to do service to his country in war nor peace, for the law enables him not so much as to serve in a jury, and the wars design him but to the galleys or the gallows. So if the liberty of the subject be in this point impeached [...] then they are [...] little better than the king's bondmen, which will so discourage them and so abase and deject their minds, that they will use little care or industry to get that which they cannot keep and so will grow both poor and baseminded like to the peasants in other countries, which be no soldiers nor will be ever made any, whereas every Englishman is as fit for a soldier as the gentleman elsewhere." (Foster, 1966, p. 195)[2]

Hedley does not define Englishness as a special relation to liberty. Rather, the economic and military prowess fostered by England's "laws, liberties, and government" (Foster, 1966, p. 195) distinguishes her subjects from the "bondman or peasants in other places." Hedley recognizes that liberty is a necessary condition for the active citizenship he values, but it doesn't follow for him that liberty is separable from – or more important than – active citizenship.

So far, I have tried to demonstrate that Smith and Hedley attribute equal value to participating in public life and to possessing liberty. The rest of this chapter pursues two arguments. The first is historical: some early modern political thinkers,

---

2   For Skinner's analysis of Hedley's speech, see Skinner (2003, p. 14; 2002a, p. 311; 2002b, p. 260-61).

I claim, figured active participation in legislation as necessary to liberty. They were not, however, democrats: they believed that the people of the realm were free because they consented, *through their parliamentary representatives*, to the laws that bound them. This apparently paternalistic republicanism, in which a select group of citizens actively participate in political life and secure liberty for all, came with a twist: an ideology that universalized participation because it conflated absolutely representatives and those they represent. The second argument is theoretical: I suggest that Skinner and Pettit's shared commitment to a particular construction of negative liberty entails a preference for representative democracy over direct democracy. Shakespeare's *Coriolanus* figures explicitly in the first argument as a rare early modern identification of liberty and direct participation in political life but also shadows the second argument: Shakespeare's radical critique of political representation troubles the ideology of representation in his time and in our own.

I

The antonym of freedom, Pettit argues, is domination: that is, "subjection to an arbitrary power of interference on the part of another – a *dominus* or master – even another who chooses not actually to exercise that power" (Pettit, 2002, p. 340; cf. Pettit 1997, p. 5). Pettit thus rejects one negative construction of freedom – the liberal definition of freedom as freedom *from* interference – for another: freedom is freedom *from* domination. Pettit argues that whereas non-arbitrary interference – for example, laws to which the governed consent – merely *conditions* freedom, even non-interfering domination *compromises* freedom: if I recognize that "agents and agencies [...] have a power of arbitrary interference in [my] life," my consciousness of that power will lead me "to make efforts to keep them sweet, tailoring [my] actions to their expected wishes" (Pettit, 2001, p. 137) and make me a slave even if the dominating agent or agency never actually interferes with me (Pettit, 2002, p. 347; cf. 2001, p. 145).

Skinner has traced the definition of freedom as non-domination to seventeenth-century neo-Roman writers such as Henry Parker, John Marsh and John Goodwin, who argued that "if you live under any form of government that allows for the exercise of prerogative or discretionary powers outside the law, you will already be living as a slave [even if your] rulers [...] choose not to exercise these powers, or [...] exercise them only with the tenderest regard for your liberties" (Skinner, 1998, pp. 68-69). We can trace this ideal of freedom as non-domination, on Skinner's account, back to Hedley's great 1610 speech. Interference –

even the catastrophic seizure of all one's weath – does not in itself enslave a man, Hedley argues; rather, the monarch's arbitrary power to interfere in the subject's life and the subject's recognition of that power make him a slave: "it is not so much to lose all a man's wealth as the power of holding it, for that is nothing else but bondage, or the condition of a villein, whose lands and goods are only in the power of his lord, which doth [...] abase his mind" (Foster, 1966, p. 195).

Pettit, too, argues that for seventeenth-century English republicans domination, rather than interference, compromises freedom: a citizen subject to the interference of non-arbitrary laws is free; to be subject to domination, even in the absence of interference, is to be a slave (Pettit 2002, p. 344). For example, Harrrington's "contrast between someone who lives in Turkey, subject to arbitrary rule [...] and the citizen of republican Lucca," Pettit claims, turns on the neo-Roman ideal of freedom:

""the greatest bashaw is a tenant, as well of his head as of his estate, at the will of his lord, [but] the meanest Lucchese that hath land is a freeholder of both". [...] The crucial phrase here is "at the will of his lord": no matter how permissive the lord is, the fact of depending on his grace and favor, the fact of living under his domination, entails an absence of freedom." (Pettit, 1999, pp. 32-33).

The great bashaw who must keep the sultan sweet and the humble Lucchese subject to a non-arbitrary rule of law exemplify what Pettit identifies as "the two themes that distinguish the ideal of political freedom" in "the republican tradition": "the non-interfering master takes away the subject's freedom [but] the non-mastering interferer does not" (Pettit, 2001, p. 145; cf. 2002, p. 345).

To be free is to not be a slave; that is, not to be under domination; that is, as Pettit puts it, not to "live at the will of another – the arbitrary will of another – in the manner of a slave" (Pettit 1999, pp. 32-3). If we are tempted to supply a positive definition of freedom, we will likely find ourselves listing those actions that only free citizens in free states may pursue: dispose of his or her labor as he or she sees fit; speak his or her mind without fear of punishment; advocate for political policies; vote; run for office; petition elected officials; organize a social agency; and so on. Before long, we will have come back round to Collinson's citizen-subjects and the Ciceronian ideal that "vertues holle praise consisteth in doing." (Grimaldi, 1566, fol. 8.v). According to Pettit and Skinner, however, leading political actors and recluses alike are free or unfree only as a function of their relation to domination. Pettit explains that the republican tradition with which he, "Skinner, Sunstein, and Braithwaite [...] identify is not that sort of tradition – ultimately, the populist tradition – that hails the democratic participation of the people as one of the highest forms of good and that often waxes lyrical, in communitarian vein, about the desirability of the close, homogeneous society that popular participation is often taken to presuppose" (Pettit, 1999, pp. 7-8). For Pettit, participation is not a "bedrock value"; rather, "[d]emocratic participation *may be essential* to the republic" only in so far as "it is necessary for promoting the enjoyment of freedom as non-domination, not because of its independent attractions" (Pettit, 1999, p. 8, my emphasis).

Skinner attributes far more value to widespread participation in political life, but he, too, argues that the opportunity to exercise rights – rather than the actual exercise of rights – defines freedom. Seventeenth-century neo-Romanists, Skinner argues, didn't believe that "liberty *consists in* membership of a self-governing state" or that "individual freedom" could be "equated with virtue or the right of political participation" (Skinner, 1998, p. 74 n.38; cf. Skiner 2002a, p. 212). Moreover, the theory that domination – rather than interference – causes unfreedom requires that the actual exercise of rights be forcefully put in its place: for if "it is possible to enjoy your liberties to the fullest degree without being a free-man," then we must always be on guard against the misrecognition that to exercise liberties – to be free from interference – is to be free. What makes a person free is the absence of a dominating agent or agency with the power to interfere arbitrarily in his or her life *and* the recognition, the secure belief that no such power hangs over him or her.

II

Looking for the neo-Roman ideal of freedom in Elizabethan England may seem quixotic, but the queen's subjects routinely claimed that they were not under domination. For example, in a 1593 speech defending the Commons' right to advocate for a more perfectly reformed ministry, James Morice reminded his fellow MPs that they were the free subjects of a monarch rather than the slaves of a tyrant:

"Behold with us the sovereign authority of one, an absolute prince, great in majesty, ruling and reigning, yet guided and directed by principles and precepts of reason which we term the law. No Spartan king, or Venetian duke, but free from account and coercion of any, equal or superior; yet firmly bound to the commonwealth by the faithful oath of a Christian prince, bearing alone the sharp sword of justice and correction, yet tempered with mercy and compassion; requiring tax and tribute of the people, yet not causeless, nor without common assent. Wee again the subjects of this kingdom are born and brought up in due obedience, butt far from servitude and bondage, subject to lawful authority and commandment, but freed from licentious will and tyranny; enjoying by limits of law and justice our lives, lands, goods and liberties in great peace and security, this our happy and blessed estate." (Hartley, 1995, p. 35)

Morice is no rebel: Parker admires the Venetians for curbing the power of their dukes; Morice is glad that Elizabeth, unlike a "Venetian duke," is an "absolute prince." Morice, however, does anticipate Parker's definition of freedom as the absence of domination: to live under a prince merely "guided" – rather than "guided *and directed*" – by law, to rely merely on the prince's "mercy and compassion" would leave the subject entirely dependent on her will (and thus a slave); but Elizabeth's power to interfere in the lives of her subjects is limited by law and requires their "common assent." To enjoy one's "liberties *in great peace and security*" is precisely to recognize that one's liberties are not subject to arbitrary acts of interference.

Morice's Englishman is only modestly involved in securing his "happy and blessed estate": he "assent[s]" to the laws he obeys and the taxes he pays. By contrast, Speaker Christopher Yelverton, in his speech to Elizabeth I at the closing of Parliament in 1598, attributes the subject's freedom to active participation in fashioning laws:

"If that comon wealth (most sacred and most renowned Quene) was reputed in the world to be the best-framed, and most likely to flurishe in felicities, where the subjects had their freedom of discourse, and their libertie of likeing, in establishing the lawes that should governe them; then must your Majestie's mighty, and most famous realme of England (by your most gracious benignity) acknowledge it self the most happie of all the nations under heaven, that possessth this favour in more frank and flowing manner than any kingdome doth besides. Singuler was the commendation of Solon that set lawes among the Athenians; passing was the praise of Licurgus that planted lawes among the Lacdemonians and highly was Plato extolled that devised lawes for the Magnesians: but neither yet could the inconveniences of the state be so providently forseene, nor the reason of lawes be so deeply searched into, were they never so wise, nor the course of them be so indifferent, or so plausible; nor the people be so willing to put themselves under the dutie of them, as when the people themselves be agents in the frameing of them. And where the rules of government in some comon wealths have been setled only by some fewe magistrates, there divers varieties of mischeifes have allso many times befallen them." (Hartley, 1995, p. 197)

Yelverton offers two reasons for preferring collective lawmaking to lawgiving by a singular titan or "some fewe magistrates." The first is pragmatic: the wisest individuals – Solon, Lycurgus, Plato, and Elizabeth – are incapable of foreseeing all "the inconveniences of the state." Yelverton's account of parliamentary legislation institutionalizes Smith's reconciliation of monarchism and republicanism: "Smith described the queen as 'the life, the head and the authorite of all things that be done in the realme of England," Collinson observes, and "defined England, politically, as 'a society or common doing of a multitude of free men collected together" (Collinson, 2002, p. 36). Yelverton's England is the "best-framed" commonwealth because its head and body legislate collaboratively: "the whole state of [the] kingdome [...] assemble[s], consult[s], and resolve[s] uppon some fewe petititons"; Elizabeth's assent "geve[s] full life and essence unto" those parliamentary bills and makes them laws (Hartley, 1995, p.198).[3] Elizabethan MPs had long argued that the queen, in fact, *depended* on the collective doing of the entire political nation. In a 1566 speech, an MP argued the necessity of the Commons from the monarch's natural limitations: because "his eye and eare cannot be in every corner of his kingdome and dominions at one instant," he must rely on the "counsel" of MPs who come from "everie part of the same absent from the king's eye and eare" (Hartley, 1981, p.129-30; cf. a similar speech from 1571 in ibid., p. 227). In *The order and usage of the keeping of a Parliament in England* (1571), John Hooker figures the MPs as a whirl of collective doing: they "are as it were one body, having many eyes to se, many feet to go, and many heads to labour withal, and so circumspect they are for the government of the commonwealth that they see all things, nothing is hid or secret, nothing is straunge or new" (Hooker, 1977, p. 117). Collective law*making*, then, is simultaneously more effective than monarchic law*giving* and is the collective product of princely wisdom, parliamentary knowledge and activity, and the "consent of the whole bodie" of the realm.

Yelverton's second reason for preferring collective legislation returns us to the neo-Roman ideal of freedom: the English people owe their exceptional happiness to their "libertie of likeing, in establishing the lawes that should governe them." Like Morice, Yelverton defines freedom as non-domination: if a man is bound by laws to which he does not consent, then he is not free; if, by contrast, the people consent to the laws that they are bound to obey, then they may be said to be the authors (the "framers") of the non-arbitrary interference those laws visit upon their lives and thus free men (See Skinner, 2007, p. 237; Skinner, 2005, pp. 156-157). The same principle – the neo-Roman ideal that "each law must be

---

3   Parker, of course, would argue that the necessity of Elizabeth's assent to parliamentary legislation made Yelverton, his fellow MPs, and all the men and women they represented slaves: her veto power made all law-making dependent on her will.

enacted with the consent of those who will be subject to it" (Skinner, 2007, p. 205) – runs through almost all orthodox Elizabethan political philosophy, from Smith to Richard Hooker, who argued that

"the lawful power of making laws to command whole politic societies of men belongeth so properly unto the same entire societies, that for any prince or potentate of what kind soever upon earth to exercise the same of himself, and not either by express commission immediately and personally received from God, or else by authority derived at the first from their consent upon whose persons they impose laws, it is no better than mere tyranny. Laws they are not therefore which public approbation hath not made so." (Hooker, 1989, p. 93)

Morice and Hooker recognize "common assent" and "public approbation" as sufficient guarantors of the subject's liberty, but Yelverton's emphasis on the people's role in "establishing" and "framing" the laws that govern them seems to suggest that active participation in lawmaking secures freedom.

"Framing" is an especially resonant description of the people's agency. From the beginning, "to frame" named a high order of making: the earliest meanings refer not simply to building and carpentry but to uniting parts into the frame of a ship or house (*OED* II.4). "To frame" quickly acquired meanings proper to intellectual and artistic endeavors – for example, to perfect something (a law, a poem) by bringing it into proper balance; and by the 1580s, many of these meanings had coalesced in the "framing" of pictures and miniatures. "When the people themselves be agents in the frameing of" the laws that govern them, then, they secure their own freedom by *participating* in an exalted kind of fashioning.[4] In Yelverton, we finally have an early modern who not only values active participation – perhaps as highly as liberty – but claims that active participation produces freedom. The subject's obedience *and* freedom depend on his recognition that he is not under domination because he is himself the author of the laws that condition his freedom.

III

Yelverton was not a populist. The "people themselves be agents in the frameing of" law, but their agency, Yelverton acknowledges, is mediated by representation:

---

4   See Skinner (2005), pp. 162-3 for a very keen discussion of the way the political and aesthetic intersect in "representation."

"According [...] to your Majesty's most wide and princely commandment, and according to the ancient and well-ruled freedome of the subjectes of England, hath the whole state of your kingdome (represented here by Parliament) assembled, consulted, and resolved uppon some fewe petitions, thought fitt for lawes to them by your Majestie to be established" (Hartley, 1995, pp. 197-98). The English subject enjoyed an "ancient and well-ruled freedome" not to participate directly in the making of law but to empower representatives who did so on his behalf. In this respect, Yelverton's position – an entirely orthodox Elizabethan account of parliamentary representation (see, for example, Smith, 1583, pp. 34-35; Hooker, 1989, p. 182) – fits neatly into the neo-Roman tradition that Skinner has recovered.[5] Parker, Milton, and Nedham argued that to be free one "must live...under a system in which the sole power of making laws remains with the people *or their accredited representatives*" (Skinner, 1998, p. 74, my emphasis). Thus, to say that a state is free only when "*all* individual members of the body politic [...] remain equally subject to whatever laws *they choose to impose upon themselves*" (ibid., my emphasis) is "not to say that individual freedom [...] can in some sense be *equated* with virtue or the right of political participation": rather, Skinner cautions, the "writers [he is] discussing merely argue that participation (at least by way of representation) constitutes a necessary condition of maintaining individual liberty" (1998, p. 74-5 n38).

Skinner's work on representation is often wonderfully illuminating, but he misses something here: representation does not minimize the importance of participation; rather, it makes universal participation the positive condition of freedom because the ideology of representation in early modern England insists that there is no "or" between "the people" and "their accredited representatives," between "participation" and "participation [...] by way of representation." Skinner himself argues that some "English political writers" in the 1640s conflated "the people" and their MPs: Parker, for example, insisted that Parliament is "vertually the whole kingdom it selfe'" (see Skinner, 2005, pp. 155 and 164). Given the full original force of "virtually" ("[i]n respect of essence or effect" [*OED* 1]), to "say that Parliament is virtually the people," Skinner observes, "is to say that, so far

---

5   Thus, Richard Hooker argues that only "public approbation" legitimates a law, but "approbation not only they give who personally declare their assent by voice sign or act, but also when others do it. [...] As in parliaments, councils, and the like assemblies, although we be not personally ourselves present, notwithstanding our assent is by reason of others agents there in our behalf. And what we do by others, no reason but that it should stand as our deed, no less effectually to bind us than if ourselves had done it in person" (Hooker, 1989, p. 93).

as its essential qualities and powers are concerned, Parliament is no different from the people in any way at all. Its voice can be regarded as strictly equivalent to 'the voice of the whole Kingdom,' and its recommendations" (2005, p. 164).

Skinner has shown that Charles I's defenders sought to delegitimize the Commons' authority on the grounds that MPs only imperfectly represented the people: Digges pointed out that women did not vote; even among men, Spelman remarked, Parliament was elected by "a miner number of the people" (qtd. in Skinner, 2006, p. 160). Digges and Spelman, then, do not question the efficacy of representation *per se*; rather, they merely claim that limits on the franchise leave many men and women unrepresented. Long before the crisis of the 1640s, Charles I's father articulated a vastly more devastating critique of parliamentary representation. As he brought the first session of his first parliament to a close, James I admonished the MPs: "This house doth not so represent the whole commons of the realm as the shadow doth the body but only representatively. Impossible it was for them to know all that would be propounded here; much more all those answers that you would make to all propositions" ("Speech at the prorogation of parliament, July 7, 1604," Kenyon, 1966, p. 36). "[B]ut only representatively": James insists on the very difference between real and representative presence that Parker aims to efface.

James was reacting to Jacobean MPs who, like their Elizabethan predecessors, sometimes attributed to political representation a kind of secular magic that matched the mysticism of divine kingship. In 1593, for example, Francis Bacon argued that every man in England was personally present in the Commons' chamber in St. Stephen's Chapel. During the Commons' consideration of a bill to settle the countess of Cumberland's jointure, Sir Thomas Heanage reported that Francis Clifford, a party with an interest in the proposed settlement, had assured him that he "was contented" that it pass. A few MPs objected that Heanage's report of Clifford's speech was immaterial, but Bacon successfully persuaded the House that reported speech introduced into Commons' proceedings could not be considered hearsay: "Mr. Francis Bacon in this pointe shewed there was a difference betwixt this Courte [...] and other inferiour courtes [...] for there they are not to credit report or information, but the party to be bound must be brought *coram* and be present. But in this Court representatively all men are present, wherfore this scruple needs not that the party to be bound should be here seene, for all men are here present representatively. So this bill passed currant" (Hartley, 1995, p. 122). How can the claim that "all men are here present representatively" answer the charge of hearsay? The juridical "scruple" of disregarding hearsay rests entirely on a distinction between actual presence and representative presence. Bacon dismisses the distinction between direct testimony and reported speech because the magic of political representation has effaced the difference between being present in one's own person (coram) and being "present representatively."[6] Bacon does not exempt Parliament from hearsay rules; he claims that such rules are irrelevant to Parliament because political representation produces something like the "real presence" of the people of the realm in their parliamentary representatives.

What we might think of as conservative critiques of political representation *per se* could be found even among MPs. For example, Arthur Hall, who frequently disparaged the body in which he served, mocked the Commons' claims to represent the entire realm: "your number of Parliament men you see in your house are fewe to the huge multitude of them whose consents are bounde by your agreemente." (Hall, 1576, Eii^r). Was there a radical critique of political representation in early modern England? Occasionally, even MPs who promoted the Commons' importance tacitly allowed that there was a difference between the MPs and the people themselves. During the 1572 debates over the fate of Mary, Queen of Scots, Robert Snagge proposed that the entire realm be canvassed: "He would have every man which is absent likewise to declare their consent as we have don, and therefore requireth a generall oath" (Hartley, 1981, p. 392). Outside of St. Stephen's, a few voices argued that customs were as good as statutes because they more perfectly expressed the people's consent (Anon., 1584, pp. 3-6). The crises of the 1640s tended to confirm rather than pressure the fundamental soundness of political representation as the proper mechanism by which the subject secured his freedom. For example, Parker argued that direct democracy not only was impractical – the "reall body of the people, is too cumbersome and irregular in its movements to be capable of acting for itself" (qtd. in Skinner, 2005, p. 163) – but also unsound: "by virtue of election and representation, a few shall act for the many, the wise shall consent for the simple, the virtue of all shall be reduced to some, and the prudence of some shall redound to all" (ibid. p. 164). Even Rainsborough was on board: when he famously claimed at Putney that "the poorest he [...] that is to live under a government ought first by his own consent to put himself under that government," he was arguing for a wider franchise rather than questioning the legitimacy of representation *per se* (Firth, 1891, p. 301).

---

6 The Latin preposition "coram" means "before" and was widely used to indicate personal presence before a juridical body. Richard Huloet and John Higgins define "coram" as "In my presence. Ante oculos. Coràm me, Sub oculis" (Higgins, 1572, kkijr).

IV

Did anyone in early modern England believe that in order to be free, a citizen had to participate in political life *in his own person*? It would seem not: from Smith to the Levellers, English champions of freedom accepted voting – or, even, the condition of being represented – as sufficient. For critiques of representation as an impediment to liberty, we have to look beyond England to Rousseau, to some of the anti-Federalists, to Robespierre. With one exception: in *Coriolanus*, Shakespeare, that most English of writers, posits a necessary relation between freedom and mass participation; Rome's common citizens win true liberty through collective action, and they lose it when they cease to act for themselves but act instead through – and under the dominion of – political representatives.

In the first scene of the play, Rome's starving citizens – outraged by rampant usury and exorbitant grain prices – rebel against the Senate. Although these plebeians enjoy the status of citizens, they do not have any effective political rights; instead, they depend wholly on the "mercy and compassion" of the patricians: "What authority surfeits on would relieve us," the First Citizen complains in the unmistakable rhetoric of early modern charity; "if they would yield us but the superfluity, while it were wholesome, we might guess they relieved us humanely" (1.1.12-15).[7] The rebellion is necessary, the First Citizen tells the patrician Menenius, precisely because the Senators regard the plebeians not as rights-bearing citizens but as "poor suitors" spouting words: "Our business is not unknown to the senate; they have had inkling this fortnight what we intend to do, which now we'll show 'em in deeds. They say poor suitors have strong breaths: they shall know we have strong arms too." (1.1.50-51). The revolt ends when the besieged Senators grant the citizens the right to elect tribunes who will make their voices heard in Rome's political sphere. Prior to the rebellion, then, "citizen" is worse than an empty title: it is a veil of servitude. Indeed, because the senators exercise absolute control over the distribution of grain, the plebeian citizens' very lives depend on their masters' wills.[8]

The tribunate seems to secure for the people both real freedom and the opportunity to participate actively in political life. To be sure, the tribunes fear that their "office may [...] go sleep" if Coriolanus has his way (2.1.209), but the suspension of the tribunate would now be a coup rather than the exercise of an already constituted prerogative: the citizens are not under domination because

---

7   All quotations from *Coriolanus* follow Shakespeare, 1986. For the rhetoric of relief, distribution, superfluity, and sufficiency, see Smith, 1592, A5 v, A6 v. C2 r, C1 r.
8   For the master's power over the slave's life, see Skinner, 2002a, p. 9-10.

the Senate no longer possesses an arbitrary power to interfere with them. Thus, when Coriolanus seeks to reduce the people to their former status, the tribunes accuse him of treason: "We charge you, that you have contrived to take / From Rome all seasoned office and to wind / Yourself into a power tyrannical; / For which you are a traitor to the people" (3.3.66-68). Despite the seeming provocation of "seasoned" (the tribunate is still in its infancy), even Coriolanus' friends offer no defense against the charge of innovation.

Shakespeare departs from North's Plutarch, his principal source, to forge an exceptionally clear link between revolutionary political action and the transformation of Roman citizenship. In Plutarch, the plebeians rebel after the Senators break their promise to restrain rapacious creditors; the Senate finally begins to debate measures against usury only after the plebeians refuse to help defend the city against its enemies; the people, tired of waiting for a do-nothing Senate to act, leave Rome, encamp themselves on Mons Sacer, and contemplate the possibility of permanently abandoning Rome for greener pastures. The citizens return to Rome after Menenius, acting on behalf of the Senate, agrees to the establishment of the tribunate. In Plutarch, revolutionary violence fizzles, but a walk-out brings victory. Shakespeare, by contrast, makes the citizens' attempt to occupy the Capital the effective cause of change. The citizens we see in Act 1 mock Menenius's Fable of the Belly – he assures the citizens that the Senatorial belly selflessly distributes nourishment to the plebeian members – and, as they prepare to resume their assault on the Capitol, we learn that the senate has acceded to the demands of another mass of rebelling citizens (1.1.39).

Shakespeare's model for citizenship *is* revolutionary action: the citizens win rights by acting, and only active participation will maintain their rights. If we're hoping to see in the rest of the play a kind of institutionalized revolutionary citizenship, we'll be disappointed. As soon as the tribunate is created, the citizens are transformed into passive and mostly mute pawns of their representatives. The tribunes Sicinius and Brutus muster the people when they need muscle to back up their proclamations against Coriolanus, but they seek to exclude the people from political participation as much as possible: "Go home," they urge the citizens again and again (see, for example, 4.2.1-8); and they congratulate themselves on creating a Rome in which "tradesmen," rather than "pestering [the] streets," stay in "their shops [...] going / About their functions friendly," a Rome in which the citizens no longer run "about the streets, / Crying confusion" (4.6.5-9 and 4.6.29-31). The tribunes, the relieved patricians come to realize, are the new "masters o'th'people" (2.2.51; cf. 2.2.77); and, indeed, the citizens now submit themselves on bended knees before the men whom they have empowered (see 2.1.67-76; 4.1.22-27).

Even when the citizens do reappear on the political stage, they no longer conceive of themselves as agents capable of autonomous action: when Coriolanus defies the tribunes' authority, the First Citizen warns that the intemperate general "shall well know / The noble tribunes are the people's mouths, / And we their hands" (3.1.270-72). The First Citizen, who once wittily thwarted Menenius' attempts to figure the plebeians as the extremities of the body politic, now figuratively incorporates the people as the tribunes' hands and acknowledges that the people depend on the tribunes to speak for them. Thus, in the great scene of Coriolanus's expulsion from Rome, the tribunes make the people their puppets:

Sicinius: [...] in the name o'the'people,
    And in the power of us the tribunes, we
    E'en from this instant banish him our city
    In peril of precipitation
    From off the rock Tarpeian, never more
    To enter our Rome gates. I'th' people's name
    I say it shall be so.
All: It shall be so, it shall be so! Let him away!
    He's banished, and it shall be so!
[...]
Brutus: There's no more to be said, but he is banished
    As enemy to the people and his country.
    It shall be so!
All: It shall be so, it shall be so!
[...]
Aedile: The people's enemy is gone, is gone.
All: Our enemy is banished, he is gone. Hoo-hoo.
Sicinius: Go see him out at gates, and follow him,
    As he hath followed you, with all despite.
    Give him deserved vexation. Let a guard
    Attend us through the city.
All: Come, come, let's see him our at gates. Come.
    And the gods preserve our noble tribunes! Come. (3.1.103-09, 120-23, 140-47)

Before they trade their own voices for political representation, the people deliberate amongst themselves (1.1.1-29), collectively resolve a course of action (1.1.30), and counter patrician ideology with their own entirely coherent analysis of inequality (1.1.15-17 and 70-76). "Hoo-hoo": if the citizens can speak only words supplied by their tribunes, they have no voice of their own; if they can only participate in political affairs by way – and on the say so – of the tribunes, they have lost their capacity for active citizenship; if the citizens are a hand moved by the will of others, they have lost their freedom.

V

In *Coriolanus*, *Titus Andronicus*, and *Julius Caesar*, political representation invariably monopolizes participation for the representing class and *necessarily* diminishes the freedom of the represented. On Shakespeare's account, political representation is incompatible with an ideal of freedom as non-domination because political representation – as a practice and as a mystification – makes those who are represented dependent on those who represent them. Skinner shares some of Shakespeare's anxiety about representation:

"It is [...] open to us to meditate on the potential relevance of a theory which tells us that, if we wish to maximise our own individual liberty, we must cease to put our trust in princes, and instead take charge of the public arena ourselves. It will be objected that this is the merest nostalgic antimodernism. We have no realistic prospect of taking active control of the political processes in any modern democracy committed to the technical complexities and obsessional secrecies of present day government. But the objection is too crudely formulated. There are many areas of public life, short of directly controlling the actual executive process, where increased public participation might well serve to improve the accountability of our *soi disunt* representatives [...] unless we place our duties before our rights, we must expect to find our rights themselves undermined." (Skinner, 1986, pp. 249-50)

Skinner is kin to those republicans who recognize representation as, at least potentially, a threat to liberty, who would nod their heads to the American politician Al Smith's great prescription that the "cure for the defects of democracy is more democracy."[9]

Pettit, by contrast, suggests that the ills of representative democracy can be cured by more representation. Pettit is a Madisonian in so far as he believes that democracy is both impractical and undesirable: "I assume that the prospect of plebiscitary government is infeasible and indeed that it would be wholly inimical to the cause of deliberation, so that democratic government is inevitably representative government" (Pettit, 2004, p. 52). Pettit, then, simultaneously denies the possibility of democracy and (unconvincingly) redefines democracy as

---

9   Smith's remark was first recorded in 1923; I quote here from Smith, 1932, p. XX2.

representative government: "Systems of representative government, I shall assume, are designed to give control over government to the people. Far from being an alternative to democracy [...] they embody an institutional framework or rather a family of frameworks for realizing the democratic ideal of giving *kratos* to the *demos*, power to the people" (Pettit, 2010, p. 61; Pettit, 2004, p. 59).

Pettit tames democracy by subsuming it within a system of representation, but he wants to defang it further because too much democracy – at least of the Athenian sort – is inimical to fostering deliberation. Deliberative democracy diverges from "the most familiar conception of the role of democracy...as the means whereby a people as a whole asserts its collective will" and instead embodies "an alternative conception [that] represents democracy, not as a regime for the expression of the collective will, but rather as a dispensation for the empowerment of public valuation" (Pettit, 2004, p. 58). Deliberative democracy requires, first of all, that we institute the most mediating form of political representation:

"Indicative representers *stand for* the representees in the sense of typifying or epitomizing them; how they act is indicative of how the representees would act. Responsive representers *act for* or *speak for* the representees, playing the part of an agent in relation to a principal; how they act is responsive to how the representees would want them to act. Both sorts of representation, so I shall assume, have to be authorized by the representees. Authorized indicative representers I describe as proxies, authorized responsive representers as deputies. Deputies divide, in a traditional distinction, into delegates who are more or less explicitly directed by representees and trustees who have interpretive discretion in determining how to construe their representees." (Pettit, 2010, p. 65)

To serve the aims of deliberation and depoliticization, Pettit argues, "all public deputies will have to be interpretive trustees rather than directed delegates" (ibid., p. 78).

Pettit's preference for "interpretive trustees" further qualifies the limited role he assigns the *demos*. Democracy, Pettit argues, has "two dimensions": "First, democracy has to orient government to all common, recognizable interests of its people. And, second, it has to orient it only to such common, recognizable interests" (Pettit, 2000, p. 114). Pettit suggests that we think of these two dimensions as, respectively, authorial and editorial. The authorial dimension is positive: "ordinary people" participate by "searching out and generating a rich supply of presumptive common-interest policies" (ibid., p. 116). However, Pettit's citizens will not directly articulate such policies; rather, the "authorial role has to be implemented, clearly, by electoral institutions whereby policies and policy-making agencies are thoroughly discussed" (ibid., p. 116). Thus, the people are "the indirect, electoral authors of [...] policies" that achieve articulate form only when "interpretive trustees [...] construe their representees."[10]

Mediating the people's authorial role is still an insufficient containment of the dangers of democracy in its "familiar" form: if "deliberation is to predominate, then the power of those representatives must be passed on in various areas to appointed boards and officials" (Pettit, 2004, p. 59). Editorial control – the "negative scrutinize-and-disallow dimension" of democracy – "cannot be exercised collectively, in the manner of electoral, authorial control" because "whatever problems arose in the first dimension will recur in the second. The editorial control that democracy requires [...] has got to be exercised by individuals or groups at a noncollective level" (Pettit, 2000, p. 118).[11] All of the ills of Pettit's Republic can't be cured by more representation; some ills require the more radical cure of granting to non-elected "individuals and groups" something very like a negative voice in the legislative process. In 1642, Henry Parker claimed that Charles' power to veto bills passed by the Lords and Commons "subjects [the English people] to as unbounded a regiment of the Kings meere will, as any Nation under Heaven ever suffered under"; when, in 1649, Charles doggedly refused to part with the negative voice, the champions of liberty parted his head from his body.[12]

---

10 Pettit believes that the people can trust that their own ideas will survive the mediation of representation because their representatives "have an incentive to enhance their chances of election and reelection by promoting any cause that can attract general support" (Pettit, 2000, p. 125).

11 It is not particularly important to Pettit that such bodies be established by collective consent (ibid., p. 119).

12 For Skinner on Charles' "Negative Voice," see Skinner, 2007, p. 238. Pettit insists that his non-elected editors would not possess a negative voice: "while editorial control must operate at noncollective levels, it cannot plausibly take the form of a veto" (Pettit, 2000, p. 118). But the editorial agencies that Pettit envisages could indeed thwart the will of the elected bodies whose purpose it is to generate policies for editorial consideration. Such agencies would not resemble the Supreme Court – a check, that is, on the legislative branch; rather, they would be part of the legislative process and could prevent collectively generated "policy ideas" from becoming law (ibid., p. 120).

REFERENCES

[Anon.] (1584). *A Breefe discourse declaring and approving the necessarie and inviolable maintenaunce of the lawdable Customes of London*. London.
Collinson, P. (2002). *Elizabethans*. London: Hambledon and London.
Higgins, John. (1572). *Huloets dictionarie*. London.
Firth, C.F. (Ed.) (1891). *The Clarke Papers: Volume 1*. London: The Camden Society.
Fortescue, J. (1997). In Praise of the Laws of England. In S. Lockwood (Ed.). *On the Laws and Governance of England*. Cambridge: Cambridge University Press.
Foster, E.R. (Ed.). (1966). *Proceedings in the House of Parliament. Volume 2: The House of Commons*. New Haven: Yale University Press.
Grimaldi, N. (1566). *Marcus Tullius Ciceroes thre bokes of duties, to Marcus his sonne, turned oute of latine into english*, by Nicolas Grimaldi. London.
Hall, A. (1576). *A letter sent by F.A*. London.
Hartley (Ed.), T.E. (1981). Proceedings in the Parliaments of Elizabeth I. Vol 1: 1558-1581. London: Leicester University Press.
Hartley (Ed.), T.E. (1995). *Proceedings in the Parliaments of Elizabeth I. Vol 3: 1593-1601*. London: Leicester University Press.
Hooker, J. (1977). The order and usage of the keeping of a Parliament in England. In V. Snow (Ed.), *Parliament in Elizabethan England*. New Haven: Yale University Press.
Hooker, R. (1989). *Of the Laws of Ecclesiastical Polity*, ed. A.S. McGrade. Cambridge: Cambridge University Press.
Kenyon, J.P. (Ed.) (1966). *The Stuart Constitution, 1603-1688*. Cambridge: Cambridge University Press.
Peltonen, M. (2002). Citizenship and Republicanism in Elizabethan England. In M. van Geldern and Q. Skinner (Eds.). *Republicanism: A Shared European Heritage. Volume I: Republicanism and Constitutionalism in Early Modern Europe*, pp. 85-107. Cambridge: Cambridge University Press.
Pettit, P. (1999). *Republicanism: A Theory of Freedom and Government*. Oxford: Oxford University Press.
Pettit, P. (2000). Democracy, Electoral and Contestator. *Nomos*, 42.
Pettit, P. (2001). *A Theory of Freedom: From the Psychology to the Politics of Agency*. Oxford: Oxford University Press.
Pettit. P. (2002). Keeping Republican Freedom Simple: On a Difference with Quentin Skinner. *Political Theory*, 30, 339-356.
Pettit, P. (2004). Depoliticizing Democracy. *Ratio Juris*, 17, 52-65.

Pettit, P. (2010). Varieties of Public Representation. In Ian Shapiro et al. (Eds.). *Political Representation.* Cambridge: Cambridge University Press.

Shakespeare, W. (1986). *The Complete Works*, ed. Stanley Wells et al. Oxford: Clarendon Press.

Skinner, Q. (1986). The Paradoxes of Political Liberty. In Sterling M. McMurrin (Ed.), *The Tanner Lectures of Human Values, Vol. 7* (pp. 225-250). Cambridge: Cambridge University Press.

Skinner, Q. (1998). *Liberty Before Liberalism.* Cambridge: Cambridge University Press.

Skinner, Q. (2002a). *Visions of Politics. Volume 2: Renaissance Virtues.* Cambridge: Cambridge University Press.

Skinner, Q. (2002b). A Third Concept of Liberty. In *Proceedings of the British Academy* 117, 237-68.

Skinner, Q. (2003). States and the Freedom of Citizens. In Q. Skinner and B. Stråth (Eds.) *States and Citizens: History, Theory, Prospects* (pp. 11-27). Cambridge: Cambridge University Press.

Skinner, Q. (2005). Hobbes on Representation. *European Journal of Philosophy* 13, 155–184.

Skinner, Q. (2006). Rethinking Political Liberty. *History Workshop Journal* 61, 156-170.

Skinner, Q. (2007). The Monarchical Republic Enthroned. In John F. McDiarmid (Ed.), The *Monarchical Republic of Early Modern England: Essays in Response to Patrick Collinson* (pp. 233-260). Ashgate: London, 2007.

Smith, H. (1592). *The poore mans teares opened in a sermon.* London.

Smith, A. (1932). *The New York Times.* 31 January.

Smith, T. (1583). *De republica Anglorum. The maner of gouernement or policie of the realme of England.* London.

Unfreedom, Servitude, and the Social Bond

SUSAN MASLAN

"L'homme fut toujours dependant; par conséquent jamais libre, dans le sens de l'illustre citoyen de Genève," declares P.L de Bauclair in his 1765 refutation of Rousseau's *On Social Contract* ("Man has always been dependent and consequently, man has never been free in the sense of the illustrious citizen of Geneva," n.p. [p. 3]).[1] Because human beings reproduce sexually and because the impulse to reproduce is an essential need, Bauclair explains, each human being necessarily depends on another. Sexual reproduction creates a society; the force of life propels human beings into society and society is unfree since it is coextensive with dependence:

"L'intérêt de la multiplication lui ayant suscité une campagne qu'il dut envisager comme une autre lui-même, ses besoins naturelles exigerent bientôt qu'il devint esclave, si cependant l'esclavage peut consister dans les égards qu'on rend aux individus de son éspèce [...] On conçoit aisément que la femme n'est pas plus maitresse de son sort: ses besoins et ses affections voluptueuses, sa faibless, ses infirmités lui firent sentir qu'elle n'était que la moitié d'un tout dont l'autre partie avantages." (Bauclair, 1765, pp. 3-4)

"The desire to multiply provoked him to acquire a companion that he must have had to consider as a second self; his natural needs soon required that he become a slave, if, that is, slavery can be said to consist in the consideration that one owes to individuals of one's species [...] We can easily conceive that woman is even less mistress of her destiny: her needs and her voluptuous longings, her weakness, her infirmities caused her to feel that she was half of a whole whose other part lay outside her. She accepted the yoke with considerable pleasure since she perceived its many advantages to her."

---

1 All translations are my own unless specified otherwise.

"Slavery" here is nothing other than the work required to obtain and keep a sexual partner. The "slavery" that nature imposes on us, Bauclair writes, is the necessity to please and satisfy other human beings. And although such a necessity would seem to be a fundamentally social compulsion, in fact it rests on an essentializing notion of human beings as, above all bodies. Any social relations or social obligations spring immediately from basic bodily drives. Bauclair's vision is strangely egalitarian, despite its assumption of the natural inequality of men and women, because it proposes that unfreedom is a form of mutual self-binding that does not regard sex or class but instead all humans as (mere, unqualified) humans.

Of course Bauclair's opening sentence is meant to echo and overturn Jean-Jacques Rousseau's celebrated phrase "Man is born free and everywhere he is in chains." Rousseau's assertion provokes questions immediately: if man is born free, why is he in chains? How did this transformation occur? Can it be made right? Rousseau offers answers in *The Discourse on the Origin of Inequality* (1754) and in *On Social Contract* (1762). But to pose the question is to posit a story of loss – of a movement that begins with a free, autonomous individual and ends with a miserable slave. Bauclair's response is simple: we do not need to ask for an account, or a justification, because an autonomous individual never existed: man's nature is to live in society and society means unfreedom.

Rousseau's great text and Bauclair's slightly silly one both emerge out of a profound consciousness of society as, in Keith Baker's words, "the essential frame of human existence" and the "essential domain of human practice" (Baker, 2001, p. 84). Many, although certainly not all, enlightenment accounts of society's institution posited a process whereby free individuals jointly bound themselves to a whole. The theory, although with tremendous variation, presumes a loss of individual freedom and an acceptance of constraint. The forms, limits, and practices of constraint would dictate a given society's degree of freedom or unfreedom. For if wholesale subjection might logically seem a necessary correlative of society, it was less clear why the shape and experience of that subjection should be variable. Put another way, why do some (and not others) command, and some (but not others) obey? If individuals are equally free prior to entering into society why should they be unequally unfree upon joining it?

This question was posed prior to the Enlightenment – surely Etienne de la Boétie and Montaigne come to mind – but it was posed with increasing frequency, urgency, and even with more concreteness during the Enlightenment. Many answers were offered. Of course, some argued that inequality in society was simply an extension of inequality in nature; Rousseau rejected this explanation most famously in *The Discourse on the Origin of Inequality*. Others argued that social inequality was a vestige of ancient conquests. No matter which account was offered, one thing was clear: if a divine explanation was "set aside," as Rousseau put it, some other explanation was required. Moreover, historical description could purport at best to detail how social inequality and the servitude that was its corollary arose and was institutionalized; it could not lend it legitimacy.

In this essay, I would like to explore one writer's response to this impasse. In *L'Île des esclaves* (*Slave Island*, 1725) Pierre Carlet de Chamblain de Marivaux, one of France's greatest comic playwrights, suggests that there is no way out. The social institutionalization of servitude lacks legitimacy, and yet, the play's plot and its denouement appear to conclude that servitude must persist, for it is synonymous with society itself. Political terms, like legitimacy, cease to make sense in Marivaux's world and in their place Marivaux's characters adopt the unreasoned language and action of affect and sacrifice. But Marivaux's yoking of unfreedom and society differs importantly from that of Bauclair. Marivaux's society, the society whose preservation trumps all other values, has no natural or bodily basis at all. It is absolutely anti-foundational. Marivaux repeatedly introduces bodies in his play in the form of hints of love or accounts of physical suffering only to reject the body as an agent, cause, or origin. Instead, human beings are above all formed by society itself.

Marivaux's relentless identification of society as cause, effect, and sole aim of human "nature" and human action allows him to concentrate on society's fundamentally unequal distribution of unfreedom and to explore some of its ramifications. Marivaux was concerned with the relation between class position and personal identity throughout his career. Many of his plays turn on cross-dressing masters and servants. But the stakes of Marivaux's canonical plays differ dramatically from those of *Slave Island*: in *The Game of Love and Chance*, for example, disguise risks but also ensures a successful, class-appropriate betrothal. *Slave Island*, however, puts at stake the problem of social cohesion and its relation to subordination. In *Slave Island*, Marivaux asks how social relations can be maintained given the fact of servitude and, conversely, how social relations can be maintained in the absence of servitude. In this one-act play, Marivaux seems to represent the fall of voluntary servitude. Given the chance afforded by the utopian, green world of the island, the servants, seemingly good students of La Boétie, declare their servitude at an end. They cease to recognize their master's dominion over them. The play then presents a difficult social problem: how to reestablish relations of mastery and servitude in the full recognition that those relations are without political or moral legitimacy or efficacy.

Servants offer a remarkably literal example of voluntary servitude: for them this was no metaphor. Slavery and servitude are resonant terms in the figural language of politics in eighteenth-century France. Rousseau's great axiom – "man is born free and everywhere he is in chains" – is only the most famous example. But servants were not just figures or metaphors; they made up roughly one-tenth of the population of Paris and something like one-thirteenth of the population of France. Servants were both utterly familiar and uncannily unfamiliar. They were emphatically visible in public and of course ever present in the home. Yet servants were overwhelmingly strangers: nearly all were migrant workers from the countryside come alone to towns and cities in search of work; turnover was remarkably high and a source of persistent annoyance to masters. Servants often stood apart from their working class fellows geographically since they lived with their masters; sartorially, since they often wore livery or their masters' cast-off clothes; even linguistically, since they might speak a different dialect. They were also nearly universally unmarried. Nor was there necessarily much society among servants since the vast majority of them did not work in large multi-servant homes. In all these ways, servants' social bonds seem more tenuous, more modest than do those of many other groups: artisans, for example, had customers, employees, landlords, guilds, and families of their own. Contemporaries seemed obsessively interested in the one bond into which servants entered: that with masters (Maza, 1983 and Fairchild, 1984).

A wealth of writing – religious tracts, conduct books, treatises on household management, etc. – sought to explain the correct relation and reciprocal obligation of masters and servants. Much of that literature suggested a paternalistic relation. That is, the master-servant bond could be understood only by way of a figural assimilation to what was a putatively natural relation: masters were like parents; servants were like children. On this account, masters owed protection and servants owed obedience and fidelity. The metaphor of the family, of course, could be put to work to explain nearly all social structures: kings are like fathers, fathers are like kings; children are like servants; fathers are like masters, etc. In other words, all these relations could be understood as constructing and participating in a metaphorical, rather than a natural or literal system. The presence of a social term like the servant in such a system simply underscores the artificiality, the sociality of the system as a whole even as the purpose of this figural system is precisely to naturalize relations. The servant relation reveals the essential truth of all these relations: they are all figural. There is no prior literal, natural, transcendent term to serve as a stable point from which to derive the metaphor. To propose that the relation between servants and masters was paternalistic, in other words, is just to reframe rather than answer the question (Maza, 1983, pp. 7-18 and pp. 317-318; Fairchild, 1984, pp. 5-6 and pp. 137-144; Montesquieu, 1951, bk 23, chs 1-7, pp. 682-87; and Rousseau, 1997, bk 1, ch 2).

If some commentators assimilated servants to the model of the family, others understood them in relation to slavery (Sarti, 2005). On the one hand, the racial nature of contemporary slavery helped clarify the difference between white domestic servants in France and enslaved African servants in the colonies. On the other hand, slavery was still largely theorized in relation to the classical world – where slaves and masters might *not* be distinguished from one another by what the French revolutionaries called the "aristocracy of color" – rather than in relation to contemporary practices. That servants were not slaves seemed clear; yet that both groups were characterized by their state of personal servitude sometimes made this distinction less than absolute (Linguet, 1767). Nor did consent draw a bright line between slavery and servanthood in early modern France. Slavery in the classical world was often seen as having an origin in consent: people were enslaved when, after a military defeat, they consented to exchange their liberty for their life. Moreover, servants themselves understood that their own consent was not necessarily freely given; necessity compelled many to become servants. Once engaged as household servants, their freedom to leave their masters was curtailed by law and they were not legally protected from physical punishment (Fairchilds, 1984, pp. 123-124).

The anonymous poet who gives voice to a male servant in "L'État de servitude, ou la misère des domestiques," ("The State of Servitude, or the Servant's Misery," 1711), and who may have been a servant himself, at once assumes and disowns responsibility for having become a servant:

"[…] je suis un grand benais [sic],
Je suis un grand faquin de m'être mis laquais:
Quand un sort malheureux la cruelle inconstance
Aurait versé sur moi sa maligne influence,
Quand le Ciel justement irrité contre moi,
M'aurait laissé sans bien, sans crédit, sans emploi,
Fallait-il pour cela par un esprit de rage,
M'empêtrer dans les fers d'un si rude esclavage,
Et sur ce vil état fondant tout mon appui,
M'asservir lâchement au caprice d'autrui?" (Anon., 1711, n.p. [p.2]).

"[…] I am a great fool,
I am a great idiot to have made myself a lackey:
When a miserable fate and cruel deception
Enveloped me with its evil influence,
When heaven, justly angry with me,

Left me without property, help, or occupation,
Was it necessary, nonetheless, that in a rage,
I bound myself with the irons of such a brutal slavery,
And relying for all my support on this vile condition,
I have, like a coward, subjected myself to the caprices of another?"

The servant partly blames forces beyond his control ("un sort malheureux," "le ciel") for the desperate straits in which he found himself, but he attributes his "vil état" to his own agency: "de m'être mis lacquais"; "m'empêtrer dans les fers." The servant, then, allows that he serves a master by his own consent, and yet he describes his service as "rude esclavage." To be subject to the "caprice d'autrui," the servant suggests, is to inhabit a servitude no different from that of slavery even if one has submitted oneself to this subjection. The condition of being bound by the will of another, regardless of the circumstances of its institution, is sufficient to unsettle the distinction between servant and slave. And, for this poet, such a fate merits the language of tragedy. While this speaker is a great fool and of lowly position hence suitable for comedy, he is also sufficiently dignified to have earned the wrath of heavens – a position usually reserved for tragic, not comic figures. The tragic language, seemingly misplaced in the mouth of a lackey, might make the domestic servant more ridiculous – but it might also ennoble the suffering of servitude. If tragic heroism seems to depend on possessing a self-directed will, this poet's appropriation of tragic language to describe the misfortunes of heteronomy would seem to create a new kind of tragic subject (Arnold, 2007).

Servants resemble slaves not only because of the type of labor they perform but, more significantly, because they must obey the "caprice d'autrui," the will of another. Certainly this was a widely held conception of servants. When politicians in the early days of the French Revolution excluded servants from the franchise and from eligibility to hold office, they argued that slaves could not exercise political rights because they lacked a "volonté propre," that is, their own independent will. Servants act as mere means to accomplish the ends of the master: they may act as an extension or reflection of the master, or, on the contrary, as the antithesis of the master performing work the master would never perform. In all these cases, the servant's actions are willed and dictated by another. The servant is a thoroughly heteronomous subject. In a world that increasingly identifies autonomy as the chief quality and qualification of the modern subject, servants, as Sarah Maza points out, seem to be pre-modern (Maza, 1983, p. 4).

Marivaux's *Slave Island* does not focus on the political category of the will; Marivaux seems less interested in the problem of self-direction than in the psychological and material conditions of servitude. Thus the play underscores the ways in which the master-servant relation denies the servant's personhood and it insists on servitude's physical suffering. Marivaux's reflection on unfreedom in *Slave Island* is fundamentally social, not political. The play explores the ways in which lived experiences of freedom and unfreedom shape society and humanity itself. For Marivaux, modernity does not signal humanity's throwing off its shackles, but rather new organizations and practices, new consciousnesses, and new meanings of heteronomy. In this sense, servants offer new figures of humanity and modernity.

SERVITUDE AND COMEDY

Servants were not only central to Old Regime France's social order; they were central to its theatrical order. In so many of the period's plays, servants construct, unsettle, and dismantle social bonds as they ferry messages, reveal secrets, articulate truths, and conspire with and against their masters. There can be no tragedy without the stage presence of inferior confidants to hear sentiments voiced or, like Phèdre's nurse Oenone, to carry out actions beneath the dignity of their masters. There can be no comedy without the bumbling but truth revealing queries, interjections or literalisms of the servant class. While the number of servant characters who enable dramatic plots is legion, the degree to which playwrights were interested in servants is variable. And while some servants are major characters, for example, Dom Juan's servant Sganarelle, it remains nearly always the case that servants act as agents of their masters rather than agents of their own will. The abundant presence of servant characters on the French stage is not only functional in nature; instead I want to suggest that in this most social of art forms, the representation of servants also permitted authorial reflection on the practical and theoretical issues the social presence of servants and the practices of service and servitude posed.

In the first moments of *Slave Island*, a one-act play that launched Marivaux's trilogy of island plays about the constitution of human society, a male servant Arlequin, and his master Iphicrate look about themselves in the aftermath of a shipwreck that has cast them up on the shores of a remote island. Soon after, they meet a female servant Cléanthis and her mistress Euphrosine. Soon after the curtain rises, then, the audience of this comedy sees before it fissionable material that must, one would think, produce one of two dramatic resolutions: we might be on our way to radical couplings (the servant Arlequin and the mistress Euphrosine; the master Iphicrate and the servant Cléanthis) or to conventional couplings (the servants Arlequin and Cléanthis and the aristocratic masters Iphicrate and Euphronise). But *Slave Island* does not end with marriages or romantic unions of any sort, although perhaps we could call the play a comedy of remarriage that ends with servants and masters reunited after an estrangement. My point, for now, is that we expect these four characters to knit themselves together romantically, and they do not: at the end of the play, the only relationships that bind these characters are relations of servitude. Among these four protagonists, society is nothing other than the bond between masters and servants. And despite the term "esclave" and despite the background of a fictional Athens and the green world of the island, it is clear the play is set in contemporary society – the major preoccupation with gallantry, with vanity, and with superficiality are all hallmarks of critiques of French society throughout the eighteenth century – it is likewise evident that the characters Arlequin and Cléanthis are meant to be French servants, not classical slaves.

If Marivaux thwarts our generic expectations about comedy, our assumption that the two unattached men and two unattached women we meet at the outset of the play must pair off into two romantic couples, he also thwarts our generic and philosophical expectations about utopian texts and the discourse of social formation. When we discover that the island our protagonists find themselves on is inhabited and governed by slaves (or, rather, ex-slaves who are now free), we know we are in the speculative, philosophical realm – one so important to Marivaux's moment – of the social blank slate. What sort of society would ex-slaves create? The answer, it seems, is a utopia that seeks to eradicate, rather than reproduce in a different form, the relations of servitude under which the slaves once suffered. Trivelin, who is the representative of the island's political order and the only inhabitant of the island we ever see, explains to the new arrivals that the ex-slaves have constituted themselves as a Republic of equal citizens: fate may have given them the opportunity to be free, but their own actions and choices have maintained them in freedom. The citizens of the island even have an unusual scheme to spread freedom: they enslave any masters whom shipwreck brings to their shores, but the period of enslavement is limited to three years and its aim is therapeutic rather than exploitive. The ex-slaves temporarily enslave masters only to humanize them:

"Nous ne vengeons plus de vous, nous vous corrigeons; ce n'est plus votre vie que nous poursuivons, c'est la barbarie de vos coeurs que nous voulons détruire; nous vous jetons dans l'esclavage pour vous rendre sensibles aux maux qu'on y éprouve. [...] Votre esclavage, ou plutôt votre cours d'humanité, dure trois ans, au bout desquels on vous renvoie. [...] Vous voilà en mauvais état, nous entreprenons de vous guérir; vous êtes moins nos esclaves que nos malades, et nous ne prenons que trois ans pour vous rendre sains, c'est-à-dire humains, raisonnables et généreux pour toute la vie."

"We no longer take revenge on you; we correct you. We no longer pursue your life; we seek to destroy the barbarity of your hearts. We enslave you in order to make you more sensitive to the sufferings felt by those in servitude. [...] Your enslavement, or rather your course in humanization, lasts three years at the end of which we send you back . [...] You are in a bad condition, we undertake to cure you; you are less our slaves than our patients and we only require three years to make you healthy, that is to say, human, reasonable, and generous for the rest of your lives." (Marivaux, 1955, p. 430)

Much could no doubt be said about how the two great secular discourses of improvement, education and medicine, have replaced Christian morality and conversion here. Indeed, the play retains the Christian theme of suffering only to turn it to this secular account. Marivaux, however, was apparently dubious about the fruits of sentimental education: at the end of the play, Iphicrate and Euphrosine have not been educated out of their desire to have others serve them; the play does not dwell at all on the "hearts" of the masters, it does not stage a process of "sensibilization." For despite the importance of the language of feeling in this play, the characters' interior affective states do not really matter and are not explored onstage. Ironically, Arlequin and Cléanthis are the ones who become good, sentimental subjects. They take pity on Iphicrate's and Euphrosine's "suffering," which is identical to their loss of status – though Marivaux, in yet another case of withholding, never shows us the masters serving the ex-slaves – and, rather than stay on the island, they sail back to civilization willingly with their masters, sustained by the modest hope – and it is only a hope – that their servitude will now be gentler.

To understand the play's disappointments – no romantic unions, not even a glimpse of the Republic of ex-slaves, no transformation in which Iphicrate and Euphrosine learn to abhor subjecting Arlequin and Cléanthis to their wills – we have to take stock of Marivaux's radical privileging of servitude as the foundation of society and of his equally radical account of the bond between master and servant as the essence of the social bond. Marivaux's entire oeuvre reveals a fascination with servants. In Marivaux's most celebrated plays, masters and mistresses often temporarily exchange clothing and places with their servants as they pursue love and marriage; this theatrical probing of the fragility of class identity is replaced in the island plays by a more transparent meditation on the relation between servants and social order, on the place of servitude in the foundation of society. We can see this shift in the very populations of the island plays. In Marivaux's comedies with conventional settings, the masters always outnumber the servants; the servants, after all, merely further the plots of their masters and so that servants' other relationships – with fathers, mothers, and siblings – are not represented. Those potential social bonds have been displaced by domestic service. In *Slave Island*, by contrast, humanity always appears in two, equally represented forms: servant and master. Thus, *Slave Island* stages a primal scene: with Trivelin as an onstage spectator, Iphicrate, Euphrosine, Arelquin and Cléanthis play out the formation of social order. How, Marivaux asks, can humanity – in the sense of a bond shared by all human beings – itself be preserved? How, in other words, can the dispersion of humanity into solitary, indifferent atoms be prevented?

Dispersion, rather than physical violence (Hobbes' state of war), is the unspeakable threat. When Arlequin learns that he has been washed up on the island of slaves, he announces that he is going to leave his master, Iphicrate. "Chacun à ses affaires," he announces, "que je ne vous dérange pas," ("to each his own, don't let me bother you," Marivaux, 1955, p. 427). When Arlequin takes his leave – "Adieu, mon ami," ("farewell, my friend") – Iphicrate pursues him sword in hand (ibid., p. 428). As we shall see, it is telling both that Iphicrate assumes that only physical violence could enforce servitude and that the drawing of his sword has no effect. Arlequin does not offer any physical threat to his (perhaps now former) master; he simply refuses to recognize him as his master and, in the absence of some external structure to enforce servitude, it seems that simply refusing to recognize a social bond is sufficient to efface it.

Iphicrate's desperate need for Arlequin's help seems to anticipate a Rousseauian analysis: being a master has made Iphicrate the needy dependent of his servant. Moreover, that it also goes without saying that Arlequin does not share Iphicrate's desire to leave the island – why give up being a citizen in a Republic to return to servitude in a hierarchical society? – suggests that the asymmetry between the master's interest and the servant's interest is (or should be) intolerable and unsustainable. Since it is clearly in the servants' interest to remain on the island and the master's interest to leave the island, resolution can be found only by superseding the category of interest. As we shall see, the rhetoric of sentiment, of the heart, of "sensibilité" is offered as just such a supercession.

Neither the sword nor interest can produce social formations among the four protagonists, but feeling eventually does. This feeling is purportedly created by the former servant's witnessing of the former masters' suffering. But strangely, the only suffering the masters are forced to undergo on stage has nothing to do with the physical burdens of servitude. Rather, Iphicrate and Euphrosine suffer a dissolution of identity – an identity which consists solely in their status as master and which therefore, ironically, is once again utterly dependent on Arlequin and Cléanthis. The masters suffer when they are forced to listen as their former slaves describe their characters and habits.

Trivelin: il est nécessaire que vous m'en donniez un portrait, qui se doit faire devant la personne qu'on peint, afin qu'elle se connaisse, qu'elle rougisse de ses ridicules, si elle en a, et qu'elle se corrige.
[...]
Cléanthis: Vaine, minaudière et coquette, si cela la regarde? Eh! Voilà ma chère maitresse; cela lui ressemble comme son visage.
[...]
Euphrosine: Je n'y saurais tenir. (Marivaux, 1955, p. 433)

Trivelin: you must depict her character for me and you must rehearse this description in the presence of the person you depict so that she can come to know herself, to blush for her foolishness if she is foolish, and to correct herself.
[...]
Cléanthis: Vain, affected, a flirt, does that describe her? That's my dear mistress, that is her to a tee.
[...]
Euphrosine: I cannot withstand this.

These portrait scenes – although quite mild in their criticism – are portrayed as indescribably painful for the masters. Arlequin and Cléanthis describe their masters' vanity, silliness, and pettiness. The pain these scenes produce is that of the destruction of the masters' narcissistic satisfaction. Under the regime of servitude, Arlequin and Cléanthis serve as flattering mirrors for their masters. By offering undistorted images in the portrait scenes, the servants not only dissolve their masters' sense of self, they annul the bond between them precisely because that bond had been predicated on the servants' distortingly reflective function. The portrait scenes also underscore the tight relation between servants and comedy itself since dramatic theorists in the seventeenth and eighteenth centuries continued to argue that comedy was a social mirror: comedy showed audiences their faults so that they might correct them.

The relation between masters and servants supports the masters' social identities and in so doing sustains their deepest subjectivities. But this same relation works to deprive the servants of any inter-subjective recognition at all. Indeed, the masters deny the servants what we might well think of as the most fundamental attribute of personhood: a name. When Trivelin asks Arlequin "Comment vous appellez-vous?" ("what is your name?") Arlequin makes clear that names are the property of masters alone:

Arlequin: Est-ce mon nom que vous demandez?
Trivelin: Oui, vraiment.
Arlequin: Je n'en ai point, mon camarade.
Trivelin: Quoi donc, vous n'en avez pas!
Arlequin: Non, mon camarade, je n'en ai que des sobriquets qu'il m'a donné; il m'appelle quelquefois Arlequin, quelquefois Hé. (Marivaux, 1955, p. 428)

Arlequin: Are you asking my name?
Trivelin: Yes, of course.
Arlequin: I don't have one my friend.
Trivelin: What do you mean you don't have one!
Arlequin: No my friend. I only have nicknames that he has given me. Sometimes he calls me Harlequin, sometimes he calls me Hey You.[2]

The master, on the other hand, has a proper name just as he has property in himself: speaking of Iphicrate, Arlequin explains "il s'appelle par un nom lui," ("him, he's got a name"). Despite the depersonalizing practices of servitude, Arlequin and Cléanthis are represented as full, morally autonomous beings: they know their own minds; they observe social relations accurately; they express their own judgments clearly and forcefully; they make decisions. The masters, on the contrary, are seemingly ineffective and often speechless.

While Marivaux shows masters' selves predicated entirely upon their mastery over others, he represents slaves/servants' selves as grounded in their humanity, a humanity understood as a kind of affective self-presence and thus outside and beyond the seemingly closed system of servitude and hence autonomous. But the autonomy of this humanity is also resolutely social since it requires a "coeur bon" – that is, a sympathy with the sufferings of others in order to come into being.

What can establish a lasting social bond? Marivaux immediately dismisses the notion of a legitimate, or for that matter efficacious, social bond based on force. Marivaux was not making his point subtly here: while Arlequin and Trivelin

---

2   Marivaux might have found inspiration for this exchange on names from the practice, common at the time, of servant's employers to rename them and refer to them by the name of the province from which they came. Both Maza (1983) and Fairchilds (1984) discuss this practice.

are traditional names of *zani* from the *commedia dell'arte* repertory, the male master Iphicrate is named for an Athenian general – ironically, a man of humble birth – and his name literally means "rule by force." Arlequin reminds Iphicrate repeatedly that his characteristic mode of relation to him has been physical violence:

Iphicrate: Mais je ne te comprends point, mon cher Arlequin.
Arlequin: Mon cher patron, vos compliments me charment; vous avez coutume de m'en faire à coups de gourdin […] et le gourdin est dans la chaloupe.
Iphicrate: Eh! Ne sais-tu pas que je t'aime?
Arlequin: Oui; mais les marques de votre amitié tombent toujours sur mes épaules, et cela est mal placé. (Marivaux, 1955, p. 427)

Iphicrate: But I do not understand your point my dear Arlequin.
Arlequin: My dear boss, your compliments are charming; your custom usually is to make them with blows from a club […] and the club is in the boat.
Iphicrate: But don't you know that I love you?
Arlequin: Yes; but the marks of your affection always fall on my shoulders and that is a bad place for them.

The reversal of position demonstrates the bankruptcy of the argument that might can make right: Iphicrate recognizes no legitimate authority in Arlequin once their roles are switched. Force may create servitude but it cannot create right or obligation and it is therefore prone to produce not only suffering but instability: "Tu me traitais comme un pauvre animal," ("you treated me like a poor animal,") muses Arlequin, taking up arguments that Montesquieu had worked through just a few years earlier in his tales of the Troglodytes, "et tu disais que cela était juste, parce que tu étais le plus fort. Eh bien! Iphicrate, tu vas trouver ici plus fort que toi," ("and you used to say that that was just because you were the strongest. Oh well, Iphicrate, you will find something stronger than you here", Marivaux, 1955, p. 427).

But Arlequin's quick political-philosophical awakening is more profound; he recognizes that his own participation, indeed his own consent, endowed Iphicrate with the power of mastery: "Doucement," he warns the threatening Iphicrate, "tes forces sont bien diminuées, car je n'obéis plus," ("be careful, your forces are greatly diminished because I no longer obey you," Marivaux, 1955, p. 428). Arlequin explains, in other words, that he had delegated his own power and agency to his master and that Arlequin's power was the source of his master's power over him. Arlequin's consent to his servitude constituted the bond between them, and his refusal to consent to his own disempowerment dissolves that bond.

If social relations maintained by coercion are neither a legitimate nor a stable foundation for a social order, what might produce more felicitous, more efficacious social cohesion? The answer Marivaux seems to entertain is the force of love. A new society which has overcome the obstacles of social hierarchy that separated its members and is newly bound by love, would seem to fulfill perfectly the generic requirements of comedy. Marivaux tantalizes us with the possibility that the four castaways might pair off into cross-class couples: the servants cook up a plot to order Euphrosine to marry Arlequin and Iphicrate to marry Cléanthis, but Marivaux then stages the unspeakable impossibility of such a resolution. Nor does Marivaux develop the more conventional prospect of ending his play with the marriage of Iphicrate and Euprosine and the marriage of the servants Arlequin and Cléanthis. Such a resolution would posit a sexual or romantic satisfaction as a substitute for a political one. Such a solution would elevate the transcendent value of love in and for itself above worldly values of rank or power; such a revaluation too would seem to provide a suitable comic reshaping of the play's social world. But Marivaux offers none of that. The play's structure keeps reminding us of the possibility that the society of masters and slaves could be united by ties of love, desire, and even kinship, but Marivaux relentlessly presents only one social relation, only one social bond – the bond between master and servant, and makes the possibility of society depend upon it. Marivaux's exclusive representation of the master servant bond as the sole social bond and the foundation of society itself begs the question of how, exactly, society is to reproduce itself. The exclusion of reproductive sex, indeed all sex, in this comedy, underscores the purely social, rather than natural, account of human relations.

To achieve a resolution the play must re-establish and re-affirm a bond among subjects who have no bond. Marivaux rejects something like a natural basis for subjection: nothing that happens on the island affirms that masters are naturally superior to their servants. He rejects another possible natural bond when he rejects sexual desire as the basis for a social bond. The play goes out of its way to negate any basis for affection between master and servant. And yet the resolution to the crisis is nothing other than an explosion of sentiment: "Que vois-je? vous pleurez mes enfants; vous vous embrassez," ("what do I see? You are crying my children, you embrace each other," Marivaux, 1955, p. 451), Trivelin asks rhetorically as both servants are on their knees before their masters, kissing their hands, and they all embrace as the final scene begins.

The play makes this sentimental outpouring and resolution dependent on Arlequin's unearned, unmerited and therefore absolutely freely given compassion. Upon seeing Euphrosine's unhappiness, Arlequin is moved and when his master Iphicrate reproaches Arlequin for his lack of affection and fidelity, despite Arlequin's clear-sighted understanding that his master has never shown him anything but violence and scorn – "tu disais bien que tu m'aimais, toi, quand tu me faisais batter," ("sure, you used to say you loved me when you were having me beaten," Marivaux, 1955, p. 447) – he is moved to accept once again his subaltern position, to pardon his master's past faults, and to leave the island of the slaves and to return with his master to resume their former life together. When Cléanthis sees this reconciliation between Arlequin and his master, she follows the example, despite her own mistress's lack of repentance for her cruelty. The masters in turn appear to be moved by their servants outpouring of sentiment: Iphicrate exclaims "Mon cher Arlequin, fasse le ciel, après ce que je viens d'entendre, que j'aie la joie de te montrer un jour les sentiments que tu me donnes pour toi!" ("My dear Arlequin, after what I have just heard, may heaven someday allow me the joy of showing you the feelings you have inspired in me!" Marivaux, 1955, p. 448). But Iphicrate's "someday" seems a meager guarantee of change. In the final scene Trivelin congratulates the servants on their successful conclusion to the social experiment and everyone on their good feelings and he counsels the masters to learn to be less cruel.

For those seeking a representation of social change, this conclusion is obviously a disappointment. It is also less than compelling dramatically since it is at odds with all that comes before. We can, of course, read the sentimental conclusion as a kind of ideology, a way to mask real social conflict. But what is striking is precisely the anti-foundational nature of that sentiment. No change, no revelation, no act inspires the servants to love their masters. For Marivaux, the sentiment that re-forms the bonds between master and servant is nothing other than the recognition that nothing links them and the recognition that such a nothingness is impossible. Iphicrate argues repeatedly to Arlequin that they are bound by affection, friendship, and love. He invokes too the ethical weight of duty that, he believes, should tie Arlequin to him. But Arlequin refutes all these claims with ease and in each case points out the pure violence of the relation between them. Yet, precisely because Arlequin perceives the lack of any ethical or affective basis for the social bond between master and servant, he is never convinced by his master's claims, he alone freely chooses to resume that relation:

"Tu me remontres bien mon devoir ici pour toi; mais tu n'as jamais su le tien pour moi. [...] Tu veux que je partage ton affliction, et jamais tu n'as partagé la mienne. Eh bien!

Va, je dois avoir le cœur meilleur que toi; car il y a plus longtemps que je souffre, et que je sais ce que c'est que de la peine. Tu m'as battu par amitié: puisque tu le dis, je te le pardonne. [...] Je parlerai en ta faveur à mes camarades, je les prierai de te renvoyer, et s'ils ne le veulent pas, je te garderai comme mon ami; car je ne te ressemble pas, moi; je n'aurai point le courage d'être heureux à tes dépens."

"You remind me of my duty to you here but you never knew your duty to me. [...] You want me to share your affliction and you never shared mine. Oh well, so be it! I must have a better heart than you do because I have suffered for a long time and because I know what pain is. You beat me out of friendship, since you say so, I forgive you for it. [...] I will talk to my comrades on your behalf, I will beg them to send you back and if they will not I will keep you as my friend because I do not resemble you. I will not have the courage to be happy at your expense." (Marivaux, p. 448)

Arlequin refutes the very idea of a shared human commonality, "je ne te ressemble pas," and makes this lack the basis and the engine for a social bond, "je te garderai comme mon ami *car* je ne te ressemble pas," ("I will keep you as a friend because I do not resemble you.") Unlike Iphicrate, Arlequin cannot establish his "happiness," that is his freedom, at the expense of the freedom of another--by expropriating the will of another. But the initial plan, to send Iphicrate back or to remain on the island with him bound by friendship, is immediately and without elaboration or explanation altered. Indeed, in the very next exchange with Iphicrate, Arlequin abandons the familiar "tu," resumes the hierarchical "vous" along with his slave costume, and asks Trivelin for a boat so he and Cléanthis can go back to Athens with their masters. In other words, once the lack of any real social bond is recognized as fact and once that fact is rejected not as untrue but as unsustainable, the only way the social bond can be resumed is in the form of subordination and servitude. The emotional force that explodes onstage is the force of the simultaneous admission and refusal of the impossibility of a social bond based on subordination. The libidinal source of that emotional energy is the force of terror and necessity.

Arlequin apprehends the absence of any basis for a bond; by willingly accepting his subjection, he manages to stave off the terror of the absence of social bonds. The ability to see for humanity, as it were, while the other characters perceive and act as atomized individuals, makes Arlequin the embodiment of the human and the founder of society. Arlequin renounces his own pursuit of happiness. He willingly accepts the expropriation of his will in favor of society – "je n'aurai point le courage d'être heureux à tes dépens," ("I will not have the courage to be happy at your expense.") He accepts, in other words, that a constitutive heteronomy is the norm of a social order that sees itself precisely as based on the will of its members – here invoked by that most political of eighteenth-century words: "happiness." In a sense, Arlequin reveals by literalizing the fundamental and inescapable truth not only that to live with others is to be unfree, but that society survives only because of the consensual assumption of an unequal unfreedom.

REFERENCES

Anon. (1711). "L'État de servitude, ou la misère des domestiques." Troyes, France.
Arnold, O. (2007). *The Third Citizen: Shakespeare's Theater and the Early Modern House of Commons*. Baltimore, MD: Johns Hopkins University Press.
Baker, K.M. (2001). "Enlightenment and the Institution of Society." In S. Kaviraj and S. Khilnani (Eds.). *Civil Society: History and Possibilities*. Cambridge, UK: Cambridge University Press.
Bauclair, P.-L. (1765). *Anti-contrat social*. The Hague, Netherlands.
Fairchilds, C. (1984). *Domestic Enemies: Servants and their Masters in Old Regime France*. Baltimore, MD: Johns Hopkins University Press.
Linguet, S.N.H. (1767). *La Théorie des loix civiles*. London, England.
Marivaux, P. de C. (1955). *Théâtre complet*. Paris: Gallimard (La Pléiade).
Maza, S. (1983). *Servants and Masters in Eighteenth-Century France*. Princeton, NJ: Princeton University Press.
Montesquieu, C. de (1951). *Oeuvres complètes*. Paris: Gallimard (La Pléiade).
Rousseau, J.-J. (1997). *The Social Contract and other Later Political Writings*. Cambridge, UK: Cambridge University Press.
Sarti, R. (2005). "Freedom and Citizenship? The Legal Status of Servants and Domestic Workers in Comparative Perspective, 16th-21st Centuries." In S. Pasleau and I. Schopp (Eds.) *Proceedings of the Servant Project*. Liège: Editions de l'Université de Liège, 2005.

Naturally free, politically unfree

Voltaire's Quakers and the modern discourse of human rights

INGVILD HAGEN KJØRHOLT

A recurring question echoes through the seemingly endless volumes that constitute Voltaire's *œuvre*: how might freedom materialize in real historical societies? The Enlightenment *philosophe* repeatedly defined "freedom" as a matter of tolerance. Tolerance not only ensures individual freedom; as tolerant religious or political authorities do not interfere in the citizens' thoughts and actions, they encourage a dynamic public sphere and, consequently, tolerance also furthers societies' economic as well as intellectual growth. In well-known works such as *Lettres philosophiques* (1734) or *Candide* (1759), Voltaire shows how religious and political tyranny constantly lead to conflicts while unhindered commerce and scientific progress are the true sources of prosperity and peace. Such an inclination to correlate freedom with the absence of external intervention – thus emphasizing a liberal concept of freedom as non-interference – becomes visible in the author's representations of ideal societies, such as the legendary Eldorado or contemporary England. It has led, among scholars, to the generally accepted view of Voltaire as an early liberal thinker.

Yet, a more thorough inquiry of the author's notion of freedom implies that this view needs to be modified. *Candide*'s Eldorado – the incarnation of an enlightened society – or indeed the London Exchange scene in the sixth philosophical letter – where Presbyterians and Jews cooperate to further the common good – each clearly illustrate that Voltaire pictures a state of non-interference in utopian terms. He represents both the fictional land of gold and the actual Exchange as communities too good to be true. From a realist point of view, both world history and contemporary European politics continually reveal to Voltaire that freedom should rather be regarded as absence of domination. This view is predominant in *Lettres philosophiques* where the author convincingly argues that English citizens are free due to the British constitution, while, on the other hand,

Frenchmen are not free as their lives depend upon arbitrary power – the will of the Prince.

In defining freedom as non-domination rather than non-interference, Voltaire relies on classical republicanism and the Roman conception of freedom, according to which the distinction between free subjects and slaves is of crucial importance. While free men enjoy certain individual rights within a legal constitution, slaves are dependent on the will of their masters. "Unfreedom" thus means to be subordinated to arbitrary power (cf. Skinner, 2003).

Nevertheless, the obvious contrast between free English citizens and unfree French slaves is not the only configuration of a republican notion of freedom in Voltaire's philosophical letters. The kind of unfreedom that will be questioned in the following is not contrary to, but, rather, an inherent part of the idea of freedom as non-domination: i. e. the idea of "natural liberty." More specifically, I will argue that the representation of the Quakers in *Lettres philosophiques* exposes the shortcomings, or rather the unfreedom, of natural liberty. By illustrating how freedom necessarily follows from citizenship and the citizens' participation in political life, the Quaker letters reveal that non-domination does not necessarily equal freedom. The letters indicate that Voltaire's *œuvre* touches a problem inherent in 18th century discourses on liberty and human rights, and that it ought to be discussed within the framework of classical republicanism.

THE DIFFERENTIATION OF FREEDOM: ANALYTICAL AND HISTORICAL FRAMEWORK

Hannah Arendt's political philosophy offers an analytical framework for a discussion of the notion of natural liberty and the difficulties it entails with respect to a political concept of freedom. In Arendt's view, freedom is not only a question of domination. Taking a specific historical notion of political organisation as her point of reference, the city state or *polis* in ancient Greece, Arendt stresses the crucial association of freedom with politics as she emphasizes that "[t]he meaning of politics is freedom" (Arendt, 2005, p. 108). Individuals gain freedom by fulfilling their citizen duties inside the walls of a delimited *polis*. Furthermore, she argues that freedom is what defines human beings as different from other creatures. In other words, it is only as a citizen, a political agent, that an individual may achieve its humanity. Freedom thus constitutes both citizens and human beings, and Arendt's critical idea is that the notion of "human rights" is worthless in cases where human beings lack citizenship. In order to have "the rights to have rights", one ought to be a citizen. It is only as *bios politikos* that human life has purpose and value beyond fulfilling biological needs (Arendt, 1998). How did the Greek citizen become a *bios politikos*? Arendt identifies three essential activities which describe the human condition: "labour", "work" and "action". In ancient Greece these activities had their clearly defined purposes as well as distinct localizations. While labour and work primarily were located within the family sphere (*oikos*) and contributed to the provision of material necessities, action was the only activity located in the *polis*, which also explicitly involved freedom. Arendt's (and the Greek) concept of "action" is a complex one. Action is first and foremost interaction, an activity conditioned by the gathering of a plurality of viewpoints. Such a plurality would never exist within families or other hierarchical or doctrinal communities, she argues, in as far as all the members of such groups automatically represent the same subject and thus hold identical viewpoints. Arendt considers the ability to "act in plurality" as the crucial quality that distinguishes human beings from other species. In acting, man exceeds the bare necessities of life by leaving his immediate existence as *zoe*, naked life, and entering the political community as a political agent, *bios politikos* (Arendt, 1998).

This notion of politics and of man as a political being was a Greek invention that would soon evaporate. Even the Romans were unfamiliar with the formerly sharp distinctions between labour, work, and action. Consequently, the borders between a political and a non-political space became blurred, thus altering the meaning of freedom. Instead of equalling freedom with action, in other words, to understand freedom as the possibility to act politically, Arendt argues that freedom in fact soon became associated with the opposite – withdrawal from politics (Arendt, 1998, 2005).[1] Politics thus lost its purpose as the specific space of freedom; it was, so to speak, deterritorialized and depoliticized.

17th and 18th century discourses on natural law explicitly articulate this depoliticization of freedom. They invigorate the Stoic idea that man is born free and, consequently, that freedom is a natural quality independent of historical and political conditions (cf. Hunt, 2007, pp. 117cc.). Natural law theory and its idea of natural freedom, or liberty, made a crucial impact on modern notions of universal human rights, as the first article of the United Nation's 1948 *Universal Declaration of Human Rights* makes clear: "All human beings are born free and equal in dignity and rights. They are endowed with reason and conscience and

---

1 Cf. the notions of religious and academic freedom understood as a freedom from politics (Arendt, 2005, p. 136).

should act towards one another in a spirit of brotherhood."[2] Arendt emphasizes that the individual's affiliation with and participation in the *polis* defines him as a citizen and bestows upon him the ability to rise above mere biological existence and, thus, that citizenship is the condition for his freedom. Human rights discourses, on the other hand, argue that all men are born free and consequently demand that freedom should be available in every circumstance. Even though the idea of natural liberty has greatly impacted modern notions of rights and politics, it has not entirely displaced the idea of political liberty. Following Susan Maslan (2004, 2006), I would argue, rather, that these two varieties illustrate a differentiation of the republican notion of freedom as non-domination, which emerged in the 17th and 18th centuries and became emblematic of the modern era's political and judicial institutions.

The explicit and politically potent distinction between political rights and human rights and, consequently, between political and natural freedom, emerged in the 18th century (cf. Hunt, 2007). As the name reveals, the French revolution's *Déclaration des droits de l'homme et du citoyen* (1789), a precursor of the UN's *Declaration* from 1948, makes a division between "the rights of man" (natural rights) and "the rights of the citizen" (political rights). While all men are born free, that is, endowed with natural rights, not all men are citizens of France enjoying the freedom of the French Constitution. The 1789 *Déclaration* clearly states that some liberties are exclusively reserved for the latter, and it thus draws a fundamental demarcation line within the category "human being" – here, a distinction between citizens and foreigners. It emphasizes the citizen's right to take part in the general will and thus in the making of the law. Additionally, it claims that "[t]ous les Citoyens étant égaux à ses yeux, sont également admissibles à toutes dignités, places et emplois publics, selon leur capacité, et sans autre distinction que celle de leurs vertus et de leurs talents" ("[a]ll citizens, being equal in the eyes of the law, are equally eligible to all dignities and to all public positions and occupations, according to their abilities, and without distinction except that of their virtues and talents", *Déclaration des droits de l'homme et du citoyen de 1789*, article 6). Likewise, only citizens may "parler, écrire, imprimer librement" ("speak, write, and print with freedom", *Déclaration des droits de l'homme et du citoyen de 1789*, article 11). Consequently, the citizen's rights are not designated by his natural liberty due to the rights of Natural Law, but are instead associated with and defined by what we, following Arendt, may call the freedom to act politically inside a delimited political sphere – in this case:

---

2   United Nations, *Universal Declaration of Human Rights* (1948), article 1.

France. In the *Déclaration* this implies the right to hold public positions and the right to distribute one's thoughts within the French public space.

The *Déclaration* thus activates two different significations of freedom as non-domination: the right not to be a slave and the right to be a citizen, to participate in the construction and conservation of a democracy. This distinction within the republican concept of freedom is of crucial importance in 18th century discourses, as the two articles "Liberté naturelle" and "Liberté politique," both signed by Louis de Jaucourt, in Denis Diderot and Jean le Rond d'Alembert's *Encyclopédie* (1751-1772), signal.

Jaucourt considers natural liberty to be human beings' ultimate right, a kind of liberty given to man in his natural state:

"Le premier état que l'homme acquiert par la nature, & qu'on estime le plus précieux de tous les biens qu'il puisse posséder, est l'état de liberté; il ne peut ni se changer contre un autre, ni se vendre, ni se perdre; car naturellement tous les hommes naissent libres, c'est-à-dire, qu'ils ne sont pas soumis à la puissance d'un maître, & que personne n'a sur eux un droit de propriété."

"The first state that man acquires through nature, and that we esteem the most precious of all things, is the state of liberty; he can neither be traded for another, nor sold, nor lose his person; because naturally all men are born free, that is to say, they are not subject to the power of a master, and no one else has a proprietary right over them." (*Encyclopédie*, Louis de Jaucourt, LIBERTÉ NATURELLE)

Natural liberty ensures every individual the right to pursue happiness as long as he does not contradict governmental laws. It is considered a sort of premise based on a law given by nature and thus a matter that exists before and beyond any political sphere. Political liberty, on the other hand, is a question of the political division of powers:

"la liberté politique d'un état est formée par des lois fondamentales qui y établissent la distribution de la puissance législative, de la puissance exécutrice des choses qui dépendent du droit des gens, & de la puissance exécutrice de celles qui dépendent du droit civil."

"the political liberty of a state is shaped by fundamental laws which establish therein the distribution of the legislative power, the executive power in matters of public law, and the executive power in matters of civil law." (*Encyclopédie*, Louis de Jaucourt, LIBERTÉ POLITIQUE)

While Jaucourt in line with the Roman division between slaves and free subjects thus defines natural liberty as non-domination, his definition of political liberty emphasizes that freedom originates from membership in the *polis* or the *res publica*. Finally, Jaucourt turns to history and asserts that England is the ultimate historical manifestation of this latter kind of liberty.

LETTRES PHILOSOPHIQUES' TWO ASPECTS OF REPUBLICAN (UN)FREEDOM

Lettres philosophiques, also known as *Lettres Anglaises*, was first published in an English translation in London in 1733 (*Letters Concerning the English Nation*), then in Paris in 1734. Voltaire's letters on England anticipate Jaucourt's articles. In a peculiar potpourri of satire, historiography, Enlightenment propaganda, and personal anecdotes, the letters discuss the rather abstract notions of natural and political liberty within a number of specific historical contexts. While the English publication went unheeded, the French reception of the 24 letters has become legendary: The work, published without approbation, was immediately censured. Authorities confiscated the edition, arrested the publisher, and issued a proscription and warrant of arrest against Voltaire, who was immediately recognized as the author. The Parisian parliament accused the letters of subverting religion and manners, as well as the government, and ordered a public book burning at the stairs of the Palais Justice. A Jansenist pamphlet referred to them as "lettres diaboliques." The author had to flee Paris.

The strong censure indicates that the letters were considered a threat to both the political and religious order. A few decades after its publication, *Lettres philosophiques* was nearly canonized as revolutionary. "Cet ouvrage fut parmi nous l'époque d'une revolution" ("This work would start the era of a revolution among us"), Condorcet stated in his biography *Vie de Voltaire* (1787) (Condorcet, 1994, p. 46), a view the French literary historian Gustave Lanson would adopt more than a century later, confirming that the letters were "la première bombe lancée contre l'ancien regime" ("the first bomb directed towards the Old Regime", Lanson, 1910, p. 52). Voltaire's work was seen as an intervention in an emerging and changing public space. It not only provoked public reaction, but also participated in the construction of the public sphere as such. Thus it was, as a later critic, Shirley Jones, has put it, "a political act" (Jones, 1982, p. 149).

The *Lettres philosophiques* are imbued with a critical agenda. Under the pretext of describing the ways and customs of France's most important neighbour and political opponent in the European power play, the author represents England in most ways as a positive contrast to France. Voltaire introduces a comparative figure, and a dichotomy of freedom and "unfreedom," that would become a leitmotif in his works: England is, compared to France, the land of freedom. Its governmental system explains this freedom. Unlike France, England has not been subjected to an absolutist Prince. The country's constitutional monarchy guarantees the freedom of its inhabitants by stimulating religious tolerance, commercial life, scientific progress, and intellectual achievements. In other words, the author represents the citizens' freedom as founded in English politics. The comparative representation apparently makes England the home of the free while in France, in harsh contrast, unfreedom – such as religious persecutions and restrictions on the freedom of the press – reigns due to the absolutist regime. But it turns out that the dichotomy between freedom and unfreedom is not only a question of non-domination or domination. Even a state of non-domination, like the one found in England, may imply unfreedom.

In later editions of *Lettres philosophiques*, the author added a 25th letter which complicates the work's overall significations. I would suggest that this letter is a key to get a grip on Voltaire's discussion of natural liberty and its shortcomings. In the last letter, somewhat surprisingly entitled "On the *Pensées* of M. Pascal" ("Sur les *Pensées* de M. Pascal"), he leaves his main theme, England as France's positive contrast, in favour of a dialogue ridiculing the Jansenist philosopher's Augustinian theory of predestination. 20th century scholars seem to agree that this added letter serves to emphasize the work as, first and foremost, a religious critique: either as a commentary to the still ongoing quarrel between Jesuits and Jansenists, or as a critique of the Jansenist conception of human life, or finally as an attack upon Christianity in general (cf. Cassirer, 1968, p. 145-148; Desné, 1972, p. 43; Pomeau, 1995, p. 233-234). Still, this interpretation sounds less than satisfying as little in the earlier letters' way of argument appears to convincingly anticipate such a critique as the work's essential agenda.

"Tout le malheur des hommes vient d'une seule chose, qui est de ne savoir pas demeurer en repos dans une chambre" ("All of man's misfortune comes from one thing, which is not knowing how to sit quietly in a room"), Blaise Pascal states in one of *Pensées*' well-known dictums. In the 25th letter Voltaire, on the contrary, insists that man is born to act in society, not to contemplate in an ivory tower:

"Qu'est-ce qu'un homme qui n'agirait point, et qui est supposé se contempler? Non seulement je dis que cet homme serait un imbécile, inutile à la société, mais je dis que cet homme ne peut exister." (Voltaire, 1994, p. 173)

"What sort of thing is a man who doesn't act and yet supposedly contemplates himself? I say not only that such a man would be an imbecile, useless to society, but that such a man cannot exist." (Voltaire, 1961, p. 132)

The citation activates two key motives not only in the Pascal letter, but also in the *Lettres philosophiques* as a whole: the importance and value of the civic virtues *action* and *usefulness*. I will suggest that the insistence on the ability to act in society as the human being's most fundamental quality is not only a rejection of Pascalian theology; in addition, Voltaire, from the viewpoint of political theory, criticizes the notion of the passive subject. He argues that man is a political agent, defined by the liberty to take part in a political process. As such, the last philosophical letter invites its reader to consider the work on the whole as a discussion of the citizen's relations to the *polis*. The letters discuss how England values certain social identities like intellectuals, merchants, and religious minorities differently than France. They reveal how the citizens' freedom always depends upon how they are treated by their government. In addition to its insistence on England's superiority, *Lettres philosophiques*' central message is this: that freedom results from actions which are located within a political sphere. From the point of view of the Pascal-letter, a chief question in the letters consequently seems to be whether one is included in or excluded from the *polis*.

It is on this point that Voltaire's Quakers become an interesting case. Following Arendt's concepts as well as the 18th century discourse on political and natural liberty, I will in the following explore a significant differentiation in the work's treatment of the republican notion of freedom as non-domination, namely the differentiation between non-political and political societies, and, consequently, between natural and political liberty. An analysis of the so called "Quaker letters" reveals that Voltaire seems to prefer the latter and it illustrates how he uses literary conventions to represent natural liberty as a state of unfreedom.

THE QUAKER LETTERS

Recent studies have demonstrated 18th century literature's articulation and exploration of the historical emergence of the notion of human rights (Hunt, 2007; Maslan, 2004). In discussing the opposition between natural and political freedom within fictional frameworks and from a pragmatic point of view, Voltaire participates in this investigation. His representation of ideal societies – such as Eldorado or the London Exchange – demonstrates the shortcomings of natural liberty. The introductory letters in Voltaire's *Letters philosophique* reveal that the kind of freedom such societies embody, turns out to be useless – and hence in fact it ceases to be freedom – when facing the real world.

Voltaire entitled his first four philosophical letters "Sur les Quakers" ("On the Quakers").[3] Unlike the other letters, they constitute a continuous narrative in which the author explicitly becomes the personal narrator as well as one of the two main characters. The first letter opens *in medias res* as Voltaire visits a famous old Quaker who has retired to the countryside outside London. The old man invites the French *philosophe* into his home for a conversation. In the first and second letters, this particular Quaker and the Quakers in general are permitted to represent themselves directly through the old man's participation in the dialogue. The third and fourth letters leave this dialogue in favor of a narrative mode. Assuming the role of a historiographer rather than a conversation partner, the author of the last two letters gives an account of the historical background, the status quo, and even a prediction of the Quaker society's future.

In Voltaire's discourse, the old Quaker is introduced in contrast to the Jewish-Christian culture in general, and in particular to the French ideal of courteousness. His physical appearance is noteworthy – he wears a strange hat and a coat without pleads or buttons – and he does not act in line with common social rules. While the author politely addresses the old man as "Vous" and "Monsieur", the Quaker replies by calling his guest "friend" (*ami*) and "son" (*mon fils*). Still, his eccentric manners come across as admirable and the author positively describes his remarkable health and extraordinarily noble and appealing attitude. Despite the fact that the Quaker receives his guest without the slightest hint of a bow, it seems to be "plus de politesse dans l'air ouvert et humain de son visage qu'il n'y en a dans l'usage de tirer une jambe derrière l'autre et de porter à la main ce qui est fait pour couvrir la tête" ("more politeness in the openness and humanity of his expression than there is in the habit of drawing one leg behind the other, and of carrying in the hand what was made to cover the head", Voltaire, 1994, p. 20; Voltaire, 1961, p. 3). The conventional rituals of politeness are revealed as ridiculous compared to this gentleman's natural authority.

---

3   By introducing his letters with a story on the Quakers, a culturally significant but numerically marginal Christian community in the English society, Voltaire was in line with a conventional maneuver within the genre of French travel writing on England. The eccentric English Quakers constituted an object of fascination in French 17th and 18th century culture to such a degree that, as Edith Philips has put it, "[Q]uakerism was written of and defined in France almost before it was defined by its own people" (Philips, 1932, p. 2). The Quaker was thus already established as a literary type when Voltaire portrayed this peculiar group in *Lettres philosophiques*.

Nevertheless, the depiction of the old Quaker is eventually somewhat ambiguous, once the Quaker is subjected to Voltaire's familiar ironic distance. The author admires the Quaker so much that the latter almost gains superhuman qualities, explaining that the old man "n'avait jamais connu les passions ni l'intempérance" ("had always been a stranger to the passions and to intemperance", Voltaire, 1994, p. 20; Voltaire, 1961, p. 3), thus depriving him of two, in Voltaire's opinion, essential human traits. The author emphasizes the old man's idealness at the expense of his realness. Additionally, he stresses both his arrogant indulgence towards and skeptical distrust of his conversation partner by calling him a "holy man" (*saint homme*) and an "enthusiast" (*enthousiaste*), epithets with clearly negative connotations in the author's writings. Due to this distance, the glorified old Quaker simultaneously falls victim to the author's mockery and (faint) praise.

The ambivalence of the Quaker figure is echoed by the paradoxical effect of the authorial distance in the first letter, a distance which eventually allows the Quaker to give an uninterrupted speech. Consequently, the dialogue turns into a monologue while the conversation's subject changes. From discussing curious theological and cultural historical details, the Quaker turns his attention to politics and ethics. The old man regards his French guest's polite manners as the direct consequence of a hierarchically structured community and explains that his own habits, on the other hand, imply a rejection to such a notion of society. He informs the reader that the Quakers' society is truly egalitarian. Due to this sense of equality, they always use the familiar forms, whether addressing kings or shoemakers, and it also explains why everyone, even women, is allowed to speak during services. The Quakers consider all human beings their brethren, he claims, and respect no authority but the law.

Through the old man's disapproval of anti-democratic norms, it is as though the distance between the author and the Quaker character disappears. In articulating the idea of a democratic (all human beings are equal), ethic (all human beings should be treated with respect and charity), and juridical (the authority is the law, not the Prince) society, the retired Quaker gradually becomes the implied author's mouthpiece. In consequence, the author and his manners, rather than the Quaker and his eccentric society, turn out to be the proper object of satire. The irony thus works two ways in the first two letters, as the ridicule strikes the Quaker, a superstitious freak, and the narrator himself, a representative of a hypocritical and hierarchical culture that the Quaker opposes.

Within the framework of *Lettres philosophiques*' dominating comparative figure, the contrast between England and France, the question is, however, whether or how the Quakers' societal ideal corresponds with the greater English society. Rather than being an England in miniature, the Quaker society introduces a third alternative to the dichotomy between France and England, allowing a critical representation of England as well as of the Christian sect. The Quaker society functions as a vehicle for a double critique: On the one hand, by constituting a contrast to English politics, it reveals that England is not a righteous democracy. The Quakers point to a kind of unfreedom within the *polis*, that is, the fact that English politics brutally subordinates important democratic prin-ciples in order to enrich and expand its political territory. In this, England resem-bles France; it gains its strength through domination. On the other hand, the representation of the Quakers accentuates the necessary association of freedom and politics, showing the shortcoming of ethical ideals such as egalitarianism as long as they are not situated in a political sphere.

This double critique – of English politics and of the utopian aspect of the Quakers' ethical ideals – becomes acute in the letters' discussion of colonial politics. In the last paragraph of letter number one, the old Quaker expresses his egalitarian and cosmopolitan ethics within a specific political and historical context: the British colonization of America. The Quakers are a peaceable people; they refuse to engage in wars not because they fear death, but, as he explains, because:

"[...] nous ne sommes ni loups, ni tigres, ni dogues, mais hommes, mais chrétiens. Notre Dieu, qui nous a ordonné d'aimer nos ennemis et de souffrir sans murmure, ne veut pas sans doute que nous passions la mer pour aller égorger nos frères, parce que les meurtriers vêtus de rouge, avec un bonnet haut de deux pieds, enrôlent des citoyens en faisant du bruit avec deux petits bâtons sur une peau d'âne bien entendu; et lorsque après des batailles gagnées tout Londres brille d'illuminations, que le ciel est enflammé de fusées, que l'air retentit du bruit des actions de grâces, des cloches, des orgues, des canons, nous gémissons en silence sur les meurtres qui causent la publique allégresse." (Voltaire, 1994, p. 24)

"[...] we are not wolves or tigers or watchdogs, but men and Christians. Our Lord, who has commanded us to love our enemies and to endure without complaint, certainly does not wish us to cross the sea and cut the throats of our brothers because some murderers dressed in red, and wearing hats two feet high, are enlisting citizens by making a noise with two little sticks on the tightly stretched skin of an ass. And when, after battles won, all London glitters with lights, when the sky blazes with fireworks, and the air resounds with the noise of thanksgiving, of bells, of organs, and of cannon, we mourn in silence over these murders, the cause of public gaiety." (Voltaire, 1961, p. 7)

According to the old man, the Quakers are first and foremost human beings (*hommes*) and Christians (*chrétiens*) and, thus, they regard Native Americans as their brothers (*nos frères*) instead of barbaric foreigners. Consequently, they differ from the ideal of the patriotic British citizen whose primary civic virtue is the love of his own country and fellow citizens. Instead of representing the Quakers as a part of British society and the English national character, the old man emphasizes their place outside of, and in opposition to, England and its politics – they refuse to take part in the conquering of the New World. In this passage, the Quakers become the incarnation of an ethical ideal and as such, they reveal the unethical aspects of colonial politics by showing that the British Empire is far from unfamiliar with domination, and, indeed, dependent on subordination of other people.

Voltaire's Quakers have occasionally been compared to another ideal people in French 18th century literature, the Troglodytes in Montesquieu's *Lettres persanes* (1721). Both Montesquieu's archaic people and Voltaire's religious sect are associated with a moral ideal of humanity, and both groups are configured as enclaves outside of the greater society. There is, however, an important difference between the two ideals. Montesquieu situates his Troglodytes in a prehistoric, mythological and allegorical context, letting them represent a number of different social organizations, while Voltaire takes the Quakers out of the realm of the ideal and shows that the moral which they represent may be realized in a historical context (cf. Wellington, 1994, p. 37). In other words, the Quakers' ethics become a matter of politics. This "politicization" takes place in the third and fourth letters, which have resemblances to the genre of historiography, particularly in the representation of the Quaker colony.

We are told that, in 1680, William Penn, the son of a wealthy English Vice admiral, became the sovereign of a Quaker state: Pennsylvania, a truly ecumenical society and an exceptional American colony. As its chief-legislator Penn actually made a political alliance with the natives, stating they were brothers and equals:

"Il commença par faire une ligue avec des Américains ses voisins. C'est le seul traité entre ces peuples et les chrétiens qui n'ait point été juré, et qui n'ait point été rompu." (Voltaire, 1994, p. 38)

"He began by making an alliance with the Americans, his neighbors. This is the only treaty between these people and the Christians that was never sworn to and has never been broken." (Voltaire, 1961, p. 18)

Pennsylvania becomes the historical manifestation of an actual *polis* where all inhabitants enjoy both natural and political liberties. The old Quaker's cosmopolitan ethics – his ideal of democracy as well as his imperial critique – merge in the Quaker colony, wherein the egalitarianism of the Quaker Church seems to be implemented in a political community.

Pennsylvania resembles a kind of cosmopolitan state. It is built neither on a differentiation of citizens and foreigners nor social hierarchies. This is a historical innovation, the author claims:

"C'était un spectacle bien nouveau qu'un souverain que tout le monde tutoyait, et à qui on parlait le chapeau sur la tête, un gouvernement sans prêtres, un peuple sans armes, des citoyens tous égaux, à la magistrature près, et des voisins sans jalousie." (Voltaire, 1994, p. 38)

"It was quite a new sort of spectacle: a sovereign whom everyone familiarly *thee'd* and *thou'd*, and spoke to with one's hat on; a government without priests, a people without weapons, citizens all of them equals – magistrates excepted – and neighbors free of jealousy." (Voltaire, 1961, p. 18-19)

Pennsylvania is perfectly democratic and tolerant. Its inhabitants feel secure. And it also seems like the colony is fulfilling the rights of man and the natural liberty that Jaucourt defined in the *Encyclopédie*; a liberty implying that the individuals "ne sont pas soumis à la puissance d'un maître, & que personne n'a sur eux un droit de propriété" ("are not subject to the power of a master, and no one else has a proprietary right over them", *Encyclopédie*, Louis de Jaucourt, LIBERTÉ NATURELLE).

To Voltaire, the American colony appears almost too good to be true. The author emphasizes his incredulity by concluding that Pennsylvania – in contrast, we may add, to *Candide*'s well-known Eldorado – is a rare case of a historically realized utopia: "Guillaume Penn pouvait se vanter d'avoir apporté sur la terre l'âge d'or dont on parle tant, et qui n'a vraisemblablement existé qu'en Pennsylvanie" ("William Penn could boast of having brought forth on this earth the Golden Age that everyone talks so much about, and that probably never was, except in Pennsylvania", Voltaire, 1994, p. 38; Voltaire, 1961, p. 19). Despite the state's historical existence, Voltaire describes it as a Golden Age and thus as a cultural phantasm. This utopian description of Pennsylvania constitutes a turning point in the Quaker narrative. It hints at the conclusion of the Quaker letters, which makes clear that the Quakers' community is not sustainable in real life.

Similarly to Montesquieu's Troglodyte fable, Voltaire's Quaker narrative is not only the story of a society's rise and prosperity, but also of its degeneration. The fall is a consequence of isolation. Neither the English nor the Pennsylvanian Quakers exist in a vacuum. They are parts of the larger political community of 18th century imperial England. In this historical context it is as if the Quakers are deprived of the right to existence. Despite the fact that the British Toleration Act (1689) gave all dissenters, and thereby the Quakers, political liberty, that is, access to the Parliament, the Quakers continued to voluntarily exclude themselves from the *polis*. Their consequent resistance to act in Arendt's sense of the word, to participate in the political society, causes their shortcomings in *Lettres philosophiques*. This self-imposed isolation puts their ethics – moderation, incorruptibility, pacifism – in another, and more critical, light. These qualities are not only moral or ethical ideals; they also imply what we, following Arendt, may call a resistance to take part in the political community. The ideals are not situated and realized within a political sphere. Therefore they are morally deficient and even though the Quakers are certainly not dominated, they are not really free.

The letter that succeeds the four Quaker letters opens by claiming that "un Anglais, comme homme libre, va au Ciel par le chemin qui lui plaît" ("An Englishman, as a free man, goes to Heaven by whatever road he pleases", Voltaire, 1994; p. 42; Voltaire, 1961, p. 22). But in spite of religious freedom, each individual and each sect necessarily exists within larger communities: the nation and the world. The first four letters deal with a specific situation that defines the Quakers: the fact that they are a minority that only exist in the margins of the large *polis* of colonial England. This very situation, it seems, leads to their final setback in the Quaker narrative's very last paragraph:

"Par tout pays, la religion dominante, quand elle ne persécute point, engloutit à la longue toutes les autres. Les quakers ne peuvent être membres du Parlement, ni posséder aucun office, parce qu'il faudrait prêter serment et qu'ils ne veulent point jurer. Ils sont réduits à la nécessité de gagner de l'argent par le commerce; leurs enfants enrichis par l'industrie de leurs pères, veulent jouir, avoir des honneurs, des boutons et des manchettes; ils sont honteux d'être appelés quakers, et se font protestants pour être à la mode." (Voltaire, 1994, p. 40)

"In every country the dominant religion, if it does not actually persecute all the others, swallows them up in the end. Quakers cannot be members of Parliament, nor can they hold office, for in either case one must take oath, and they refuse to swear. They are reduced to making money by means of commerce. The children, made rich by the industry of their fathers, want to enjoy themselves, to acquire honours, buttons and cuffs. They are ashamed to be called Quakers, and are turning Anglican to be in style." (Voltaire, 1961, p. 21)

In the four Quaker letters, the author presents a society that, despite its moral idealness and utopian conceptions, necessarily confronts the utterly prosaic laws of history. The Quakers are overtaken by the reality that they are a part of the English political sphere, and the ideal of an ethically motivated withdrawal from politics appears to be impossible. Denying modernization, development, and, most of all, action within a larger political context, collides with the notion of political liberty – the idea that, as Arendt claims, an individual's freedom depends on citizenship and the ability, or in this case, rather, the will, to act in the *polis*. The Quakers' refusal to participate in colonial wars in the first letter may certainly express an ideal pacifism and an admirable rejection of imperial politics from the point of view of a cosmopolitan ethics. Nevertheless, it also implies a self-destroying passivity towards the larger political community in the sense that the rejection leaves the small Quaker society susceptible to the actions of stronger forces. Opposition to general European manners and customs, as well as refusal to act politically (to be politicians, or hold public positions in the English society), in fact, threaten their identity.

Voltaire's fourth philosophical letter, the last Quaker letter, concludes that, from an empirical point of view, the Quakers, with their ideal claims, have no chance to survive other than as a minor religious group with decreasing influence. Even their own children dissociate themselves from the Quaker identity by preferring the norms of wider society. And, with no political freedom to act, to take part in the general will of the *polis* they are a part of, the Quakers will, in the long run, be totally "swallowed up" by the outside world. In that case, their ideals of egalitarianism, tolerance, and pacifism become worthless. Their ethics have no political impact. From their location outside of the English *polis*, they appear to be just as "unreal" and just as excluded from historical reality as *Candide*'s Eldorado, the land of gold and perpetual peace that Candide and his companion chooses to leave in order to act within the global *polis*, i.e. to participate in the European politics of trade and colonialism.[4]

CONCLUSION

The Quakers have a double function in Voltaire's *Lettres philosophiques*. They become a complex and ambiguous figure as they embody an ideal democratic society, while at the same time they illustrate the unfreedom that follows from

---

4 Cf. the discussion of colonial politics in my article "Cosmopolitan, slaves, and the global market in Voltaire's *Candide ou l'optimisme*" (Kjørholt, 2012).

being excluded from and not taking part in the *polis*, i.e. the unfreedom of natural liberty as far as it is not situated in a concrete political sphere. Thus, the Quakers incarnate both a critical opposition to and a destructive exclusion from the *polis* they are related to: England and its colonies. The opposition makes them free in the sense that they actively refuse to behave according to the predominant societal constrains and norms. By turning their back on politics, the Quakers show that they are not dominated; they protest against status quo in a way that echoes *Lettres philosophiques*'s representation of the English political order as an alternative to that of France. However, the refusal to participate as citizens within the Commonwealth implies an unfreedom, as the Quakers thereby reduce themselves to a party without any influence on its surroundings. Their voluntary withdrawal from the *polis* makes them unfree in the sense that they never reach the level of the political agent, *bios politikos*, and instead remain passive subjects deprived of the right to act.

Following Arendt's concept of politics and 18th century discourses on political and natural freedom, I have argued that the Quakers illustrate the shortcomings of natural liberty. Their ethics and ideals of egalitarianism and pacifism are short-lived in the real world. The Quakers refuse to act and refuse to change, and are therefore a more or less meaningless part of the political England. They thus illustrate a general maxim in Voltaire's work: the primacy of politics to ethics. The only freedom that matters in real life is political freedom, which allows the individual to act as a citizen in order to influence society's constitution. Ethics have no functionality outside a political sphere, and according to Voltaire, in this respect politics is the premise of ethics. Ethical ideals should thus be pragmatically adjusted to political reality.

A liberal concept of freedom as non-interference becomes inadequate in discussing Voltaire's Quakers. The Quaker letters reveal the necessity to examine the author within a republican tradition, while they bring his political realism to the fore. Several scholars have discussed his realistic and pragmatic notion of politics which differs from the more well-known political thinkers of the French Enlightenment, Montesquieu and Jean-Jacques Rousseau (cf. Gay, 1965; Perkins, 1965; Pomeau, 1970). As one critic has put it: "as a political thinker he tended to respond to events rather than metaphysical abstractions" (Williams, 1994, p. xiii). Voltaire's pragmatic, realistic and situational approach to political subjects makes his literature an extraordinary archive for the study of early modern politics. To quote Nicholas Cronk:

"True, no single one of Voltaire's writings on political theory is as celebrated as Montesquieu's *De l'esprit des lois* or Jean-Jacques Rousseau's *Contrat social*; on the other hand, his voluminous political writings – and activities – had an immediate and practical impact which arguably the works of Montesquieu and Rousseau did not." (Cronk, 2009, p. 4)

The practical and immediate scope allows a focus on the functionality of republican concepts such as natural and political liberty, or the distinction between man and citizen, in the century that paved the way for the French Revolution and its *Déclaration des droits de l'homme et du citoyen de 1789*. Using Arendt's concept of the political as an analytical tool, I have suggested that *Lettres philosophiques*'s main concern is the investigation of the relations between individual identity, ethics, and politics, and thus my aim has been to call attention to this functionality.

The Quaker letters reveal that it is only as political liberty that freedom may be realized in a historical society. Last, but not least, they demonstrate the crucial importance of politics in Voltaire's literary work. The representation of the Quakers is only one of numerous examples of the author's tendency to emphasize the constraints of reality at the expense of the ideal, or the historical fact rather than the utopian imagination.[5] The focus on political reality thus affected Voltaire's poetics, a fact that scholars seem to have surprisingly left unexplored, and which deserves further attention in academic research. Hopefully, this article provides one possible example of how this political poetics could be approached.

REFERENCES

Arendt, H. (1998). *The Human Condition* [1958]. Chicago: University of Chicago Press.
Arendt, H. (2005). *The Promise of Politics*. New York, NY: Schocken Books.
Cassirer, E. (1968). *The Philosophy of the Enlightenment* [1932]. A. Koelln and J.P. Pettegrove (transl.). Princeton: Princeton University Press.
Condorcet, N. de (1994). *Vie de Voltaire* [1790]. Paris: Quai Voltaire.
Cronk, N. (2009). Introduction. In N. Cronk (Ed.) *The Cambridge Companion to Voltaire* (pp.1-15). Cambridge: Cambridge University Press.
Déclaration des Droits de l'Homme et du Citoyen de 1789. Retrieved from http://www.legifrance.gouv.fr/Droit-francais/Constitution/Declaration-des-Droits-de-l-Homme-et-du-Citoyen-de-1789

---

[5] Another obvious example is the representation of the utopian Eldorado in *Candide* (cf. Kjørholt, 2012).

Desné, R. (1972). The Role of England in Voltaire's Polemic Against Pascal: Apropos the Twenty-fifth *Philosophical Letter*. In P. Gay (Ed.) *Eighteenth-Century Studies. Presented to Arthur M. Wilson* (pp. 41-57). Hanover / New Hampshire: The University Press of New England.

Diderot, Denis & Jean le Rond D'Alembert (Eds). (2011), *Encyclopédie, ou dictionnaire raisonné des sciences, des arts et des métiers, etc.* [1751-1772]. ARTFL Encyclopédie Project, Robert Morrissey (Ed.), University of Chicago. Retrieved from http://encyclopedie.uchicago.edu/

Gay, P. (1965). *Voltaire's Politics. The Poet as Realist* [1959]. New York: Princeton University Press.

Hunt, L. (2007). *Inventing Human Rights. A History*. NY/London: W.W. Norton & Company.

Jones, S.E. (1982). Voltaire's use of contemporary French writing on England in his *Lettres philosophiques*. *Revue de littérature comparée*, 56 (2), pp. 139-156.

Kjørholt, I.H. (2012). Cosmopolitans, Slaves, and the Global Market in Voltaire's *Candide ou l'optimisme*. *Eighteenth-Century Fiction*, 25 (1), pp. 61-84.

Lanson, G. (1910). *Voltaire* [1906]. Paris: Librairie Hachette.

Maslan, S. (2004). The Anti-Human: Man and Citizen before the Declaration of the Rights of Man and of the Citizen. *The South Atlantic Quarterly*, 103 (2/3), pp. 357-374.

Maslan, S. (2006). The Dream of the Feeling Citizen: Law and Emotion in Corneille and Montesquieu. *SubStance*, 35 (1), pp. 69-84.

Perkins, M.L. (1965). *Voltaire's concept of international order*. Les Délices/Genève: Institut et musée Voltaire.

Philips, E. (1932). *The Good Quaker in French Legend*. Philadelphia: University of Pennsylvania Press.

Pomeau, R. (1970). *Politique de Voltaire* [1963]. Paris: Colin.

Pomeau, R. (1995). *La religion de Voltaire* [1969]. Paris: Librarie A.G. Nizet.

Skinner, Q. (2003). States and the freedom of citizens. In Q. Skinner and B. Stråth (Eds.) *States and Citizens* (pp. 11-27). Cambridge: Cambridge University Press.

Voltaire (1994). *Lettres philosophiques* [1734]. R. Pomeau (Ed.). Paris: Garnier-Flammarion.

Voltaire (1961). *Philosophical Letters*. E. Dilworth (trans.). New York: The Bobbs-Merrill Company.

Wellington, M. (1994). Montesquieu's Troglodytes and Voltaire's Quakers: A Case of Ideological Kinship. *Dalhousie French Studies*, 28, pp. 29-41.
Williams, D. (1994). Introduction. In D. Williams (Ed.) *Voltaire. Political Writings* (pp. xiii–xxxviii). Cambridge: Cambridge University Press.

Dependency, Corruption, and Aesthetics in Denis Diderot's *Le neveu de Rameau*

ANNE FASTRUP

Denis Diderot's posthumously published satire *Le neveu de Rameau* (probably written between 1761-1772) displays a complex network of references to some of the most difficult years, 1751-1759, in the history of the great Enlightenment project *L'Encyclopédie ou dictionnaire raisonné des sciences, des arts et des metiers,* of which Diderot was co-founder and chief editor. The 1750s constituted a period of ideological tension and increasing political paranoia in France, and from being a project of national prestige, the *Encyclopédie* was by then considered a threat to the religious, social, and political order of *l'ancien regime*. As was announced in Louis XV's decree concerning the book trade in 1757, printing and diffusion of text that "tends to attack religion, to stir up the spirits, to question Our authority, and to trouble the order and tranquillity of our states" was punishable by death (quoted from Israel, 2009, p. 14). The *Encyclopedie* project was suspended more than once by the courts and, as chief editor of the *Encyclopédie,* Diderot was in a permanently dangerous situation. The police had kept an eye on him since 1749, but from 1757 onwards he felt even more unable to express his views publicly. It is therefore hardly surprising that one of the most salient themes of *Le neveu de Rameau* is unfreedom. Normally, Diderot would discuss his writings in private correspondences, but *Le neveu de Rameau* was apparently composed in utter secrecy (Freud, 1967, p. 23). This silence has, of course, prompted much speculation. Why Diderot never mentioned the satire, no sure evidence can tell us. However, since it was first published in 1805 in German by Goethe, the satire, which consists of a long, digressive imaginary philosophical conversation between two half-fictional half-authentic characters, *Lui* and *Moi,* has been regarded as Diderot's secret revenge on the opponents of the *Encyclopédie*, the so-called anti-philosophers or anti-Encyclopaedists.[1] In close cooperation with, if not simply on the orders of powerful figures of the court, parliament, and church, these enemies of the *Encyclopédie* tried to stop the publication of the great work through a mixture of negative publicity and regular smear campaigns. Of course, the attempt did not succeed. The *Encyclopédie* was published, but only just.

Picking up on Goethe, the purpose of this article is to discuss *Le neveu de Rameau* in the context of the unfreedom that Diderot experienced while editing the *Encyclopédie*. As will be clear in what follows, the nature of his unfreedom goes beyond the mere fact of being restrained by the system of censorship regulation. Furthermore, the characters in *Le neveu de Rameau* are only indirectly connected with the Encyclopaedists and the anti-Encyclopaedists. The one main character, who appears under the anonymous pronoun *Lui*, refers to Jean-François Rameau, a poor musician and nephew of the great French composer Jean-Philippe Rameau, while *Moi* is a naïve and idealistic version of Diderot, himself. The central music and opera theme – which ranges far more widely than the reference to France's then leading composer Rameau – has a crucial role to play in the satire's interpretation of the anti-philosophers' attempt to obstruct the publication of the *Encyclopédie*. There is a connection between what we, with Goethe, may call the vengeance function of *Le neveu de Rameau*, and the theme of unfreedom. However, there may be said to be a complex correlation. *Le neveu de Rameau* intervenes in its historical context in a number of ways and at many levels. In addition, Diderot is an inexorable dialectician. The subjects he takes up refuse to fall easily into stable categories and unequivocal meanings, just as unfreedom itself is dealt with in *Le neveu de Rameau*.

The theme of unfreedom is signalled from the very beginning. The prologue is adorned with an epigraph by Diderot's favourite poet Horace, which translates into English as: "Born under the evil influence of every Vertumnus." Vertumnus was the Roman god of the change of the seasons, and it is *inter alia* in this meaning – changeability – that we should look for the epigraph's signalling effect on the first page of the satire.[2] However, the Horatian satire cited is known as the *Saturnalian satire*, because it takes place during the period of *Saturnalia,* the

---

1 The anti-philosophers consisted of a large and quite powerful group of judges, journalists, poets, teachers, Franciscans, Jansenists, and Jesuits. All of these persons had close connections with wealthy patrons with great influence in the Court, among them Louis-August Bertin de Blagny, who plays a key role in *Le neveu de Rameau*.
2 "every *Vertumnus*" refers, of course, to the fact that Vertumnus is never the same but constantly changes shape, like the seasons.

religious Roman feast and carnival celebrated around the winter solstice. What is remarkable about this feast and carnival is that the normal social hierarchy was turned upside down during the days of the carnival. The feast commenced with a procession led by a person of very low rank disguised as a king, which set the scene for the slaves to exchange role and place with their masters, the condemned with the judges, etc. By referring to Horace's satire and the *Saturnalia*, Diderot not only introduces a theme of freedom and unfreedom, but also warns the reader that the contents of these concepts are by no means stable or clear. Who is free and who is unfree and what it means to be unfree is left open from the outset.

Despite this openness, here *Lui* seems the unfree one, and in more than one sense. Firstly, he is slave to his "besoin" or his "appétit" – hunger, instinct, desire or lust. Secondly, he is a slave of those who can satisfy his needs and desires. Hence, *Lui* is both physically and socially unfree. As we shall see, *Lui's* social unfreedom can be described on the basis of Philip Pettit's definition of freedom (unfreedom, respectively) from his book *Republicanism: A Theory of Freedom and Government* (1997). In this book, Pettit states that freedom cannot be defined exclusively according to Isaiah Berlin's famous distinction between positive and negative liberty in *Two Concepts of Liberty* (Berlin, 1969). Freedom must also be understood as the absence of dependency and domination, as "non-domination" (Pettit, 1997, p. 5). In his introduction, Pettit makes it clear that unfreedom as non-domination has nothing to do with being restrained by the laws of a legitimate government (ibid). Quite to the contrary, the "restraint of a fair system of law – a non-arbitrary regime – does not make you unfree" (ibid). The unfreedom that Pettit has in mind consists in being subject to arbitrary sway or to the "potentially capricious will or potentially idiosyncratic judgement of another" (ibid). Although Pettit's concept of unfreedom can be politically defined or politically legitimized (as in monarchy, for instance), he is first and foremost referring to non-formal, social, or intersubjective relations. Unfreedom as domination refers to a situation in which someone is or *feels* compelled to always take someone else's will or desire into consideration.

Pettit's definition of unfreedom can be applied to the principal character of *Le neveu de Rameau*. The most striking feature of the nephew is that he lives in dependency and under the domination of others. People with money, influence and power can get him to do anything at all. In particular, *Lui* is at the beck and call of the wealthy and powerful, but also very capricious Bertin, an extremely affluent financier and a member of *l'Académie des inscriptions et des belles-lettres*. The character is based upon the real Louis-August Bertin de Blagny, who, during the *Encyclopédie's* most critical years, 1752-1765, played an important role as patron of the Encyclopaedists' enemies. In the fictional world of *Le neveu de Rameau*, the nephew gains entry to Bertin's salon and well-filled dinner table thanks to a well-developed sense of being in service to the rich and – as he himself explains to *Moi* – service is about tracking the desire of the master.

The nephew simultaneously functions as the carrier of the satirical view and tone of the dialogue. He commands the floor, and it is he who taunts and mocks and reveals what the world is like in reality. *Le neveu de Rameau* is a satire about society in general and polite society in particular, both described as being in a state of degeneration and corruption. And with his insider knowledge of Bertin's circle, the nephew is eminently placed in terms of observing the corrupt nature of the rich and powerful, indeed of the whole tissue of society. For this reason, *Moi* – the philosopher – likes to talk to someone like the nephew:

"[…] leur caractère tranche avec celui des autres, et [qu']ils rompent cette fastidieuse uniformité que notre education, nos conventions de société, nos bienséance d'udage ont introduite [referring specifically to the nephew *Moi* says:] Il secoue, il agite; il fait approuver ou blamer; il fait sortir la vérité; il fait connaître les gens de bien; il démasque les coquins; c'est alors que l'homme de bon sens écoute, et démêle son monde." (Diderot, 1989, p. 72)

"[…] their characters contrast sharply with other people's and break the tedious uniformity that our social conventions and set politeness have brought about [referring specifically to the nephew *Moi* says:] He stirs people up and gives them a shaking, makes them take sides, brings out the truth, shows who are really good and unmasks the villains. It is then that the wise man listens and sorts people out." (Diderot, 1966, p.35)

Already at this point it is clear that the "servant," or "slave," *Lui*, is superior to the philosopher, *Moi*. The slave sees the world in a clearer light than "the wise man," who sees everything through the flattering prism of his moral ideals. This brings us to the central matter of this article. In *Le neveu de Rameau* unfreedom has some "advantages" in the shape of great intellectual broad-mindedness and, what is of particular interest to me here, great aesthetic sensitivity. The nephew knows everything about both French and Italian opera – prefering the latter – goes into ecstasies when he listens to or recalls a piece of music, and formulates a new poetics for the opera that breaks with classicist doctrine – which his uncle's music respects. Diderot has, however, also equipped the nephew with a seemingly strange double competency: he has both a visionary aesthetic gift and he is a master of the art of flattery, or service. What is the logic behind this connection between social unfreedom and aesthetic sensitivity? More precisely, what is it about the nephew's servitude that makes him able to break with the classicist aesthetic and its ideals of clarity, harmony, propriety, and moderation?

LUI'S UNFREEDOM

On the general level, *Lui*'s unfreedom consists in his being governed by "external" or physical forces such as hunger: "Son premier soin, le matin, quand il est levé, est de savoir où il dînera; après diner, il pense où il ira souper" ("His first care when he gets up in the morning is to make sure where he will be dining; after dinner he thinks where to go for supper," Diderot, 1989, p. 71; Diderot, 1966, p. 34). *Lui* appears to *Moi* to be "an eating subject" rather than "a fellow thinking subject" (Zalloua, 2003, p. 198). His day passes rushing hectically from house to house, ingratiating himself here, pleasing and enthusing there, in the hope of being invited to dine. In a way, he is a caricature of the physiological determinism that Diderot – if somewhat ambiguously – professed in his materialistic writings. The nephew is carried away by every outburst of desire or passion, and in that sense he may also be said to incarnate the typical Enlightenment concept of unfreedom, understood here along with Isaiah Berlin as being governed by "irrational impulses, uncontrolled desires, my 'lower' nature [...] my 'empirical' or 'heteronom' self" (Berlin, 1969, p. 9). *Lui* may be regarded as a satirical personification of the moral, human, and political imperfections from which the philosophers of the Enlightenment wished to free the human race by lifting it up to the higher level of reason, autonomy, and self-control through upbringing and reforms. *Moi* makes several attempts to appeal to the nephew's better nature by reminding him of how disgraceful, undignified, and unhappy his life is. Instead he should instil in himself "La connaissance de ses devoirs; l'amour de la vertu; la haine du vice" ("knowledge of one's duties, love of virtue, hatred of vice", Diderot, 1989, p. 137; Diderot, 1966, p. 82). Virtue, dignity and happiness come from helping one's friends and fighting for one's country. But the philosopher is wasting his breath, because according to *Lui*: "Il n'y a plus de patrie. Je ne vois d'un pole à l'autre que des tyrans et des esclaves" ("There is no such thing left [as one's country]. From pole to pole all I can see is tyrants and slaves", Diderot, 1989, p. 114; Diderot, 1966, p. 65). If one is wealthy, one should enjoy one's good fortune; if one is poor, one must:

"faire la sa cour, morbleu; faire sa cour; voir les grands; étudier leurs gouts; se prêter à leurs fantaisies; server leurs vices; approuver leurs injustices." (Diderot, 1989, p. 115)

"Butter people up, good God, butter them up, watch the great, study their tastes, fall in with their whims, pander to their vices, approve of their injustices" (Diderot, 1989, p. 65)

What *Lui* is really saying is that one can only maintain one's dignity – understood here as working for the common good, and not allowing oneself to be pushed around by physical impulses or powerful tyrants – if one is in relationships characterised by equality. It is only if one can identify equally with others as fellow citizens that one can see common interests and a larger political community.[3] But in a world where some are rich and others are poor, and where some dominate others, there exists no equality, no common interests, and no common good. In this world, all pursue their primitive impulses and private interests with every means at their disposal.

The involuntary gestures, spasms, and pantomimes that frequently accompany the character's words and thoughts also belong to the picture of *Lui*'s unfreedom. These involuntary pantomimes, for which the nephew is famed, occur especially when he speaks about an intense desire for something – good food, a woman's breast, a glass of good wine – or when he is seized by strong feelings, such as when he talks about or recalls music. In these states, consisting of primitive impulsive desires and aesthetic emotions, all words and notions are accompanied by a gesture, thus giving us the impression of a primitive continuity between consciousness, language, and body. *Lui* cannot think, feel, or talk without leaving corporeal traces in the form of spasms, giving the feeling of a person who repeatedly travels back into the history of civilisation before language, back to the natural, gestural, and mimetic language that the philosophers of the time thought preceded conventional language. Thus, the unfreedom has connotations of belonging to a lower rung of civilisation, which may be turned into something more positive, as it is *inter alia* this spasmodic body that makes *Lui* the liberating, non-conformist character that he also is.

Finally, *Lui*'s unfreedom manifests itself in the form of the domination exercised over him by Bertin and his clique:

"J'étais leur petit Rameau, leur joli Rameau, leur Rameau le fou, l'impertinents, l'ignorant, le paresseux, le gourmand, le bouffon, la grosse bête. Il n'y avait pas une de ces epithets familières qui ne me valût un sourire, une caresse, un petit coup sur l'épaule, un

---

3 Cf. Tue Andersen Nexø: "Materially Unfree. Corruption as a societal diagnosis and the political forms of unfreedom in Machiavelli, Davenant, and Bolingbroke", in this book.

soufflet, un coup de pied, à table un bon morceau qu'on jetait sur mon assiette [...] car moi, je suis sans consequence." (Diderot, 1989, p. 88)

"I was their dear Rameau, their pretty Rameau, their Rameau the lunatic, the impertinent, the ignorant, the lazy, greedy old fool. Not one of these pet names but earned me a smile, a caress, a tap on the shoulder, a box on the ears, a kick, a toothsome morsel chucked on to my plate during meals [...] I could take without its being of any consequences, for I am a person who isn't of any consequence." (Diderot, 1966, p. 46)

Lui is defined by others. He is nothing himself but a projection of the vices, characteristics, and faults of his surroundings. It was *inter alia* this aspect of Diderot's character that caught Hegel's interest and caused him to incorporate *Le neveu de Rameau* within *Phenomenologie des Geistes*. Hegel viewed the nephew as an image of a phase in the history of the development of consciousness, where the I has not yet found itself, and is alienated in external definitions. But instead of regarding *Lui* from the perspective of Hegelian alienation, we can see him from the perspective of republican liberty. As mentioned above, Philip Pettit – in contrast to Berlin and the liberal tradition – has argued that freedom should also be understood as "non-domination," that is, the absence of dependency and domination. "Domination" should be understood here as the consequence of great inequality, of dependency relations that cause the powerless party to constantly consider the interests and wishes of the powerful (Pettit, 1997, p. 60-61). The nephew's relationship to Bertin may be said to be prototypical for such a domination and dependency relationship, and it is in the light of this unfreedom – and not because the nephew has not yet found an authentic expression of his subjectivity – that his change of identity, his "alienation", should be understood.

The relationship with Bertin implies several things, the first being that the nephew is not free to express his own honest opinions. That this is the case is shown when, in a surprising and singular attack on "dignité," he expresses his honest opinion of Bertin and his mistress. He is immediately shown the door and told never to show himself again. Like the anti-philosophers, *Lui* only has access to Bertin's food and hospitality as long as his behaviour pleases Bertin, in other words as long as *Lui* complies with the wishes of his master and mistress: "[il faut] chercer son désir dans yeux, rester suspend à sa lèvre, attendre son ordre..." ("we try to read her wishes in her eyes, hang upon her lips, wait for her orders...", Diderot, 1989, p. 124; Diderot, 1966, p. 72). As a consequence of this asymmetry, the subject or servant is morally corrupted; he invariably becomes dishonest and insincere as he is forced to speculate in how he can cheat and deceive. Although Pettit does not directly write about moral corruption, it is implicit in the quotes he uses to illustrate the social and moral effects of unfreedom. Pettit quotes John Milton, who, thinking of the monarchy, describes "the perpetual *bowings* and *cringings* of an abject people" (Pettit 1997, p. 61), and also refers to *Discourses Concerning Government* (1689) whose author Algernon Sidney claimed that: "slavery doth naturally produce meanness of spirit, with its worst effect, flattery" (ibid.). Both examples show the dissimulation, falseness, and servility, in short, the moral corruption that characterises an unfree people. The nephew himself formulates the unfree person's (his own) moral characteristics as the ability to flatter, lie, commit perjury, break promises, crawl, seduce and lead into depravity – without suffering qualms of conscience.

We read many examples of the nephew's skills at flattery. He knows precisely what to say and the posture he should adopt to satisfy his master's and his mistress's vanity. At the same time, being a *flatteur* requires great ingenuity and "versatility," because neither Bertin nor his mistresses deserve praise. In addition, the flattery must show variation:

"[...] il ne faut pas toujors approuver de la même manière. On serait monotone [...] il faut savoir preparer et placer ces tons majeurs et péremptoires, saisir l'occasion et le moment [...] il faut être placé à l'écart, dans l'angle de l'appartement le plus éloigné du champ de bataille, avoir préparé son explosion par un long silence, et tomber subitement comme une comminge [...] Personne n'a cet art comme moi [...] j'ai des petits tons que j'accompagne d'un sourire; une variété infinite des mines approbatives; là le nez, la bouche, le front, les yeux entrent en jeu; j'ai une souplesse de reins; une manière de contourner l'épine du dos, de hausser ou de baisser les épaules, d'étendre les doigts, d'incliner la tête, der fermer les yeux, et d'être stupéfait, comme si j'avais entendu descendre du ciel une voix angélique et divin. C'est là ce qui flatte." (Diderot, 1989, pp. 125-126)

"[...] you mustn't always gush in the same way. It would pall [...] you must know how to prepare and where to bring these peremptory tones in the major key, how to seize the occasion and the moment [...] Then you must take up your position some way off in the corner of the room farthest removed from the battlefield, having prepared your explosion by a long silence, and you suddenly drop like a bomb [...] Nobody has ever touched me in this art [...] I have some soft notes which I accompany with a smile and an infinite variety of approving faces, with a nose, mouth, eyes and brow all brought into play. I have a certain agility with my lips, a way of twisting my spine, raising my head, shutting my eyes and being struck dumb as though I had heard an angelic, divine voice come down from heaven. That's what gets them." (Diderot, 1966, pp. 73-74)

This rather comic passage describes how the servant must have a feeling not only for the narcissism of his master or mistress, but also for the timing, dramatic structure, choreography, and effects of his own behaviour. The servant must be empathetic, sensitive, analytical, ingenuous, versatile, and a good actor too. It may seem strange that the body is emphasised to such an extent in connection with flattery, and one could ask why flattery seems to be communicated most efficiently in pantomime language. Diderot's satire does not provide any direct answer to this, but in other works Diderot writes that gesture – and thus also pantomime – has a sublime and in principle limitless meaning, because its expression cannot be translated into unequivocal content. In his writings on dramaturgy, Diderot also recommends the use of pantomime onstage, as its affective impact on the spectators is far greater than that of spoken language (Diderot, 1988, pp. 268-279). So, gesture and pantomime do not merely provide a limitless praise, they also affect the receiver on an emotional level which – one might claim – is under the radar of critical judgement.

UNFREEDOM, CORRUPTION, AND POWER

Towards the end of the dialogue, *Moi*, who would seem to have lost his illusions about patriotism and friendship, suddenly paints a picture of a society where everyone is unfree and where, consequently, everyone adopts a posture:

"Quiconque a besoin d'un autre, est indigent et prend une position. Le roi prend une position devant sa maîtresse et devant dieu; il fait son pas de pantomime. Le minister fait le pas de courtesan, de flatteur, de valet ou de gueux devant son roi [...] Ma foi, ce que vous appelez la pantomime des gueux, est le grand branle de la terre. Chacun a sa petite Hus et son Bertin." (Diderot, 1989, p. 191)

"Whoever needs somebody else is necessitous and so takes up a position. The king takes up a position with his mistress and with God; he performs his pantomime step. The minister executes the movements of courtier, flatterer, flunkey or beggar in front of his king [...] Good heavens, what you call the beggars' pantomime is what makes the whole world go round. Every man has his little Hus and his Bertin." (Diderot, 1966, pp. 121-122)

Everyone has desire and everyone is dependent on others to satisfy this desire. This is why everyone is unfree and why everyone stages pantomimes. What *Moi* describes is, in fact, a corrupt society, that is a society in which *all* are forced to constantly take the demands and interests of others into consideration. No one dares to speak his honest opinion, no one dares to develop a free position, and everyone feels compelled to say something they do not mean. But the nephew knows that this dependency is experienced differently depending on one's place in the social hierarchy. His experience shows that there is a great difference between being an unfree master and being a servant. In short, unfreedom manifests itself differently in *Lui's* case and in the case of Bertin and his friends. If we first look at Bertin and the anti-philosophers, their lack of freedom shows itself in two similar ways, as mechanisation and animalisation. Several times *Lui* compares Bertin to a mechanical puppet: "[il] a l'air d'une pagoda immobile à laquelle on aurait attaché un fil menton" ("[he] looks like a motionless image with a string tied to its chin", Diderot, 1989, pp. 122-123; Diderot, 1966, p. 71). As for the anti-philosophers, they have according to *Lui* degenerated into animals, predators:

"Nous paraissons gais, mais au fond nous avons tous de l'humeur et grand appétit. Des loups ne sont pas plus affamés; des tigres ne sont pas plus cruels. Nous dévorons comme des loups, lorsque la terre a été longtemps couverte de neige; nous déchirons comme des tigres, tout ce qui réussit [...] Jamais on ne vit ensemble tant de bêtes tristes, acariâtres, malfaisantes et courroucées. On n'entend que les noms de Buffon, de Duclos, de Montesquieu, de Rousseau, de Voltaire, de d'Alembert, de Diderot, et Dieu sait de quelles epithets ils sont accompagnés." (Diderot, 1989, p. 134)

"We look Jovian, but in reality we are all foul-tempered and voracious of appetite. Wolves are not more famished, tigers no more cruel. We devour like wolves when the earth has been long under snow, like tigers we tear to pieces anything successful [...] Never were there seen so many wretched, spiteful, malevolent and truculent creatures in one place. You hear nothing but names such as Buffon, Duclos, Montesquieu, Rousseau, Voltaire, D'Alembert, Diderot, and God knows what epithets are coupled with them." (Diderot, 1989, p. 80)

The anti-philosophers are just as controlled by their instincts as *Lui*, just as much at the mercy of their desires and vices as he is. The difference is merely that they can afford to be so. Where *Lui* must always hide his desire to achieve his goal (a seat at the dinner table), the powerful can afford not to dissemble in this respect. The *powerful* unfree person can allow himself to indulge his natural condition, his natural impulses, while the *powerless* unfree person must constantly change identity, take on new roles, and work on his apparition to accommodate the desire of the master. However, as indicated above, this situation means that the servant or the slave remains superior in a social and aesthetic sense. He is forced to empathise with others' desires, to understand the hidden motives, the unspoken rules, the invisible hierarchy, and games of power. He must observe, understand, and be strategic.

We have now reached the point where we are able to explain why Diderot has equipped his character with this double identity of *flatteur* and musician; we are on the trail of the connection between his unfreedom and his aesthetic sensibility.

THE DEGENERATION OF SOCIETY AND THE NEW MUSIC

It has been said of Diderot's depiction of Bertin's circle (the anti-philosophers) that it appears as "une inversion du monde des salons" (Melancon 2000, p. 29). It may be viewed as a picture of the degeneration of *la bonne compagnie*. Because what *Moi* learns through *Lui's* reports from Bertin's circle is that *"les honnêtes gens"* have been replaced by "des gens de cour, des financiers, de gros commercants, des banquier, des gens d'affaires" ("court, high finance, commerce, banking, business of some kind", Diderot, 1989, p. 111; Diderot, 1966, p. 63), people who neither master the polite conversation of the salon nor live up to its social and moral ideal of self-control. Bertin's circle, however – as we saw earlier – is only a symptom of the more extensive corruption and regression of the fabric of society, as the nephew says: "Dans la nature, toutes les espèces se dévorent; toutes les conditions se dévorent dans la société. Nous faisons justice les auns des autres, sans que la loi s'en mêle" ("In nature all the species feed on each other, and all classes prey on each other in society. We mete out justice to each other without the law taking a hand", Diderot,1989, p. 111; Diderot, 1966, p. 63). No government, policy, or legislation interferes in this class warfare. Society has fallen back to a pre-political, natural state.

Why does music – opera – play such a key role in this satire about the corruption of polite society and society's general descent into a natural state? Why has Diderot created this nephew, who is both unfree and – in theory, anyway – a renewer of the opera? These questions cannot be answered within the framework of satire itself, but require an excursus on its historical context.

As a literary character, the nephew acts as a link between social satire, unfreedom, and music. Discussions of music within the satire span the nephew's criticism of French opera's tradition from Lully and Rameau, his defence of the Italian *opera buffa,* and his vision of new lyrical poetry. If we look at the satire in its historical context, there is nothing surprising in the coupling of the social and the aesthetic. Since the 17th century, "les grands," that is the Court and the urbanised nobility, have perceived themselves as the highest judges in matters of taste, and acted accordingly. It was their social, cultural and linguistic etiquette that had been elevated to the norm in the field of art. As Jolanta T. Pekacs writes: "the criteria of honnêteté in the social realm and those of a seventeenth-century work of art based on the classical doctrine [were] difficult to separate" (Pekacs 1999, p. 279). But judging from *Le neveu de Rameau,* in the middle of the 18th century we are in a new situation. The ideals of *honnêteté* has been displaced by the egoistic and vain private interests of financiers, patrons, and their allies. In *Le neveu de Rameau* Diderot thus asks what happens to aesthetic imitation when the social segment, whose rules art must respect, is corrupted. What happens to the aesthetic norms when the social norms are no longer dictated by *honnêteté*, probity, and moderation, but by the greed of the financier and his lackeys? What art does this society generate? In the first instance, Diderot answers by having the nephew expose classical French opera as a completely anachronistic genre consisting of: "les vols, les lances, les glories, les triomphes, les victoires […] féerie […] insipide mythologie…" ("rapine, lances, gloires, triumphs and victories […] fairy-tale […] insipid mythology", Diderot, 1989, pp. 162-163; Diderot, 1966, p. 101), which, however, fortunately "est au diable […] l'Académie royale du cul-de-sac n'a que fermer boutique" ("will go to the devil and the Royal Academy in the cul-de-sac will have to shut up shop", Diderot, 1989, p.161; Diderot, 1966, p. 100), as the nephew so tersely formulates it. The days of the French opera are numbered, the audience is bored. But what should take its place? The satire gives two "answers" to this question. The first answer takes the form of a pantomime, and the second is the nephew's poetics for new lyrical poetry.

Let us observe the pantomime first of all, more precisely one of the nephew's very famous pantomimes, called "l'homme-orchestre" in the reception of Diderot. Here *Lui* mimes not only a whole orchestra, but also scenes, conflicts, situations, music, and song from a great number of French and, in particular, Italian operas. Regarding *Lui's* big orchestra or opera pantomime, performed at Café de la Regence at Palais-Royale with the audience consisting of the café's guests and random passers-by, *Moi* states:

"Il commencait à entrer en passion, et à chanter tout bas. Il élevait le ton, à mesure qu'il se passionnait advantage; vinrent ensuite, les gestes, les grimaces du visage et les contorsions du corps […] Il entassait et brouillait ensemble trente airs, italiens, français, tragiques, comiques de toutes sortes de caractères […] succesivement furieux, radouci, imperieux, ricaneur. Ici, c'est une jeune fille qui pleure et il rend toute la minauderie; là il est prêtre, il est roi, il est tyran, il menace, il commande, il s'emporte; il est esclave, il obéit […] Admirais-je? Oui, j'admirais! Étais-je touché de pitié ? j'étais touché de pitié; mais une teinte de ridicule était fondue dans ces sentiments, et les dénaturait. Mais vous vous series échappé en éclats de rire, à la manière don't il contrefaisait les differrents instruments. Avec les joues renflées et bouffies, et un son rauque et sombre, il rendait les corps et les bassons [...] faisant lui seul, les danseurs, les chanteurs, les chanteuses, tout un orchestre, tout un theatre lyrique, et se divisant en vingt rôles divers, courant, s'arrêtant, avec l'air d'un énergumène, étincelant des yeux, écumant de la bouche [...] il pleurait, il riait, il soupirait; il regardait ou attendri, ou tranquille ou furieux; c'était une femme qui se pâme de douleur; c'était un malheureux livré à tout son désespoir..." (Diderot, 1989, pp. 166-167)

"He began to warm up and sang, first softly, then as he grew more impassioned, he raised his voice and there followed gestures, grimaces, and bodily contortions [...] He sang thirty tunes on top of each other and all mixed up: Italian, French, tragic, comic, of all sorts and descriptions [...] in turn raging, pacified, imperious, scornful. Here we have a young girl weeping, and he mimes all her simpering ways, there a priest, king, tyrant, threatening, commanding, flying into a rage, or a slave obeying [...] Did I admire? Yes, I did. Was I touched with pity? Yes, I was. But a tinge of ridicule ran through these sentiments and discoloured them. But you would have gone off into roars of laughter at the way he mimicked the various instruments. With cheeks puffed out and a hoarse, dark tone he did the horns and bassoons [...] a one-man show featuring dancers, male and female, singers of both sexes, a whole orchestra, a complete opera-house, dividing himself into twenty different stage parts, tearing up and down, stopping, like one possessed, with flashing eyes and foaming mouth [...] He wept, laughed, sighed, his gaze was tender, soft or furious: a woman swooning with grief, a poor wretch abandoned in the depth of his despair..." (Diderot, 1966, pp. 102-104)

Lui's body houses an insatiable appetite but also functions as a "medium of artistic self-expression, the site of amazing and captivating visual performances" (Zalloua, 2003, p. 206). As a pantomime artist, *Lui* transforms the animal unit of body and consciousness into an artistic expression with which he creates a moment of sensus communis between himself and *Moi*. Here we are faced with the paradoxical element of the nephew's body. On the one hand it forces him into dependency and social alienation, but on the other hand it serves him as an aesthetic means of expression with which he can make a personal sense experience public through his pantomimes, that is, accessible to sensory perception for *Moi* and the other guests at Café de la Regence.

But this does not exhaust the connection between unfreedom and the aesthetic pantomime. What we see in the impact of music on the nephew is, in reality, an aesthetic counterpart or aesthetic analogy to Bertin's (and *l'appétit*'s) domination. Music exercises the same domination over *Lui* as Bertin (and *l'appétit*) do. In both cases the body is both the source and the seat of the I's divestment of authority and self-determination – of freedom. If this divestment, this unfreedom or heteronomy, represents a moral problem in the social world (as it clearly does), it is on the other hand a source of pleasure in the field of aesthetic experience. Or, as Diderot writes with a mixture of fascination and condemnation about people with the gift of a special musical sensibility in *Lettre sur les sourds et les muets*:

"En musique, le plaisir de la sensation dépend d'une disposition particulière non seulement de l'oreille, mais de tout système des nerfs. S'il y a des têtes sonnantes, il y a aussi des corps que j'appelerais volontiers harmoniques; des hommes, en qui toutes les fibres oscillent avec tant de promptitude et de vivacité, que sur l'expérience des mouvements violents que l'harmonie leur cause, ils sent la possibilité de mouvements plus violents encore et atteignent à l'idée d'une sorte de musique qui les ferait mourir de plaisir [...] Ne croyez pas [...] que ces êtres si sensible à l'harmonie soient les meilleurs juges de l'expression." (Diderot, 1978, p. 582)

"In music, the pleasure of the sensation depends on a particular predisposition, not only of the ear but of the entire nervous system. If we call some heads finely tuned, there are also some bodies that I'd have no trouble calling harmonic; men in whom the fibres oscillate with such promptness and liveliness that, from the experience of violent movement that harmony brings about, they sense the possibility of even more violent movements, and arrive at the idea of a kind of music that would make them die from pleasure [...] do not believe [...] that these beings who are so attuned to harmony are the best judges of expression."[4]

Before this, Diderot has compared the three art forms and pointed out that music is different from poetry and pictorial art in that it does not exhibit an object and thus does not function as an imitative art. Instead, its sounds, timbres and harmonies play directly into the body's nervous system, to the great pleasure of the music lover. Diderot's theories about the three art forms all mark a break with classicist aesthetics, but music represents a particularly radical break in that it is thought to affect the subject on a pre-linguistic and pre-reflective physical level – beyond the control of will and consciousness. *Lui* has also exhibited music's physicality in an earlier pantomime, where he mimes a musician performing a piece of music:

---

4 I thank Christopher Prendergast for his translation of this passage.

"[...] il se démène de la tête, des pieds, des mains, des bras, du corps. Comme vous avez vu quelquefois au concert spiritual, Ferrari ou Chiabran, ou quelque autre virtuous, dans les memes convulsions [...]" (Diderot, 1989, p. 97)

"[...] head, feet, hands, arms, body, all play their part. In this very way you would have sometimes seen Ferrari or Chiabran or some other virtuoso in similar convulsions at the Concert of Sacred Music [...]" (Diderot, 1966, p. 53)

The musician, as in a pantomime, constitutes "a representation of pleasure;" he is shaken by spasms, his hands move in convulsive jerks up and down the neck of the violin, and his face assumes "an expression of ecstasy." No other art form demonstrates a similar connection between the body's automatism and spirituality. On this basis it could be said that music is an art form whose aesthetic expression – whether beautiful or not – emanates from an animal and mechanical subjectivity. Interpreted through the nephew's pantomime, music thus appears to be an art form that fits with an historical situation where civilisation has fallen back into a form of natural state and where *l'honnête homme* (and *le philosophe*) have been dislodged from the social scene by courtiers, financiers, great merchants, stockbrokers, and their gang of mediocre poets and journalists. In the context of the satire, the anti-philosophers' predatory automatism functions in a way – however paradoxical it may sound – as the moral or social argument for an aesthetics that is no longer bound to *decorum*, but instead lets the body loose in a mechanical, delightful development. The nephew's various music and opera pantomimes expose what art could be in a society that has thrown off the masks of self-control and good breeding, and left itself at the mercy of its latent animal primitivism. Diderot seems to say that this constitutes a problem for society, but an opportunity for art.

Diderot, however, did not create the opera-pantomime from his imagination alone. The pantomime contains several references to the Italian *opera buffa*, which Parisians had become acquainted with between 1752 and 1754, when the Italian composer and conductor Eustachio Bambini's troupe made a guest appearance on the stage of the *Académie royale de musique*. The comic operas came as a shock to the Parisian audiences. Historians actually speak of the Italians' guest appearance as an aesthetic earthquake in dominant French taste and listening culture. The dramaturgy was completely alien; the actors used movements, grimaces, and gestures the like of which had never been seen on the academy's "noble scene," where the actors' body language was supposed to respect the requirement of propriety ("bienséance"). The Italians' appearance *had* to spark a feud – which it also did. In autumn 1752 one of these "guerre pamphlétaire," which France was famous for at that time, broke out: *La Querelle des Bouffons*, where adherents of the Italian *opera buffa* faced adherents of the French opera, *tragédie lyrique* (Fabiano, 2005, pp. 11-12). The supporters of the Italian opera, who included all the Encyclopaedists, among others, found the Italians' physical dramaturgy liberatingly funny; opponents perceived the gestures and grimaces as inappropriate "singeries" – a scandalous degradation of the respectable Parisian opera stage. *L'opera buffa* clearly constituted a break with the doctrine of classicism, which had formed the framework of French theatre and opera since the 17th century.

Diderot's point via the nephew's pantomime could be seen as an attempt to lay bare, enlarge, and celebrate this break between *la bonne compagnie* and theatre, or opera. Simultaneously, Diderot suggests a new connection between the social world on the one hand, theatre, music, and poetic lyrics one the other. Through *Lui* and his pantomime, Diderot seems to be saying that *la bonne compagnie*, once the ideal or the norm of aesthetic imitation, has become merely an object of aesthetic depiction, or to be more precise of comic or satirical recreation. Judging from *Le neveu de Rameau*, this entails that theatre (and opera) will change radically, tragedy will be replaced by comedy and farce (like in the *opera buffa*), and heroism and *honnêtété* will have to make their way for low, simple, and primitive morals. Last, but not least, the body of the actor will be liberated from the rules of *bienséance* (decency) and become the instrument of expression – the mediator of the mechanical, animal movements, the desire, greed, and aggression that now govern society.

Lyrical Poetry: Power versus Desire

If *Le neveu de Rameau* has anything new to say about unfreedom in relation to common understandings of the concept, this stems from the interlinking of music and (moral) corruption, opera and the regression of civil society, as previously mentioned. The aesthetic potential of unfreedom is to be found in this interlinking, which we shall now examine by confronting the nephew's vision for a new form of lyrical poetry (poetry that is sung, like in the opera). What is important to understand in the nephew's poetics for the new lyrical poetry is that it tackles one of the points of contention in *La Querelle des Bouffons*, namely the extent to which song in opera is superior or subordinate to the poetical verse line. In French opera, song has to adapt to the verse line; in the Italian *opera buffa,* the opposite is the case. Not surprisingly, the nephew believes in the precedence of song. But, what is song, *Moi* asks. Song is an imitation of "the cry of animal instinct," and the nephew states that this cry must "dictate the line which suits us." An echo of the animal cry of passion can be heard in "a beggar asking for alms in the street," it can be heard in "a man in a towering rage," in a woman "mad with jealousy, a despairing lover, a flatterer – yes, a flatterer lowering his voice and dwelling on each syllable in honeyed tones" (Diderot, 1966, p. 107). Everyone has passions irrespective of rank and lineage, and the passions are apparent in the tone of voice, but at the same time the individual passions have their specific accent or tone. It is these accents that the uncle Jean-Philippe Rameau and the French opera, with its heroics and mythological universe, would seem to be deaf to:

"C'est au cri animal de la passion, à dicter la ligne qui nous convient [...] il faut que la phrase soit courte; que le sens en soit coupé, suspendu; que le musician puisse disposer du tout et de chacune de ses parties; en omettre un mot, ou le repeter; y en ajouter un qui lui manqué [...] Il faut que les passions soient fortes ; la tendresse du musician et du poète lyrique doit être extreme [...] Il faut les exclamations, des interjections, des suspensions, des interruptions, des affirmations, des negations; nous appelons, nous invoquons, nous crions, nous gémissions, nous pleurons, nous rions franchement. Point d'esprit, point d'épigramme; point de jolie pensées. Cela est trop longue de la simple nature." (Diderot, 1989, pp. 169-170)

"It is the animal cry of passion that should dictate the melodic line [...] phrases must be short and the sense cut off, suspended, so that the musician can utilize the whole and each part, omitting one word or repeating it, adding a missing word [...] The passions must be strong and the sensibility of composer and poet must be very great [...] What we want is exclamations, interjections, suspensions, interruptions, affirmations, negations ; we call out, invoke, shout, groan, weep or have a good laugh. No witticisms, epigrams, one of your well-turned thoughts – all that is far too removed from nature." (Diderot, 1989, p. 106)

The struggle of primitive forces against the pressure of civilisation is recreated in this violent confrontation between the animal cry of passion and the syntax of the sentence. It is these forces that the nephew has felt smouldering within himself, which he has heard echoes of in the voices of ordinary people, and, last but not least, which he has seen fully developed at Bertin's gatherings. And it is these forces that will dictate the melodic line and verse line in the new opera. The result will entail the liberation of passion, voice, and breathing from the rules of language, and from the defining, civilising shaping of thought.

The historical inseparability of the rules of polite society and art forms the background of Diderot's invention of a literary figure who masters both the social game and music, whose depiction includes how changes in the social register more or less automatically trigger changes in the aesthetic register. The moment when fashionable society is corrupted by unfreedom, the moment when the world of society is no longer governed by good manners, self-control, politeness, propriety, and the like, is the moment when the rules that dictate art are also challenged. Diderot, it seems, exploits this situation in an almost diabolical manner, as though he celebrates the corruption of polite society as the emancipation of art. When propriety, politeness, and rectitude do not exist, art does not have to conform to the respectful imitation of polite society's social and cultural ideals. Then it is freed to perform functions other than reflecting and supporting the dominant elite and the existing order. Then it can show the world in many perspectives. Then it can speak the language not only of the lord, but also of the slave.

AN AESTHETIC COUNTER-ATTACK

Let us finally return to Goethe's understanding of *Le neveu de Rameau* as a secret revenge on the anti-philosophers. It seems obvious by now that Goethe was right. In *Le neveu de Rameau,* Diderot organises a literary counter-attack against the anti-philosophers' smear campaigns by portraying them as unfree predators, and his need for retaliation seems all the more understandable given that the attacks on the *Encyclopdédie* were not without consequences for Diderot and his team of writers. The problem for the Encyclopaedists' opponents was that the censors, time and again, found *no* grounds to prohibit the articles in the *Encyclopédie,* and therefore had to resort to other, non-formalised, means of stopping its publication. As mentioned before, they came close to succeeding. In February 1752, the king issued a decree prohibiting the publication of the *Encyclopédie* (it was later revoked), and, in January 1759, the *procureur général* of the Parliament of Paris alleged that the *Encyclopédie* was part of a large-scale conspiracy aimed at undermining both church and state. In March 1759, the *Conseil d'Etat* took away the *Encyclopédie's* licence to print, and the work was placed on the *Index* together with d'Helvetius's *De l'Esprit* (1758), a hyper-materialistic work with far-reaching moral and political implications. In September 1759, Pope Clement XII faced all who possessed copies of the *Encyclopédie* with the choice of discarding the book or being excommunicated from the Catholic Church. As Robert Darnton remarks: "it was hardly possible for a book to be condemned more completely" (Darnton, 1979, p. 12). One could say that Diderot and the other Encyclopaedists composed the *Encyclopédie* within an atmosphere of unfreedom in almost every sense of the word.

The participation of the Encyclopaedists in *La Querelle des Bouffons* (1752-1754), wherein they unanimously sided with the Italian opera, should be viewed in the light of this unfreedom. The opera feud began immediately after the king prohibited the *Encyclopédie* in February 1752, cf. above, and therefore many think that the Encyclopaedists' participation in the feud was an attempt to counter royal prohibition. Their political indignation at *l'ancien regime*'s restrictions on freedom of thought and the press is thus transposed to an aesthetic critique of the French opera which – as formulated by Rousseau – was defended by "the great, the wealthy and the ladies" (Pekacz, 1999, p. 287).

Nor is Diderot's satire only directed at the factions that combated the *Encyclopédie* on ideological and personal grounds. Through references to the *Querelle des Bouffons*, the satire attacks the political order in *l'ancien regime*. The buffoon feud, as it appears, is not merely over the social side of taste, but also over its national political implications. As Elizabeth Cook writes, since the opera's introduction to France it had functioned as "an overt celebration of absolutism; enthusiasm for a rival, foreign style [as Italian opera] assumed a deeper symbolism [...] threatening the fabric of Ancien Régime at the mid-point of the century" (in Fabiano 2005, p. 147). The Italians' entry into the French cultural institution, known as an incarnation of royal authority and absolutist cultural policy, thus presented an obvious occasion to air criticism of *l'ancien regime* and the influence of certain powerful groups on the cultural institutions of the regime.

As editor, Diderot could not afford to counter the assaults that the antiphilosophers launched on the *Encyclopédie*, his team of writers, and his person. His enemies were too powerful. To a certain point this inequality in power appears analogous to the "bloody awful economy" to which the Nephew refers at the end of the dialogue when he complains that

"[q]ue diable d'économie, des hommes qui regorgent de tout, tandis que d'autres qui ont un estomac importune comme eux, une faim renaissante comme eux, et pas de quoi mettre sous la dent. *Le pis, c'est la posture contrainte où nous tient le besoin.*" (Diderot, 1989, p. 189)

"some men bursting with everything, while others, with stomachs just as clamorous and a hunger just as unremitting, have nothing to get their teeth into. *The worst thing is the subservient posture in which you are kept by need.*" (Diderot, 1966, p. 120)

Diderot was also in a somewhat subservient position, since the cost of expressing his honest opinion on the anti-philosophers, the king, court, and parliament in all likelihood would have been persecution or imprisonment. With Pettit, we could say that he was forced constantly to take the opinions, moves, and intrigues of others into consideration; hence he lived in a situation of domination. However, in this subservient position and all secrecy, he produced a literary work considered to be among the most audacious, vigorous, and progressive texts of French 18th century literature.

REFERENCES

Berlin, I. (1969). *Four Essays on Liberty*. Oxford: Oxford University Press.
Darnton, R. (1979). *The Business of Enlightenment. A Publishing History of the Encyclopédia, 1775-1800*. Cambridge, MA: Belknap Press of Harvard University Press.
Diderot, D. (1966). *Rameau's Nephew/D'Alembert's Dream*, London, Penguin Classics 1966.
Diderot, D. (1988). *Oeuvres esthétiques*. Paris : Editions Classiques Garnier.
Diderot, D. (1978). *Oeuvres completes*, vol. IV. Paris : Édition H. Dieckmann-J. Varloot, Hermann. Éditeurs des sciences et des arts.
Diderot, D. (1989). *Oeuvres completes*, vol. 12. Paris : Édition H. Dieckmann-J. Varloot, Herman. Éditeurs des sciences et des arts.
Fabiano, A. [Ed.] (2005). *La Querelle des Bouffons dans la vie culturelle française du XVIII siècle*, Textes réunis et présentés par A. Fabiano. Paris, CNRS Edition.
Freud, H.H. (1967). Palissot and Les Philosophes. *Diderot Studies*, 9.
Israel, J. (2009). "French Royal Censorship and the Battle to Supress the *Encyclopédie* of Diderot and D'Alembert, 1751-1759". In M. Lærke (Ed.), *The Use of Censorship in the Enlightenment*. Leiden and Boston: Brill.
Melançon, B. (2000). La ménagerie Bertin était-elle un salon littéraire? Antiphilosophe et sociabilité au Siècle des Lumières. In P. Popovic and E. Vigneault (Eds.), *Les dérèglements de l'art. Formes et procédures de l'illigitimité culturelle en France (1715-1914)*, Montréal: Les Presses de L'Université de Montréal.
Pekacz, J.T. (1999). The Salonnières and the Philosophes in Old Regime France. The Authority of Aesthetic Judgement. *Journal of the History of Ideas*, vol. 60, No 2, 277-297.

Zalloua, Z. (2003). The Mind and Body Problem in Diderot's *Le Neveu de Rameau*. *Symposium: A Quarterly Journal in Modern Literatures*, 56, no 4, Winter, 196-209.

Baudelaire and the Government of the Imagination

CHRISTOPHER PRENDERGAST

Let me begin by stating in summary mode the various frames of reference that inform the following remarks: first, an author (Baudelaire and his writings on criticism and aesthetics); second, a historical context (the insurrections of 1848, the failure of the short-lived Second Republic and the *coup d'état* of Louis-Napoleon); thirdly, a topic (theories of the Imagination); and finally, two framing questions, which stand at the centre of an extraordinarily rich intellectual history running from the early eighteenth century through to the later nineteenth century.

Simply put, the two questions are as follows: first, what did it mean or come to mean to be a free subject of aesthetic experience? I phrase the question in this way to make as clear as I can that by "subject" of aesthetic experience I do not primarily mean the artist, the figure of the sovereign creator that was so central an idea and a value in romantic aesthetics, theoretically formalized in German aesthetic thought but then travelling in various guises across much of the European romantic and post-romantic landscape. This emphasis on the sovereign artist will in fact return in the later section of my remarks, with a lethal twist in the tale that takes us to freedom's opposite, the condition of unfreedom. However, that is an endpoint. In the context of my initial framing question, by "subject" I understand not the sender but the receiver, that is, not the artist, but the spectator (or reader, or listener, etc; though here I will refer principally to the category of the spectator, mainly because, while Baudelaire's thinking on this front evolves through his writings on nearly all the arts, including poetry and music, the primary or more extended source is his essays on the visual arts, crucially modern painting). The question then, slightly reformulated, is this: how was the work of art conceived as a space for the exercise of imaginative freedom by the spectator? This was not an entirely new question in Baudelaire's time. It has an eighteenth-century lineage and, in the context of French aesthetic thinking, is particularly associated with Diderot (the Diderot of the *Salons*) and Diderot's promotion of what Michael Fried described as a new kind of spectatorial subjectivity governed by what Fried called "a state of absorption" and the nineteenth century was to call, over and over again, the condition of "rêverie" (Fried, 1980). What happens to that category in Baudelaire's thinking is very much at the heart of what I am here interested in.

The second question concerns the ways in which answers to the first (what it meant to be an aesthetically free subject) mapped onto what it meant to be a *politically* free subject, understood broadly in terms of the different and often competing currents of thought linking liberty and democracy. Concepts of freedom and imagination were natural bedfellows in European aesthetics from the early eighteenth century through to Kant, Romanticism and beyond. Freedom and imagination, the exercise of the one and the enjoyment of the other, typically came together in the notion of "imaginative free play". What the latter consisted in was variously understood, involving all manner of themes deriving largely from Kant's philosophy, to do with the subject's transcendence of the realms of coercion, necessity and instrumentality. But the notion was often inflected by, or at least related to, political conceptions of liberty, sometimes explicitly (as, for example, in the thought of Barry and Schiller), sometimes implicitly, such that there was often considerable overlap between my two questions – what it meant to be a free subject of aesthetic experience and what it meant to be free politicaly.

However, at this point a methodological caveat, elementary, even naïve, but which in connection with an inquiry of this type needs to be entered: it cannot be a matter of implying any straightforward equivalence of aesthetic values and political values, whereby one can automatically read off or derive one from the other. When, to take an example from Baudelaire's writings, in the poem "L'Idéal", the poet-narrator speaks of his search for "une fleur qui ressemble à mon rouge idéal" (Baudelaire, 1961, p. 21)[1], the adjectival noun 'red" of the sought-for poetic flower (the poem is of course from *Les Fleurs du Mal*) cannot simply be taken to signify the red flags or the Phrygian hats of the revolutionary barricades in 1848. Indeed the entire history of aesthetics as a theoretical practice and then later a constituted discipline is not only directly bound up with, but also a distinctive manifestation of, a broader history of cultural specialization in which the aesthetic was explicitly assigned a form of "autonomy" designed to separate it off from other areas of thought and practice. This, however, should

---

1 All references to Baudelaire's writings are to the 1961 Pléiade edition, except where otherwise indicated. Quotations of Baudelaire in English are from P.E. Charvet's translation (Baudelaire, 1972).

not discourage us, but merely alert us to a fairly obvious potential trap. If, bearing the caveat in mind, we were to map theories of the imagination in the eighteenth and nineteenth centuries, and in particular notions of imaginative freedom, onto a set of terms from the lexicon of politics, there are essentially two models of liberty directly pertinent to the inquiry – the republican and the liberal conceptions (to which in the later nineteenth century will be added the utopian, the communitarian and the mass-democratic).

Republican conceptions of liberty (so-called "positive liberty")[2] impacted on aesthetics in different places at different times, but was perhaps most consistently a preoccupation of eighteenth-century English aesthetic thought (as described for instance by John Barrell in connection with eighteenth-century painting-theory, above all in the *Discourses* of Joshua Reynolds). In this context "freedom" was tied to ideas and ideals of citizenship, the active, equal and freely assenting participation of the person in the self-governing republic. According to this model, art – both its production by the artist and its reception by the viewer – has a properly public function; and in subordinating private interests to public ones, it is a conception that encourages a focus on the general and the universal, what can be seen, held, and enjoyed in common. The free exercise of the Imagination in the virtuous republic of taste comes down to everyone concerned (let us say, before a painting in an exhibition) seeing and experiencing the same, as the aesthetic equivalent of the common good in the political sphere. One indication of what such an aesthetic can look like is Reynolds' prohibition on ambiguity as encouraging "division" (its effect, in Reynolds's words, is "to divide the attention", both of the individual viewer and across the collection of viewers that make up a "public"). Ambiguous pictures are to be deplored because they encourage multiple seeing, different points of view, and thus the fragmentation of a community of shared taste into a collection of purely private interests and pleasures.[3]

---

2 The expression is famously Isaiah Berlin's. In terms of contemporary re-thinking of republicanism, "positive liberty" is generally associated with Pocock's version of republican freedom, a version rooted in the "Aristotelian" conception (as distinct from Skinner's 'neo-Roman' version, which Skinner describes as "third concept of liberty" situated in a space beyond or to the side of the narrow "negative/positive" polarity).

3 "A painting that is ambiguous on the level of form will have one of two effects, either of which will disable it from performing the function of creating a public. Either it will divide the attention of the individual spectator, in such a way as to leave him at a loss as to how to respond to it – for he will not know where to look first, or in what proportion to bestow his attention on the various images it contains; or else it will

On the other hand, what the eighteenth-century republican or civic-humanist way of thinking deplored or feared as the enemy of true freedom (ambiguity and multiplicity), in the early nineteenth century acquired a different value under the influence of the other dominant model, historically and ideologically the great rival of the classical-republican conception, the one based on the liberal-individualist idea, which Benjamin Constant placed at the very heart of what he called "modern" liberty. This was the version favoured by romantic liberalism (in the writings of, for example, Hazlitt and Stendhal), according to which free imaginative play is basically the freedom of *individuals*, often based on a modern notion of "rights" accorded to subjects in their particularity and their differences.

One can see from even this schematic snapshot the outlines of a vast intellectual-historical narrative, with many different chapters. The particular chapter that interests me is one that comes later, the one centred on the pivotal example of Baudelaire. Baudelaire is pivotal for several reasons. The first is that aspects of the history I have just summarized flowed, if sporadically, quirkily and non-systematically, into his thinking about the fate of modern art in modern commercial society. However, the second reason – and what for the purposes of this collection I shall foreground here – concerns a set of developments that involve a radical break with the tradition linking freedom and imagination: developments which brought Baudelaire in his critical and theoretical writings to close down the spaces for the autonomous exercise of the imaginative faculty, in a manner which replaced an imputed condition of freedom with an imposed condition of *unfreedom*; where the "subject" becomes a subject in the sense familiar to political thought (namely as understood in relation to forms and agencies of subjection).

ART AND IMAGINATIVE FREEDOM

This however was an outcome, not a point of departure. Getting from one to the other means tracing a complex, uneven, and often darkly signposted journey. Baudelaire's "politics", and a fortiori their relation with both his aesthetic ideas and his poetic practice, present his biographers and critics with many problems, crucially three. The most basic concern factual gaps in the historical record, especially at the critical time of the 1848 insurrections (where he was when, with whom he was consorting, what he was thinking, whether or not contributions to ephemeral radical newspapers can be reliably attributed to him). A second diffi-

---

divide one spectator from another, but permitting each to interpret it as he wishes" (Barrell, 1986, p. 101).

culty turns not just on the contradictory nature of the record of Baudelaire's thoughts, opinions and allegiances, but on their *wilfully* contradictory nature. Let us not forget Baudelaire's unusual way with that centerpiece of modern democracy, the discourse of "rights", his own distinctive contribution to it being that there are only two inalienable rights: the right to commit suicide and the right to contradict oneself (*Etudes sur Poe*, Baudelaire 1976, vol. 2, p. 306). The third general difficulty revolves around a number of irresolvable interpretive enigmas. In his writings Baudelaire is notoriously a man of masks. What is seriously (i.e. directly) meant and what is tongue-in-cheek provocation cannot always be distinguished. When, for example, Baudelaire speaks in praise of Robespierre, it is not at all obvious what is to be taken at face value and what is poker-faced irony.[4] Similarly, when in later years he both recalls and reaffirms his earlier revolutionary allegiances as if he were bizarrely drawing on the works of the reactionary theocrat, Joseph de Maistre, there is an opaqueness that borders on the impenetrable:

"Mais moi je ne suis pas dupe, je n'ai jamais été dupe! Je dis *Vive la Révolution!* Comme je dirais: *Vive la Destruction! Vive l'Expiation! Vive le Châtiment! Vive la Mort!* Non seulement je serais heureux d'être victime, mais je ne haïrais pas d'être bourreau, – pour sentir la Révolution des deux manières!
Nous avons tous l'esprit républicain dans les veines, comme la vérole dans les os, nous sommes démocratisés et syphilisés [...]" ("Pauvre Belgique", Baudelaire, 1961, p. 1456)[5]

"But me, I'm no dupe, I never was a dupe! I say *Long live the Revolution!* As I would say *Long live Destruction!, Long live Expiation!, Long live Punishment!, Long live Death!* I should be glad to be the victim, but equally I should not dislike the role of executioner – so as to experience Revolution in both its guises!
Every one of us has the spirit of republicanism in his veins, like the pox in our bones; we are all democratized and syphilitic [...]"

Yet, while these are unsettling and unplaceable Baudelairian utterances, there are nevertheless certain broad lines of inquiry that enable us to situate Baudelaire – or more precisely the significance of Baudelaire – in relation to the two framing

---

4 For an interesting account of Baudelaire on Robespierre, cf. Pachet (1976), pp. 41-47.
5 T.J. Clark summarises it thus: "The evidence does not add up, nor does it have to. The Baudelaire it suggests is shadowy, confused, open: fluid in his allegiances, hysterical in his enthusiasms, claiming the right to contradict himself" (Clark, 1982, pp. 141-142).

questions with which I began. Baudelaire's early aesthetic formation in 1840s was strongly influenced by the emancipatory and democratising projects that flowered intellectually from eighteenth-century republicanism to nineteenth-century liberal romanticism. His commitment to the idea of an art that would set the imagination free was reflected in his early and abiding promotion of the artistic Sketch and the category of the Unfinished. In his first *Salon* (1845) and the subsequent one (the Salon of 1846, generally held to be Baudelaire's most important theoretical intervention in the field of aesthetics), he described the painting of Corot and above all Delacroix (for Baudelaire *the* exemplary modern painter) as interestingly and productively "unfinished", in the sense of assembling colour masses which, when viewed from a certain distance, appeared somewhat indistinct and blurred: "un contour un peu indécis, des lignes légères et flottantes, et l'audace de la touche" ("shapes that are not too clearly defined, lines that are light and hesitant, and bold touches of colour," *Salon de 1846*, Baudelaire, 1961, p. 892). Unlike the prescriptive, even coercive structures of the neoclassical canon, this was a style of painting that opened the mind and the imagination of the viewer to what Baudelaire, along with many of his contemporaries, called "rêverie" and "suggestion", that is to say, an art which provokes the imagination into its own interpretive work. Delacroix, wrote Baudelaire, is "le plus suggestif des peintres" who "ouvre [...] de profondes avenues à l'imagination la plus voyageuse" ("the most suggestive of all painters who [...] creates deep avenues for the most adventurous imagination to wander down," ibid., p. 889).

The avenues down which the adventurous imagination, whether of poet or painter, would wander belong in various creative topographies. But one of the most important was the boundary-crossing landscape forged from the legacy of eighteenth-century "associationism", and whose nineteenth-century formulations derived principally from the doctrine of *correspondances* and the new interest in synaesthesia. Despite the familiarity of its main outlines, this is in fact a complex idea in Baudelaire's thinking, as it is in the nineteenth century generally. For present purposes, I emphasize the more radical aspect of Baudelaire's use of the idea. The argument from synaesthesia entails a stress on the modern work of art as inherently *mobile*. For Baudelaire the modern is or should be based on the principle of movement, and as such is held to transgress the terms and relations of an inherited neoclassical conception of art, the conception we can perhaps schematically represent as a relation of domination and subordination holding between two categories: the fixed and the free. In its commitment to the mobile, the modern work of art is opposed to fixity. Modern art, according to Baudelaire, permits a "free" circulation of categories, sensations, energies, subjectivities.

Both within the individual art work and between different art works there is a mobile play of actions and impressions that breaks up fixed form, static line and arrested "identity" (in both the generic and the psychological senses of the term). In theory, modern art proclaims everything and everybody as "free", free to enter into "association" (and that term too, at the heart of the doctrine of *correspondances*, carries various senses, on a spectrum from the psychological to the political). In the process of mobile circulation released by the modern art work, nothing and nobody is assigned any "proper" place or identity within a pre-given system of fixed and hierarchical relations. Or to put this in Baudelaire's own characteristic vocabulary, modern art is fluid, sinuous and, perhaps above all, "tumultuous". "Tumulte" is a key term that recurs throughout Baudelaire's descriptions of modern art works, and notably the paintings of Delacroix and the music of Wagner. In one paragraph of the 1855 *Exposition Universelle* it appears three times in an account of Delacroix's work, while the essay on Wagner both begins with an account of how Wagner's music expresses "les tumultes de l'âme humaine" ("the turbulences of the human soul") and climaxes in a rapid accumulation of terms to do with the ideas of turbulence and excess ("Richard Wagner et *Tannhäuser* à Paris", Baudelaire, 1961, p.1210).

In reviewing the language of Baudelaire's accounts of the synaesthetic properties of modern art, and of modern painting in particular, we may find ourselves musing on two metaphors for colour, one in English and one in French: "riot of colours" and "orgie de couleurs". If by reverse catachresis we reactivate what lies buried in these otherwise dead metaphors (the French is effectively dead in part by having been largely replaced by its semantic neighbour, "débauche de couleurs"), we come up with some interesting considerations. Both denote a mode of excess, forms of dangerous behaviour. "Riot" recalls, precisely, riotous behaviour, either in the taverns or, in the strictly political reference, in the streets and on the barricades. "Orgie" denotes another form of riotous behaviour, in the bed and the brothel. To my knowledge, Baudelaire himself does not use the expression "orgie de couleurs" in his discussions of painting and colour, although the expression does enter pictorial language in the course of the nineteenth century and is to be found, for example, in Hugo. The word "orgie" by itself, however, does have an interesting career throughout virtually the whole corpus of Baudelaire's writings, as it does in the nineteenth century generally; the tracking of the term across nineteenth-century French writing is something of a fascinating lexical adventure (the high lexical scorers include Balzac, Michelet and Flaubert).

Here are some examples from Baudelaire: in the projected epigraph poem for *Les Fleurs du Mal* he refers to his own book of poems as "ce livre saturnien, orgiaque et mélancolique" ("this saturnine, orgiastic and melancholic book"); the great closing poem of the collection, "Le Voyage", refers – though here the perspective is a self-ironizing one – to the "Orgie de l'imagination"; "orgie" and "orgiaque" occur crucially in Baudelaire's account of Wagner's Venusberg music. More appositely, there are two instances to which we might here pay special attention. The first is from the prose poem "le Fou et la Vénus":

"quelle admirable journée [...] l'extase universelle des choses ne s'exprime par aucun bruit [...] c'est ici une orgie silencieuse. On dirait qu'une lumière toujours croissante fait de plus en plus étinceler les objets; que les fleurs excitées brûlent du désir de rivaliser avec l'azur du ciel par l'énergie de leurs couleurs [...]" (*Le spleen de Paris*, Baudelaire, 1961, pp. 236-237)

"What an admirable day [...] the universal ecstasy of things expresses itself noiselessly [...] this is a silent orgy. It is as if a constantly expanding light makes objects glitter more and more; as if the aroused flowers burn with the desire to rival the blue of the sky through the energy of their own colours [...]"

It will be noted how "orgies" generates and links a series of associations between sexuality, light and colour, a chain that is reproduced in the second example with a further extension into a fourth term, that of political rebellion. The example is from the famous poem of intoxicated rebellious fantasy, "le Vin des chiffonniers". Recall the scene of this poem: the ragpicker lurches drunkenly down the Parisian streets, surrounded by the spies ("mouchards") of the Second Empire regime, recalling the lost glories of the Napoleonic battlefields, dreaming of political revenge for betrayed promises (probably of 1848). The fantasy climaxes by bringing the political into contact with terms drawn respectively from the vocabularies of colour and sexuality: "orgie lumineuse" (*Les Fleurs du Mal*, Baudelaire, 1961, p. 101).

This metaphorical crossing of the themes of colour, politics and sexuality may well remind us of many things, specifically of that particular emphasis in traditional aesthetic systems (which, in the conservative imagination, last well into the nineteenth century) whereby two of the key terms of Baudelaire's modernist aesthetics – colour and metaphor – are commonly associated with the idea of an unregulated sexuality, a form of aesthetic "licence" held to be cognate with "licentiousness". More precisely, it is the association with the idea (or, in self-defeating paradox, the metaphor) of the Fallen Woman, the prostitute and the whore. Thus painted colours (especially in oil), by virtue of their assumed closeness to the turbulence of sensual life, are frequently compared to the make-up of the Harlot, the face and body daubed in alluring but deceptive cosmetics, suggestive of irresponsible and promiscuous sexual activity. Similarly, metaphor and more generally figurative discourse, as Todorov notes in *Théories du symbole* (1977), are from classical antiquity onwards often assimilated to the figure of the painted prostitute, producing relations or "couplings" transgressive of the stern proprieties of rational discourse and therefore appropriately an object of censure and control.

THE ARTIST AS DESPOT

Thus to praise colour and, moreover, to praise it in terms that are systematically metaphorical is to enter dangerous territory; it is to speak of and release energies (another key Baudelairian term) that are disruptive of traditional taxonomies and orderings of reality. The mobilities of the modern art work are seen by Baudelaire – to put the point in terms we are more likely to use – as radically decentering, tearing the subject out of all fixed "identity" and relation to the world, as necessarily involving excess, transgression of given proprieties and a certain violence done to fixed and fixing representations. Yet even as he championed this view of the nature and function of modern art, he had reservations. The wandering imagination, served by an art setting the imagination free from a normative body of rules to construct its own landscape of the mind, could all too easily wander dangerously far from appropriate controls. In the 1846 *Salon* there is a section on sculpture with the wonderfully nonchalant title "Pourquoi la sculpture est ennuyeuse", which recalls Reynolds disapproval of ambiguity. As a three-dimensional object in space, sculpture licences the body of the viewer to move around, to look at it from different points of view, thus permitting a form of free imaginative play seen as wanton and random free association, crucially of a spectator breaking free of the point of view selected by the artist:

"La sculpture a plusieurs inconvénients qui sont la conséquence nécessaire de ses moyens. Brutale et positive comme la nature, elle est en même temps vague et insaisissable, parce qu'elle montre trop de faces à la fois. C'est en vain que le sculpteur s'efforce de se mettre à un point de vue unique; le spectateur qui tourne autour de la figure, peut choisir cent points de vue différents, excepté le bon [...]" (*Salon de 1846,* Baudelaire 1961, pp. 943-4)

"Sculpture possesses various disadvantages that are the consequence of its medium. Brutally material like nature, sculpture is at the same time vague and elusive, because it displays too many aspects at one and the same time. It is in vain that the sculptor tries to position himself from a single point of view; the spectator who moves around the figure, can choose a hundred different points of view other than the right one [...]."

The viewing scene described here does not display the autonomy of a person participating in a rational community of equals, but an anarchy of individual taste and appetite, an instance of what towards the end of the *Salon* Baudelaire denounces as "le chaos d'une liberté épuisante et stérile," ("the chaos of an exhausting and sterile freedom,") and the "liberté anarchique qui glorifie l'individu," ("anarchic liberty that glorifies the individual," ibid., p. 948), and which was to be countered by the ideal sketched in the penultimate section of the 1846 Salon, "De l'école et des ouvriers", which revives the older model of the Master's studio and adapts it to the sponsoring of a new collective-corporatist spirit. It would, however, be a mistake to interpret this denunciation of rampant individualism as a resurrection of eighteenth-century republicanism or civic humanist thinking. Nor is it a self-affiliating with the more recent strains of nineteenth-century utopian and proto-socialist thought, both at a very general level sharing a stress on the priority of common values and shared tastes over purely individual and private ones. There were of course brief, fragmentary glimpses of these ideas and values in Baudelaire's reflections on painting and literature before and during 1848. Yet, while definitely important, they are very difficult to map as terms of a coherent outlook, and often – as in this last section of the 1846 *Salon* – they appear to anticipate what after 1848 were to become essentially terms of contempt. The denunciation of the liberal-individualist view of human liberty and what it implied for the forms in which art would be produced and consumed, became increasingly, and often hysterically, anchored in another way of thinking and feeling, authoritarian and – to use a term that will come to mean a very great deal to Baudelaire – "despotic".

In 1859, Baudelaire published the last of his Salons. In it are two chapters or sections on the nature and functioning of the Imagination ("La Reine des facultés" and "Le Gouvernement de l'imagination"). In the second of the two section headings, the preposition "of" is at once a subjective and an objective genitive; both active and passive, nominative and accusative. Government of the imagination is to be understood in the accusative sense of what governs it, the sense of the law-bound processes and disciplinary regimes to which the imagination, in order to function at all, must be subordinated. Baudelaire works hard to specify what he thinks these are, largely as a rule-governed form of mental discipline that distinguishes "imagination" from its weaker brother, mere "fancy", subject only to the wayward free associations of the undisciplined mind (in many respects this is a continuation of the line of thought that goes back to Coleridge's

Biographia Literaria; Baudelaire refers to Catherine Crowe, a disciple of Coleridge).[6] But one is also to read the preposition as carrying the more active sense of government *by*, the imagination as governing rather than as governed. Imagination "governs" by virtue of being primordial and sovereign, originator and organiser of the synaesthetic and metaphoric unity of experience:

"C'est l'imagination qui a enseigné à l'homme le sens moral de la couleur, du contour, du son et du parfum. Elle a créé, au commencement du monde, l'analogie et la métaphore. Elle décompose toute la création, et, avec les matériaux amassés et disposés suivant des règles dont on ne peut trouver l'origine que dans le plus profond de l'âme, elle crée un monde nouveau, elle produit la sensation du neuf. Comme elle a créé le monde (on peut bien dire cela, je crois, même dans un sens religieux), il est juste qu'elle gouverne [...]." (ibid., pp. 1037-38).

"It is the imagination that has taught man the moral significance of colour, contour, sound and scent. At the beginning of the world, it created analogy and metaphor. It decomposes all creation, and with the riches accumulated and arranged according to rules whose origin can be found only in the depths of the soul, it creates the sensation of the new. Since it created the world (one can, I think, maintain that even in a religious sense), it is right that it should govern [...]."

This is the metaphysical warrant ("même dans un sens religieux") given to the regal place of the imagination in the hierarchy of the faculties ("the queen of the faculties"), at the apex of the division of mental labour, orchestrating the different tasks of the mind and their collaborative contribution to the whole: "Sans elle, toutes les facultés, si solides et si aiguisées qu'elles soient, sont comme si elles n'étaient pas [...] Aucune ne peut se passer d'elle, et elle peut suppléer quelques-unes," ("Without her all the faculties, however firm and sharpened they might be, are as though they did not exist [...] None of them can do without her, but she can take the place of some of them," ibid., p. 1038).

Here then are two models or analogies for the work of the Imagination: a monarch and a government. These are terms that clearly resonate with political connotation. Baudelaire's text does not itself assign explicitly political meanings to the terms. Their universe of reference is cognitive, psychological and aesthetic; and in order to be convincing, any attempt to carry these references over into the sphere of political discourse would obviously require far more than a simple analogy. On the other hand, the analogical web woven by Baudelaire's

---

6   *Salon de 1859*, pp. 1040-41. On Crowe and Coleridge, see Clapton (1930).

text is very dense and massively overdetermined: in the two extracts from the 1859 Salon, the personified imagination attracts, along with queen and government, the images of a warrior, an army commander, a cardinal (with crimson robes), and a deity (with the power and authority conferred by having a divine origin). Above all perhaps, it attracts a term that recurs across the whole corpus of Baudelaire's later writings: "despot". Imagination, Baudelaire writes in *L'Oeuvre et la vie d'Eugène Delacroix* (Baudelaire, 1961, p. 1119), is "la grande faculté despotique" ("the great despotic faculty"). And it is despotic not only in ruling the potentially unruly life of the mind; but also in ruling the whole human and social universe of the experience of art.

Baudelaire's late theory of the imagination is expressly designed to ensure a form of "government" that will dominate a community of readers, spectators and listeners. The imagination as despot is crucially, and only, the imagination of the sovereign Artist, conceived as a Master-figure who guides, controls, and dictates. Under this regime the Spectator is disenfranchised, robbed of all rights to the exercise of imaginative autonomy. The spectator is positioned as entirely subordinate to the will of the master, the passive recipient of a transmission from the Artist, the transmission of what Baudelaire calls the artist's "intention"; the spectator is no longer imaginatively free (to dream, to interpret, to construct), but is the prisoner of the intentional disposition of another. Indeed it is not only that the Spectator's autonomy evaporates under this regime, but even the reality of the created art work itself; as handmaiden to the artist's intention, it becomes a mere vehicle of transmission, the dematerialized medium for the despotic projection of one state of mind onto another. The envisaged communicative scenario is stated thus: the Master artist is the one who says: "Je veux illuminer les choses avec mon esprit et en projeter les reflets sur les autres esprits," ("I want to illuminate things with my mind and cast its reflection on other minds," ibid., p. 1044). In short, what had originally been conceived as an art of "suggestion" ("an art that would free the imagination") is replaced by an art of suggestibility, an art of manipulation.

This was an extraordinary place for aesthetic theory to end up in, with a hundred-year history of attempted democratic emancipation of imaginative life reaching a dead-end, a point of exhaustion. I have not the slightest doubt that this was in part Baudelaire's reaction (and I mean "reaction" in the sense of reactionary) to the failure of 1848, in which the discourses of republic, democracy and liberty were stress-tested to breaking point, progressively hollowed out, and decisively routed by the counter-revolutionary *coup d'état* and the Napoleonic dictatorship of the Second Empire. It was an experience that in many ways broke Baudelaire. One consequence was a turning against the whole post-

Enlightenment configuration of aesthetics and politics, whether liberal, republican or utopian, in favour of a new aesthetic, based on fear of freedom and hatred of democracy, crucially a theory of the imagination which has no place for the active exercise of freedom by the viewer. Baudelaire, who himself sketched a version of artistic modernity, is often seen as one of the fathers of artistic modernism. That is correct, and it is also true that what he fathered *for* modernism was varied, complex and contradictory. But one of the things he bequeathed was a contribution to the framework for the emergence of an anti-democratic modernism of the autocratic Right, the tradition of right-wing cultural critique that starts with Joseph de Maistre and runs through Dostoievsky, Nietzsche, to Heidegger (for suggestions along these lines, see Burton, 1991, pp. 356-366).

As I have said, substantiating these claims demands a lot more work than an analogical move reading the political into Baudelaire's use of the term "government" in his theory of the imagination. Mere analogical reasoning is vulnerable to precisely the criticisms of Baudelaire and his predecessors of unregulated free association as a symptom of wanton individualism. Nevertheless, as a sort of coda (or prologue to further, more detailed investigations of text and context), let me conclude with an invitation to ruminate on the dense analogical dynamic surrounding a further account of the operations of the imagination, in a passage from another late text, *Le Peintre de la vie moderne*, the essay that more than any other is Baudelaire's programmatic statement of the aesthetic of "modernité". The passage concerns the "mutinous" claims of the "detail" on the modern art work, and in many ways its terms repeat (or evoke) the contrast drawn way back, in the 1845 *Salon*, between the "finished" and the "complete". The invitation is to consider whether or not, as he speaks unobjectionably of artistic matters, Baudelaire's terms are such that he is also speaking of political matters, a set of terms gathered in a small textual space, all with a lineage in the discourse of art criticism and art history (the subordination of "detail" to a master-design), but which here, in their concentrated in-gathering, are also expressive of fears and anxieties manifestly centred on the political: "riot", "mob", "equality", "justice", "usurpation", "anarchy", "hierarchy" and "subordination":

"Un artiste ayant le sentiment parfait de la forme, mais accoutumé à exercer surtout sa mémoire et son imagination, se trouve alors comme assailli par une émeute de détails, qui tous demandent justice avec la furie d'une foule amoureuse d'égalité absolue. Toute justice se trouve forcément violée; toute harmonie détruite, sacrifiée; mainte trivialité devient énorme; mainte petitesse, usurpatrice. Plus l'artiste se penche avec impartialité vers le détail, plus l'anarchie augmente. Qu'il soit myope or presbyte, toute hiérarchie et toute subordination disparaissent [...]" (*Le Peintre de la vie moderne,* Baudelaire, 1961, p. 1167)

"An artist with a perfect sense of form but particularly accustomed to the exercise of his memory and his imagination, then finds himself assailed, as it were, by a riot of details, all of them demanding justice, with the fury of a mob in love with absolute equality. Any form of justice is inevitably infringed; any harmony is destroyed, sacrificed; a multitude of trivialities are magnified; a multitude of little things become usurpers of attention. The more the artist pays impartial attention to detail, the greater does anarchy become. Whether he be short-sighted or long-sighted, all sense of hierarchy or subordination disappears [...]"

REFERENCES

Barrell, J. (1986). *The Political Theory of Painting from Reynolds to Hazlitt.* New Haven: Yale University Press.

Baudelaire, Ch. (1961). *Oeuvres complètes* (Pléiade). Paris: Editions Gallimard, 1961.

Baudelaire, Ch. (1972). *Writings on Art and Artists*, translated and introduced by P.E.Charvet. Cambridge: Cambridge University Press.

Baudelaire, Ch. (1976). *Oeuvres complètes*, 2 volumes (Pléiade), Paris: Editions Gallimard, 1976.

Burton, R.D.E. (1991). *Baudelaire and the Republic. Writing and Revolution*, Oxford.

Clapton, G.T. (1930). "Baudelaire and Catherine Crowe", *Modern Language Review*, Vol. 25, No. 3 (July), pp. 286-305.

Clark, T.J. (1982). *The Absolute Bourgeois: Artists and Politics in France 1848-1851*, London: Princeton University Press.

Compagnon, A. (2005). *Les antimodernes*, Paris: Gallimard.

Fried, M. (1980). *Absorption and Theatricality: Painting and Beholder in the Age of Diderot.* Berkeley: University of California Press.

Pachet, P. (1976). *Le premier venu: Essai sur la politique baudelairienne*, Paris: Denoel.

Todorov, T. (1977). *Théories du symbole*. Paris: Editions Seuil.

Unfreedom and the Crises of Witnessing
A Republican Perspective on the African American Slave Narratives

CHRISTIAN DAHL

At the end of his famous *Narrative of the Life of Frederick Douglass, An American Slave* (1845), Douglass writes about his first participation at an Abolitionist convention, in Nantucket four years after his flight from slavery in Maryland, where he was invited to tell about his former life in slavery:

"I felt strongly moved to speak, and was at the same time much urged to do so by Mr. William C. Coffin, a gentleman who had heard me speak in the colored people's meeting at New Bedford. It was a severe cross, and I took it up reluctantly. The truth was, I felt myself a slave, and the idea of speaking to white people weighed me down. I spoke but a few moments, when I felt a degree of freedom, and said what I desired with considerable ease." (Douglass, 1845, p. 117)

However brief and impersonal, the address marks a decisive moment in the symbolic transformation of the author from slave to citizen as he enters a political arena for the first time. This transformation is symbolic in at least two senses, one strong and one weak. In the strong sense, the Nantucket address marks the beginning of Douglass's life-long career as a political speaker and writer that made him famous as "The Representative Negro" in America and Britain. However, his transformation is also symbolic in the weak sense that it was neither effective nor binding from its beginning. In the 1840s the legal status of runaway slaves like Douglass was complicated and quite uncertain, and further aggravated by the Fugitive Slave Act of 1850 which stipulated that fugitive slaves residing in the North were still the property of their owners who could legally restore them to slavery. As a consequence, Douglass was forced to flee to Britain, having become vulnerable in his position as a person of public renown.

In yet another sense, we can also interpret the situation of his witnessing, the act through which his civic transformation is performed, as symbolic in so far as it represents a certain conflict within the act of witnessing. By referring to his act of witnessing as "a severe cross," Douglass symbolically addresses a constraint within the testimonial situation that has been the subject of much critical attention in studies of witness literature. It consists in the witness's expectation or experience of estrangement towards his audience due to the content of his testimony. While Douglass apparently did not feel any inhibitions when he told his story to other blacks in the Massachusetts city of New Bedford, who were familiar with the experience of slavery, he instantly feels reduced again to the status of a slave at the prospect of a white audience on Nantucket, until his words finally restore him to "a degree of freedom." This chapter will investigate the act of witnessing in the antebellum slave narratives as an attempt to transcend the condition of unfreedom, and reach for a freedom that can be asserted only gradually, in the process of speaking.

The Antebellum slave narratives constitute a body of literature centrally concerned with the problems of unfreedom. First of all, they portray the deprivations of American slaves from an autobiographical point of view. Second, the narratives were written and published with the explicit purpose of bringing an end to American slavery. Third, many of the slave narratives were authored by men and women who had escaped enslavement in the South but were not legally free and, therefore, remained dependent on the patronage and protection of white abolitionists for publication. It is thus a body of literature which struggles to affirm the witness as a free person who is fit to invest his or her testimony in political agency. These factors can, I think, explain some of the peculiarities of the slave narratives in comparison to other testimonial or autobiographical literature.

The slave narratives' struggle with unfreedom as a political and personal condition is also decisive for their literary status today, which is a mixed one. On the one hand, the slave narratives are now recognized as not only important documents in a decisive chapter in American history,[1] but also as the beginning of Afro-American literature. For these reasons, slave autobiography has become an integrated part of the American canon and is taught in most American schools.

---

1   In a wider perspective, abolitionist literature of the 18th and 19th century, to which the slave narratives contributes substantially, is responsible for changing the Western opinion on slavery, from accepting it as an unquestioned fact of life to considering it to be a violation of natural law (Davis, 2006, p. 331).

On the other hand, slave narratives have not benefitted much from the current critical prominence of witness literature, as they do not conform very well to the dominant critical demands of that genre. Contemporary discussions of witness literature have concentrated on testimony from the great political catastrophes of the 20th century, in particular the Holocaust, and reflect the so-called end of ideology following the end of the Cold War. "The witness produces no theory, teaches no doctrine, does not attempt to convince one of his own world view" writes Renaud Dulong in his book *Le témoin oculaire*, and his view is repeated by Horace Engdahl, former secretary of the Swedish Academy, who, in a speech on witness literature delivered at the centennial of the Noble Prize, declared that: "the persona of witness literature demands a certain loneliness or at least a withdrawal from ideological struggle" (Engdahl, 2002, p. 8).

These criteria for witness literature are certainly not met by antebellum slave narrators who are quite explicit in their ideological struggle against slavery. Though slave testimonies essentially rely upon authenticity and truthfulness, they only rarely appear as self-authenticating publications. Instead, their veracity usually depends on prefatory statements from prominent representatives of the abolitionist movement. It is therefore quite obvious that many of the narratives had been filtered and conformed to a political purpose and must be regarded with a certain suspicion. It is an indication of the difficulties faced by slave narratives in living up to contemporary criteria of witness literature that Toni Morrison, the most critically acclaimed contemporary writer directly engaged with slave narrative, in her famous novel *Beloved* draws on the experience of a historical refugee slave whose testimony was not and could never have been represented in the accepted slave narratives. The resistance to representation that follows traumatic experience is, in fact, a major theme in Morrison's novel and her ongoing engagement with the history of American slavery.

The historical veracity of the slave narratives is of course to a certain degree destabilized by their political purpose, and for this reason the quality of the narratives as source material for the study of American slavery has been the subject of much discussion, though most historians now accept the overall validity of the narratives. However, instead of reading the slave narratives for particular historical or literary reasons, as documentation of a decisive chapter in American history and African American literary history, they deserve to be read in a wider perspective as demonstrations of what it means to be unfree and what it takes to assert oneself as a free person, in other words: as a touchstone for the conceptualization of political freedom and its opposite. I will therefore suggest a reading of slave narratives which introduces republican political thinking on freedom as an alternative perspective for the "crises of witnessing" than those offered by psychoanalysis and trauma studies (for instance Felman & Laub, 1992; Caruth, 1996). In particular, I will draw on Phillip Pettit's republican theory of freedom, which stresses the importance of discursive control to the definition of personal freedom. As I will argue, the crises of witnessing in slave narratives are essentially connected to questions of discursive control, a fact which has hitherto been insufficiently conceptualized by scholarship.

SLAVERY, LITERACY, AND DISCURSIVE CONTROL

The philosophical concepts I will use in this essay are taken from Pettit's book *A Theory of Freedom. From the Psychology to the Politics of Agency* (2001), which adds a social dimension to his more famous republican definition of political freedom as non-domination.[2] As such, his analysis of freedom as discursive control aims to demonstrate that freedom requires more than the mere absence of interference that liberal political theorists assume. Central to Pettit's idea of freedom is the ability of agents to be held responsible for their actions. An action will be free in itself, Pettit argues, if it is underdetermined and thus materializes in a way that allows an agent to be held responsible. This agent can then be held responsible as a free self to the extent that his constitution allows him or her to choose in such a way so as to be fully responsible for the action (Pettit, 2001, p. 21). Yet the agent will only be a free person, Pettit holds, to the extent that their position in relation to other people allows them to choose in such a way that they are fully responsible for what they do. Personal freedom, in other words, requires not only that we are fit to be held responsible, but that others acknowledge us as fit to be held responsible for our actions.

This acknowledgment is naturally practiced through discourse, for agents can only be free persons insofar as they have the ability to discourse and access to discourse (Pettit, 2001, p. 70). In order to count as a free person, therefore, we must acquire discursive control through discourse-friendly relationships. Pettit's

---

2 Pettit's argument that republicanism involves a concept of negative liberty (i.e. non-domination), which is essentially different from that of liberalism, which conceives of freedom as non-interference (Pettit, 1993a, 1993b, 1997), was inspired by Skinner (cf. Skinner, 1984 and 1986) who has added substantially to the historical understanding of polemic differences between republicanism and liberalism (see also Skinner, 1998). Though the current essay is much indebted to Skinner's historical approach, I will focus here on Pettit whose conceptual framework of republican thought allows for a social perspective that is absent in the works of Skinner.

insistence on the importance of personal freedom through discourse control is leveled against philosophical theories that define freedom as only rational or volitional control. A stoic philosopher like Epictetus, allegedly a manumitted slave himself, would argue that freedom of the self depends only on the agent's rational and volitional capacity, not on his relationship to other people. A stoic slave can, in principle, conceive of himself as a free self by alienating himself from the world of men. Accordingly, a rational choice theorist will hold that a person who is threatened by a robber to choose between giving his money or his life is a free agent in so far as he is faced with a rational choice between his money and his life. While the slave and the victim of a robbery may be regarded as free agents in the sense that they can choose rationally, and the stoic slave may even count as a free self, insofar as he exerts rational control over his own volitions, neither can be acknowledged as free as long as they are deprived of discursive control.

Lack of discursive control is a problem familiar to all American slave narrators. Along with the oblique descriptions of physical coercion such as flogging and beating in the narratives, we find numerous accounts of ways that slaves were deprived of discursive control and thus denied even the most basic forms of individual personhood. A very important feature of American slavery, which almost all slave narrators discuss, concerns the systematic attempt to prevent slaves from learning to write. Since colonial times laws prohibited teaching slaves in Georgia and South Carolina how to write, and after the Nat Turner uprising in 1831 further legislation arose in many slave states to prevent slaves from gathering, travelling, and educating themselves (Genovese, 1974, p. 562). Without the refinement of such formal education, most slaves relied upon the assistance of white editors or ghost writers to produce their narratives. Though editors of antebellum narratives were eager to suppress any imaginative elements in the slave narratives in order to present slavery as authentically as possible, it is quite clear that the narratives' amanuenses and publishers were not always the transparent documentarians they claimed to be. Tendencies to grandiloquence and sentimental description of slaves' rustic plantation life are thus found in many narratives produced from oral statements, whereas they are absent from the autobiographies that were written by literate slave witnesses (Olney, 1984).

The prospect of achieving discursive control was considerably better for slave fugitives who managed to learn to write. Among these, none is more aware of the importance of literacy to emancipation than Douglass. In his narrative, he describes how his mistress taught him to read when he was a child, while his master taught him the consequences of literacy by reproving his wife for having spoiled a slave by teaching him the ABCs ("It would forever unfit him to be a slave", Douglass quotes his master). Concluding in a manner characteristic of his dialectical thinking, Douglass therefore acknowledges, "In learning to read, I owe almost as much to the bitter opposition of my master, as to the kindly aid of my mistress" (Douglass, 1845, p. 33). Though Douglass conceives of literacy as a requirement for freedom more clearly than any other slave narrator, his view is echoed by several less eloquent writers, many of whom acquired literacy only after their escape to the North, and his insight is endorsed by most contemporary scholars. "Sheer literacy was the very commodity that separated animal from human being, slave from citizen, object from subject", observes Henry Louis Gates, Jr. (Gates 1987, p. 24-25), while Olney stresses that literacy, identity and freedom are "altogether interdependent and indistinguishable as thematic strands" in the slave narratives (Olney, 1984, p. 53-54).[3]

In a comparative historical perspective it is interesting to see that literacy has been invested with far more importance for the struggle against American slavery than in previous historical periods. Contrary to Douglass's and his former owners' views on literate slaves, educated slaves were thus seen as valuable resources in the ancient Greek and Roman slave economies and not as threats to society. However, it was much easier to physically exclude slaves from the public sphere in an assembly democracy like classical Athens than it was to prevent slaves from political interference in a 19th century public sphere of printed discourse.[4]

We have seen that literacy and discourse-friendly relations to others were recognized as primary objectives for the enjoyment of personal freedom by the slave narrators. The dependence of many slave narrators on amanuenses and

---

3 The insistence on the importance of discursive independence, found both among slave narrators and contemporary historians, points to a distinction of discursive control, which Pettit ignores. According to his theory, the only real violation of discursive freedom consists in unfriendly coercion, and so Pettit grants that discursive control depends on discourse friendly relationship. In this respect the relationship between the illiterate slave narrators and their amanuenses can only be characterized as discourse friendly, in the sense that it depended on mutual agreement. However, we must acknowledge that illiterate narrators were not as free as the independent autobiographers to control their own discourse. Perhaps discursive independence is not a necessary requirement for discursive control, but it is certainly valuable to it.

4 It must be added that abolitionists and slave narrators have a tendency that has persisted to this day, to overemphasize the restrictions on slave education, which were not practiced in all slave states. Since freedom of speech was in no way as advanced as in the North, the association of literacy and emancipation was never universal in the South (cf. Webber, 1980).

editors was biased in many cases (Olney, 1984), but should on the other hand not be seen as something compromising their status as testimony. Though the tone and style of the narratives were often manipulated or distorted by editors and amanuenses (who rarely wanted the narratives to be as "unvarnished" as they pretended), historians of American slavery accept today that the factual statements of the narratives are relatively truthful, and it has been recognized that the editors often went at length to authenticate the veracity of the narratives (Blassingame, 1977).

RESPONSIBILITY AND AUTOBIOGRAPHY

As we have seen, Pettit argues that our capacity to exercise discourse control is dependent on discourse-friendly relations to other people. However, discourse control also depends on the capacity of the agent to count as a continuous person and self. Not only must I be able to relate to the actions I perform as owned by me, I must also be able to relate them to my previous doings. This is the reason why autobiography becomes such an important genre in the slaves' struggle for discursive freedom. Since Augustine's *Confessions*, autobiography has been concerned with the question how agents can change and still remain the same person. How can consciousness be continuous while the self changes over time?

Though Augustine does not talk of personal identity, it is from his *Confessions* that we have come to think of personal identity as something established by subjective acts of imaginative memory relating the past to the present. For this reason, memory often becomes the very subject of autobiography, as when writers conjure past moments in acts of present imagination. James Olney, a distinguished scholar of autobiography, has noted that such authorial acts by which the autobiographer relates past events to the moment of recollective writing ("I can see even now") are curiously absent from the slave narratives whose status as autobiography he denounces (with the sole exception of Douglass). Because the slave narratives were written to document slavery rather than the personal lives of narrators, the ex-slave was, in Olney's words "debarred from the use of a memory that would make anything of his narrative beyond or other than the purely, merely episodic, and he is denied access, by the very nature and intent of his venture, to the configurational dimension of narrative" (Olney, 1984, p. 150).

Though it would be tempting to explain the lack of imaginative subjectivity in the slave narratives by reference to the reification of slaves, Olney is right to argue that the imaginative deficit in the narratives derives from their deliberate rhetorical purpose, which was to document slavery rather than recollect and interpret individual lives. However, we must add that there is a real struggle for personal identity (between the slave's former and present self) in many of the narratives, which Olney ignores because he is too concerned with a traditional, hermeneutic understanding of selfhood and identity.

This struggle concerns the accountability of the narrators for past actions. For while slaves may alienate themselves from actions they were coerced to perform (since their lack of freedom is equivalent to a denial of responsibility), the slave narrators, in their insistence on their accountability as free persons, are often eager to confess transgressions they performed or suffered as slaves in order to avoid coercion. Harriet Jacobs (1861) felt so ashamed of the sexual harassments she had suffered as a slave that she could only publish her narrative pseudonymously, but her most daring confession is found in her account of how she debased herself morally by taking a black lover in order to cool her master's sexual desire for her. William Brown Wells (1847) confesses how he tricked a fellow slave into receiving flogging intended for him, but only much later regretted his deception. And Henry Bibb (1849) blames himself for having bred children to slavery and betrayed his family back in Kentucky by fleeing to the North. That discussions of the slaves' personal responsibility are required in the narratives is perhaps best attested by Douglass' discussion of why he did not regret having stolen another man's horse during his flight.

Clearly, these moral considerations are meant to prove the narrators' status as responsible agents over time in spite of conditions that forced them to transgress their own moral standards. If the slave narrator is not permitted to lapse into imaginative reconfigurations of his former life, he can instead affirm his status as a continuous person who is responsible for both his present and past actions. Again, Pettit's theory demonstrates why this element in the narratives must be seen as an attempt to assert freedom on the side of the slaves. In his attempt to avoid a definition of freedom that is rooted in the mind, Pettit discards the definition of personhood as continuity of consciousness in favour of a forensic definition of personhood. In order to count as a person, Pettit holds, an agent must be recognized as capable of being held responsible. For without the capability to square their feelings and doings over time agents cannot be fit for discursive control, Pettit argues. This definition of personal identity he derives from John Locke who in his *Essay Concerning Human Understanding* argues as follows:

"Where-ever a Man finds what he calls himself, there I think another may say is the same Person. It is a Forensick Term appropriating Actions and their Merit; and so belongs only to intelligent Agents capable of a Law, and Happiness and Misery. This personality extends it *self* beyond present Existence to what is past [...] it becomes concerned and accountable, owns and imputes to it *self* past Actions, just upon that same ground, and for the same reason, that it does the present." (Locke, 1975, p. 26)

I have quoted Locke at length because his definition of personhood gives a clear description of what is at stake in the slave narrators' attempt to assert themselves as persons who must "impute" their past actions in order to count as responsible and free persons in the present. The forensic definition of personhood is especially relevant for our present case because slaves were not accepted as full legal subjects. Colonial slave laws defined slaves as the chattel of their owners, thus refusing any rights of legal protection to slaves, and, though slaves in the antebellum period were allowed a minimal protection by the law and could in some cases even defend themselves in court, the idea that slaves were mere chattel persisted in antebellum law, where slaves could not witness against white men in court (Finkelman, 2010, p. 437). Correspondingly, the Fugitive Slave Act of 1850 permitted slave owners and their representatives to arrest fugitive slaves in free states without having to prove the identity of their prisoners in court. Some abolitionists therefore encouraged trials against fugitive slaves, as in the case of Margaret Garner (famous thanks to Toni Morisson's account, *Beloved*) who committed infanticide in a desperate attempt to save her children from slavery when she and her children were arrested by their owner. Abolitionists who saw her case as an extreme proof of the desperate condition of slaves were eager to have her tried for infanticide, but eventually Garner was returned without trial to her owner who restored her to slavery. Like other fugitive slaves, she was not granted the legal status of personhood and was legally debarred from giving evidence in her own case (see Reinhardt, 2002 for a detailed discussion of the Garner case). As Morrison reminds us, Garner was never permitted the minimal discursive control to tell her own story, which only survives through external sources.

From a theoretical perspective, it is important to notice the difference between the forensic definition of personal identity found in Locke and Pettit on the one hand and the more traditional Augustinian understanding of personal identity on which Olney draws on the other. While the latter bases personal identity on our internal mental capacity to recollect past experiences, the former offers an external and social definition of identity which relies on our capacity to answer to past actions. The former concerns only the continuity and changeability of the self, while the latter concerns the person in his or her relation to other people.

Personal Freedom

The question of personal identity as a requirement for freedom is further complicated in the case of fugitive slaves, for, after their escape, they had to change their names and hide their previous identity in order to avoid slave searchers. Taking a new name and a new identity is a commonplace climax in the narratives which marks the transition from bondage to freedom. Often the slaves bore the names of their masters, and for this reason they detested their family names. In some cases, as that of the mulatto William Wells Brown, the slaves were even fathered by their masters. In his narrative, Wells Brown describes how he was forced by his owner and biological father to change his first name to Sandford when the latter begot a legitimate son who, for inscrutable reasons, was also baptized William. Here is Brown's sardonic comment:

"It is sometimes common at the south, for slaves to take the name of their masters. Some have a legitimate right to do so. But I always detested the idea of being called by the name of either of my masters. And as for my father, I would rather have adopted the name of "Friday," and been known as the servant of some Robinson Crusoe, than to have taken his name. So I was not only hunting for my liberty, but also hunting for a name." (Brown, 1847, p. 98)

Douglass changed his name several times in the immediate aftermath of his flight, thus skipping from Frederick Bailey to Frederick Stanley and Frederick Johnson. Upon his arrival in New Bedford, he discovered that Frederick Johnson was such a common name that he asked his host to give him a new name, finally settling on Douglass (Douglass, 1845, p. 112). More self-consciously, Henry Box Brown promoted his own fugitive narrative by choosing a middle name referring to the legendary three-foot container in which he was mailed to the North.

If the fugitive slaves saw their new names as a promise of freedom, the change of identity was also a challenge to their freedom for reasons that must be fairly obvious from our argument. In order to be accountable as a free person and enjoy discursive control, one must, as we have seen, be able to endorse the legacy of one's accumulated personal history.[5] However, this also means that hiding or losing one's previous identity becomes a predicament for personal freedom. "It is common for slaves to answer to any name, as it may suit the humours of

---

5 This explains why the slave narrative was always more than just a weapon to fight slavery. In fact autobiography has remained a decisive means in African-American literature to affirm the free self.

the master," remarks one John Brown, not the infamous abolitionist of Harpers Ferry, about his dizzying past (Brown, 1854, p. 1).

Because the personal identity of fugitive slaves was so fragile, slave narrators make extraordinary paratextual efforts to prove their identity in their books. The typical slave autobiography of the 1840s and 1850s contains signed photographs or engraved portraits of the narrators and testimonials and letters by persons of public renown, such as editors, writers, abolitionist politicians, and clergymen, who validate the identity and reliability of the narrator. Without this external bestowal of discourse control, the narratives were simply not taken seriously by the public, whereas narratives introduced by major public figures like William Garrison, Wendell Phillips or Harriet Beecher Stowe easily became bestsellers. Douglass' autobiography, prefaced by both Garrison and Wendell Phillips, was issued in 13 editions in between 1845 and 1847, and by 1860 sold 30,000 copies, while William Wells Brown's autobiography from 1847, endorsed by the antislavery leader Quincey Jones, went through four editions in its first year of publication. The best selling narrative by far, however, was *The Life of Josiah Henson* (1849) whose sale figures rose to 100,000 copies after Harriet Beecher Stowe claimed she had based *Uncle Tom's Cabin* (1851) on Henson's autobiography (cf. Foster, 1979, p. 22).

Alongside these paratextual efforts, we also find substantial efforts by slave narrators to identify themselves in the narrative texts. The very opening sentence of the vast majority of narratives begins with a statement locating the place and (lack of) known circumstances of the narrator's birth: Case in point, Douglass's introit: "I was born in Tuckahoe, near Hillsborough, and about twelve miles from Easton, in Talbot county, Maryland. I have no accurate knowledge of my age, never having seen any authentic record containing it" (Douglass, 1845, p. 1). As slaves were often separated from their closest family early in life, the only record that could identify the slave narrators' past was the names and locations of previous masters.

The scarcity of evidence of the slave narrators' past identity explains the use of declarative speech acts with which the narrators identify themselves, as when Douglass solemnly ends his narrative with the words: "I subscribe myself, Frederick Douglass [facsimile of signature], LYNN, Mass., April 28, 1845" (Douglass, 1845, p. 125). As Olney correctly insists, the slave narratives distinguish themselves from all other autobiographical writings by their unusual insistence that their authors actually exist. We should perhaps add that this is also a distinguishing feature in respect of other pieces of testimonial literature which is usually more concerned the veracity of its testimony than proving the actual existence of the witness.[6] It only stresses that the writing self in slave autobiography is defined in legal rather than subjective terms. What matters even more than the veracity of the narratives' content (which is certainly important too), is the witness' capacity to assert him- or herself as a person capable of discursive control, a person who can witness and publicly answer to his or her testimony.

A BLACK ATLANTIC REPUBLICAN TRADITION?

As we have seen, Pettit's theory of freedom is largely compatible with the experience, thoughts and intentions found in American slave narratives. There can be no doubt that slave narrators took considerable and conscious efforts to assert discursive control by establishing their identity as responsible agents. Respectively, the slave narrators' political struggle for freedom is driven by a conception of freedom which is consistent with Pettit's republican understanding of freedom as non-domination rather than non-interference. While proponents of slavery protested against limitations of slavery as an illegitimate interference (either as federal interference with state legislation or as governmental interference with private liberty), the slave narrators and black abolitionists protested against the arbitrary domination that was forced upon slaves as a violation of their freedom.

Does this suggest that we can distinguish a black Atlantic tradition of republican thought? Or to put the question differently: does the fact that the slave narratives can be read in accordance with republican ideas of freedom suggest that the narratives were consciously written along republican figures of thought? There is no straightforward answer to this question. With the exception of Douglass, the poorly educated slave narrators were not political thinkers and spend little time on political and constitutional reflections in the narratives which are, as we have seen, closely bound to personal experience. Nonetheless, there are distinctly republican elements in the rhetorical exposition of slavery. First of all, massive descriptions of arbitrary coercion and its corruption of virtue are

---

6   This is not a categorical distinction, however, but one of degree. Thus, the fear that traumatic experience may lead to social death is not unusual in witness literature, especially among Holocaust survivors. Primo Levi writes of his worst nightmare as a prisoner in Auschwitz, in which he survives and is restored to his former life but realizes that even his closest relatives are indifferent to his story and act as if he still was not there (Levi, 2008, p. 66). Still, the efforts taken by the slave narrators and their supporters to prove their very existence is quite exceptional.

found in all narratives, which invoke a deep-seated concern in American political ideology and rhetoric that is intimately connected with the Atlantic republican tradition (Pocock, 1975; Dickson D.B. Jr., 2007, p. 38). Second, slave narrators persistently define themselves by their lack of civic and legal status, and their exposure to arbitrary domination, not by their race or cultural identity. Though the fugitive slave writers were well aware that racism persisted in the abolitionist North, the defining category for them concerns their civic status rather than colour or socio-cultural background. For strategic reasons, questions of black identity are played down in the narratives which were primarily intended for a broad white audience. After the Civil War, however, freedom in the republican sense as non-domination was replaced by racial equality as the primary political objective of black writers, who found the freedoms of emancipation slowly eroded by the implementation of depriving Jim Crow laws. By then the republican notion of freedom had lost its rhetorical sway.

If we look from a broader perspective at the antebellum slavery debate, it furthermore becomes clear that the slave narratives were also rhetorically influenced by proslavery pamphlets, even as they sought to refute them. Recently, the historian Carl J. Richard has observed how advocates of slavery like John C. Calhoun, leader of the pro-slavery faction in the Senate in the 1830s and 1840s, drew extensively on classical political philosophy. In particular Aristotle's definition of the "natural slave" as a person who is intellectually and morally incapable of liberty appealed to southern arguments and was twisted racially (pace Aristotle) to become a vindication of white supremacy (Richard, 2009, p. 189). In this way, Aristotle's political philosophy was used as evidence against the hypothesis of the state of nature, seen by many southern intellectuals as the root of abolitionism, in which modern political thinkers like Hobbes, Locke, and Rousseau had argued that men were originally free and equal individuals (Richard, 2009, p. 192).

The slave narrators were not in a rhetorical position to dispute the "neo-Aristotelian" vindication of natural slavery among writers like Calhoun by arguing in terms of the state of nature hypothesis, bound as they were to statements of experience rather than theoretical convictions. However, what they could do instead, and with greater authority, was rebuke the very idea of the natural slave by portraying their own struggle for freedom, and, secondly, portray the morally and economically corrupting power of slavery that they had witnessed. Douglass speculates that it was slavery which brought about the fall of classical Athens (Richards, 2009, p. 194), and in the narratives we find several reflections on the ways in which domination depraves the slaveholders, who are portrayed as unproductive, hypocritical, and victims of their own desires. Interestingly, the antebellum slave narrators, in contrast to their white abolitionist allies, rarely conceive of freedom as an inalienable right. Instead they are consistent in their criticism of the corrupting power of domination and their conception of freedom as the opposite of domination. In this sense, they furnish the Atlantic republican tradition with a valuable appendix.

In relation to the republican tradition, it is interesting to find republican figures of thought among the slave narrators expressed from a perspective which, for once, is the very opposite of that of the free citizen. Nonetheless, there is, as we have seen, a thorough convergence between the modern republican conception of freedom as non-domination and the beliefs and experiences found in slave testimony. I see this as an argument that Pettit's theory of freedom is not only philosophically, but also empirically, valid. However, there is another conclusion we might draw from the present analysis, which concerns the understanding of the witness as an autobiographical person. There is a tendency in much scholarship on autobiography and witness literature to emphasize the inner, psychological, and mental aspects of the witness's memory at the expense of its external agency. The aim of the slave narratives, however, was not to recover or represent the minds of the slaves but to fight slavery by asserting the discursive freedom of the slave narrators as witnesses. Their notion of personal identity is therefore a legal one which urges us to acknowledge the witness as a responsible agent rather than a mere victim. Certainly, this is an aspect of witnessing that antebellum slave narratives can help us recognize and understand in other kinds of autobiography where it appears less obvious.

REFERENCES

Slave Narratives Cited[7]

Bibb, H. (1849). *Narrative of the Life and Adventures of Henry Bibb, an American Slave. Written by Himself.* New York, NY: Published by the author.
Brown, H. "Box" (1849). *Narrative of the life of Henry Box Brown, Who Escaped from Slavery, Enclosed in a Box 3 Feet Long and 2 Wide. Written*

---

7 Cited from full-text versions and facsimiles of the original editions of slave narratives at the homepage Documenting the American South, Scholarly Bibliography of Slave and Ex-Slave Narratives edited by Professor William L. Andrews: docsouth.unc.edu/neh/

from the Statement of Facts Made by Himself. With Remarks Upon the Remedy for Slavery. By Charles Stearns. Boston, MA: Brown and Stearns.
Brown, H.W. (1847). *Narrative of William W. Brown, a Fugitive Slave. Written by Himself*. Boston, MA: The Anti-Slavery Office.
Brown, J. (1855). *Slave Life in Georgia. A Narrative of the Life, Sufferings, and Escape of John Brown, a Fugitive Slave, Now in England*. London: W.M. Watts.
Douglass, F. (1845). *Narrative of the Life of Frederick Douglass. Written by Himself*. Boston, MA: The Anti-Slavery Office.
Jacobs, H.A. (1861). *Incidents in the Life of a Slave Girl. Written by Herself*. Edited by L.M. Child. Boston, MA: Published by the Author.
Northup, S. (1853). *Twelve Years a Slave: Narrative of Solomon Northup, a Citizen of New York Kidnapped in Washington City in 1841, and rescued in 1853*. Auburn, NY: Derby and Miller.

Other references

Blassingame, J. (1977). *Slave Testimony. Two Centuries of Letters, Speeches, Interviews and Autobiographies*. Baton Rouge, LA: Louisiana State University Press.
Caruth, C. (1996). *Unclaimed Experience. Trauma, Narrative and History*. Baltimore, MD: Johns Hopkins University Press.
Davis, D.B. (2006). *Inhuman Bondage. The Rise and Fall of Slavery in The New World*. Oxford: Oxford University Press.
Dickson, B.D. Jr. (2007). Politics and Political Philosophy in the Slave Narrative. In Fisch, A. (Ed.), *The Cambridge Companion to The African American Slave Narrative* (pp. 28-43). Cambridge: Cambridge University Press.
Dulong, R. (1998). *Le témoin oculaire. Les conditions sociales de l'attestation personelle*. Paris: Éditions de l'École des Hautes Études en Sciences Sociales.
Engdahl, H. (2002). Philomela's Tongue. In H. Engdahl. (Ed.): *Witness Literature*. Proceedings of the Nobel Centennial Symposium (pp. 1-14). Singapore: World Scientific Publishing.
Gates, H.L. Jr. (1987). *Figures in Black. Words, Signs and the "Racial" Self*. Oxford: Oxford University Press.
Genovese, E.D. (1974). *Roll, Jordan, Roll. The World the Slaves Made*. New York: Pantheon Books.
Felman, S. & Laub, D. (1992). *Testimony. Crises of Witnessing in Literature, Psychoanalysis, and History*. New York: Routledge.

Finkelman, P. (2010). United States Slave Law. In R.L. Paquette & M.M. Smith (Ed.). *Slavery in the Americas* (pp. 424-446). Oxford: Oxford University Press.

Foster, F.S (1979). *Witnessing Slavery. The Development of Ante-bellum Slave Narratives*, Westport, CT: Greenwood Press.

Locke, J. (1975). *An Essay Concerning Human Understanding*. Oxford: Oxford University Press.

Olney, J. (1984). "I Was Born": Slave Narratives, Their Status as Autobiography as Literature. *Callaloo. A Journal of African American and African Arts and Letters*, 7.1 (Winter), 46-73.

Pettit, P. (1993a). Negative Liberty, Liberal and Republican. *European Journal of Philosophy*, 1, 15-38.

Pettit, P. (1993b). Liberalism and Republicanism. *Australasian Journal of Political Science*, 28, 162-89.

Pettit. P. (1997). *Republicanism: A Theory of Freedom and Government*. Oxford: Oxford University Press.

Pettit, P. (2001). *A Theory of Freedom. From the Psychology to the Politics of Agency*. Cambridge: Polity Press.

Pocock, P.G.A. (1975). *The Machiavellian Moment. Florentine Political Thought and the Atlantic Republican Tradition*. Princeton, NJ: Princeton University Press.

Reinhardt, M. (2002). Who Speaks for Margaret Garner? Slavery, Silence, and the Politics of Ventriloquism. *Critical Inquiry*, vol 29, no. 1 (Autumn), 81-119.

Richard, C.J. (2009). *Golden Age of the Classics in America: Greece, and Rome and the Antebellum United States*. Cambridge, MA: Harvard University Press.

Skinner, Q. (1984). The Idea of Negative Liberty: Philosophical and Historical Perspectives. In R. Rorty, J.B. Schneewind and Q. Skinner (Ed.), *Philosophy in History. Essays in the Historiography of Philosophy* (pp. 193-221). Cambridge: Cambridge University Press.

Skinner, Q. (1986). The Paradoxes of Political Liberty. In Sterling M. McMurrin (Ed.), *The Tanner Lectures of Human Values, Vol. 7* (pp. 225-250). Cambridge: Cambridge University Press.

Skinner, Q. (1998). *Liberty before Liberalism*. Cambridge: Cambridge University Press.

Webber, T. (1980). *Deep like Rivers. Education in the Slave Quarter Communities 1831-65*. New York, NY: W.W. North & Company.

About the Authors

Arnold, Oliver is associate professor at the English Department, University of California, Berkeley. He has published extensively on the political contexts of Shakespeare, including the monograph *The Third Citizen: Shakespeare's Theater and the Early Modern House of Commons* (Johns Hopkins University Press, 2007).

Celikates, Robin is associate professor of political and social philosophy at the University of Amsterdam, vice-director of ASCA, and an associated member of the Institute for Social Research in Frankfurt. His main areas of interest include critical theory and democratic theory, especially civil disobedience. Some recent and forthcoming papers are available at *http://uva.academia.edu/RobinCelikates*.

Dahl, Christian is associate professor at the Department of Comparative Literature, University of Copenhagen. His research concentrates on classical and early modern theatre and political culture. Publications include a book on Greek tragedy (*Tragedie og Bystat*, Museum Tusculanum Press, 2010) and Danish translations of Aeschylus and Hannah Arendt.

Fastrup, Anne is associate professor at the Department of Comparative Literature, University of Copenhagen. Her current research interests are literature and political history in Early Modern Europe. She has published books and articles on Cervantes, Calderón, Préchac, Montesquieu, Rousseau, Diderot.

Kjørholt, Ingvild Hagen is researcher at the Falstad Centre, Norway. Her PhD thesis is on Voltaire and French 18th century cosmopolitanism. She has published several articles on French 18th century literature and culture.

Lev, Amnon is associate professor at the Centre for International Law and Justice, University of Copenhagen. In addition to monographs on the political philosophy of Aristotle (Museum Tusculanum, 2008) and on the development of modern political philosophy from Hobbes to Hegel (Routledge, 2014), he has published essays on various topics relating to the history of political philosophy and international legal theory.

Maslan, Susan is associate professor at the French Department, University of California, Berkeley. She has published *Revolutionary Acts: Theater, Democracy, and the French Revolution* (Johns Hopkins University Press, 2005) and is currently working on a book-length project called "Citizen/Human: The Literary Genealogy of Human Rights in France, 1640-1795".

Nexø, Tue Andersen is associate professor at the Department of Comparative Literature, University of Copenhagen. He has mainly published on 17th and 18th century English Literature, especially on the relationship between political polemics and literature.

Prendergast, Christopher is Fellow of King's College, Cambridge and Professor Emeritus, University of Cambridge. He has published principally on French literature and cultural history. His most recent book, *Mirages and Mad Beliefs: Proust the Skeptic*, was published in 2013 by Princeton University Press. He is currently putting together a history of French literature from the Renaissance, also for Princeton.

Rostbøll, Christian F. is associate professor of political theory at the University of Copenhagen. He is the author of *Deliberative Freedom* (SUNY Press, 2009) and numerous articles on democracy theory, conceptions of freedom, autonomy, and respect.

Scurr, Ruth is Fellow, Tutor and Director of Studies in Politics at Gonville and Caius College, Cambridge. She has published extensively on the history of the French Revolution, including the monograph *Fatal Purity: Robespierre and the French Revolution* (Macmillan Publishers, 2006).